1

Social Skills
of Children and Adolescents:

Conceptualization, Assessment,
Treatment

Social Skills
of
Children and Adolescents

Conceptualization,
Assessment,
Treatment

Kenneth W. Merrell
The University of Iowa

Gretchen A. Gimpel
Utah State University

LAWRENCE ERLBAUM ASSOCIATES, PUBLISHERS

1998   Mahwah, New Jersey   London

Lawrence Erlbaum Associates, Inc., Publishers
10 Industrial Avenue
Mahwah, New Jersey 07430

Library of Congress Cataloging-in-Publication-Data

Merrell, Kenneth W.
Social skills of children and adolescents: conceptualization,
assessment, treatment / Kenneth W. Merrell and Gretchen A. Gimpel.
   p. cm.
Includes bibliographical references and index.
ISBN 0-8058-2655-6 (c : alk. paper).
1. Social skills in children—Study and teaching. 2. Social interaction in
children. 3. Social skills—Study and teaching. 4. Socialization. I. Gimpel,
Gretchen A. II. Title.
BF723.S62M47 1997
303.3'2—dc21   97-8974
                                             CIP

Books published by Lawrence Erlbaum Associates are printed on
acid-free paper, and their bindings are chosen for strength and durability.

Printed in the United States of America
10 9 8 7 6 5 4 3 2 1

Contents

Preface

The scientific study and clinical applications of child and adolescent social skills became important and well-established endeavors in the behavioral sciences as well as in the educational and human services arenas during the 1980s and 1990s. The increasing prominence of these applications of child and adolescent social skills is partly because the field has finally matured to the point that there is now an extensive literature base, making it possible to identify the most important scientific and applied components. Another reason for the surge of interest and popularity in this area has resulted from the increasing recognition of the critical importance of social–emotional development to individuals and society in general. In his 1994 best-selling popular book, *Emotional Intelligence,* Daniel Goleman persuasively argued that the social–emotional aspects of human functioning have a tremendous impact on individual lives and society and perhaps may be more important to our happiness and success in the long run than intelligence or IQ as it is traditionally defined.

Evidence of this critical impact can be found virtually anywhere in the ruined relationships, academic and occupational failure, and violence and despair that so often characterize the lives of individuals who have serious deficits in social competence or social skills. Knowing that the roots of these social–emotional problems are usually planted firmly in childhood is both troubling and promising: troubling because it underscores the failure of our institutions and families to ensure that all children will realize our hopes for them and promising because childhood provides a tremendous window of opportunity for effective assessment and intervention techniques to make an important and lasting difference in the lives of those who encounter serious obstacles to their social and emotional success.

Consequently, many books and other professional materials on the social competence of children and adolescents are available. Given that so much in this area is now available, one might ask why there should be another book on social skills. The answer to this question is twofold.

First, it is important to recognize that our knowledge regarding child and adolescent social skills is expanding rapidly, and there is a tremendous need to keep current. This book helps to meet this need not only by synthesizing a great deal of recent work in the field, but also by providing some new information and evidence that has not yet been published.

Second, with this book we have aimed to bridge an important gap that sometimes exists between research and practice. Some discussions on child and adolescent social skills are clearly written for the academician or researcher and may have little apparent application for the clinician or practitioner. Other materials are written as practical assessment or intervention guides for the clinician-practitioner but sometimes seem to be lacking in supporting scientific evidence and rationale. This volume is aimed at both arenas, and in writing it, the authors have sought to provide a solid foundation of scientific knowledge written in a manner that is accessible to nonscientists, but that also includes ample practical implications and examples for educational and clinical practice.

This volume essentially is divided into two parts. Chapters 1 to 3 provide a foundation for conceptualizing and assessing child and adolescent social skills. Chapter 1 provides a detailed introduction to the nature and importance of social skills, whereas chapter 2 is focused on developmental issues in child and adolescent social skills, including the process of social skill development, gender, and ethnocultural factors, as well as the relationship of social skills to common childhood disabilities. Chapter 3 provides an in-depth overview of methods and instruments for assessing social skills, including several new developments in this area. This chapter is intended to be not only a practical guide to assessment, but a critical survey of the current state of the art in the field. Chapters 4 to 6 are clearly focused on the arena of intervention. Chapter 4 provides a detailed basic framework for designing, implementing, and evaluating social skills interventions and includes many practical examples and suggestions that will be especially useful to clinicians and educators. Chapter 5 takes the intervention foundation of chapter 4 one step further, focusing on social skills training issues with specific problems, populations, and settings. Finally, chapter 6 provides a comprehensive overview of several widely available commercially packaged social skills training programs, providing evaluative detail aimed at being useful in the selection of intervention programs for specific needs.

The authors acknowledge the support and confidence of the editorial staff at Lawrence Erlbaum Associates in making this volume a reality and in helping them to create a product that will reach the desired end. It is hoped that this volume will achieve the goals set for it and that it will result in a valuable and unique contribution to the field. There is still much work to be done in the area of child and adolescent social skills, and this volume is intended to be a small but important step in that direction.

The Nature and Value
of Social Skills

BRANDON, SARAH, AND CASEY:
AN INTRODUCTION

Brandon, a 7-year-old boy in the first grade, was referred to the school child study team. Brandon's teacher reported that he had extreme difficulty getting along with peers and that he was often physically aggressive. The first author of this book, a member of the team, was asked to observe Brandon in the classroom and on the playground. The classroom observation took place during an academic activity in which the students were writing spelling words from the chalkboard onto their papers. Brandon quickly lost interest in the activity and tried to get the attention of a student sitting behind him. Cupping his hands to his mouth and making a strange face, Brandon repeatedly whispered "hey you!" to his neighbor. When this ploy failed to get the attention of the other student, Brandon poked him in the shoulder with a sharpened pencil, which resulted in a loud cry of "stop it!" and a warning from the teacher. The playground observation took place during morning recess on a very frigid January day. Most of the 60 or so students simply stood near the building, huddled with their hands in their pockets. Brandon and about 10 others elected to play on the jungle gym and tunnel slide. During the 10-minute observation period, it was noted that Brandon engaged in 24 different acts of physical aggression (hitting, shoving, kicking, and the like) while continually making verbal threats or insults to his peers. Within a few weeks, a full-blown special education eligibility assessment was in process. During an interview and testing session when Brandon was asked how he got along with other kids, he became stoic, appeared to hold back tears, and tersely stated, "They all hate me."

Sarah, a 10-year-old girl in the fourth grade, had been a primary concern of her homeroom teacher for most of the school year. A classic wallflower, Sarah was always on the sidelines of social activity and was described by her teachers during lunchroom discussions as being painfully shy. She seldom initiated any social interactions, and although she was never in trouble for inappropriate or antisocial behavior, she appeared to have no close friends. During the spring parent–teacher conferences, Sarah's teacher discussed her concerns with Sarah's mother, who looked as reserved and quiet as Sarah. Stating that this was Sarah's typical mode of behavior, her mother noted that Sarah had few friends, and usually became involved in solitary play activities at home, even though she seemed to want friends desperately. A few sessions with the school counselor were recommended and, with some initial hesitation, Sarah cooperated. During the third session, Sarah stated that the prospect of approaching children or initiating a conversation often resulted in such thoughts as "I don't know how to do this and I'm going to look like an idiot!"

Casey, a 16-year-old boy in the tenth grade, was referred to a clinical psychologist for treatment of depression after admission to a hospital emergency room for an unsuccessful suicide attempt. (He became unconscious after he drank several glasses of wine and took a number of his mother's tranquilizers.) During the course of treatment, some facts about Casey emerged. He had been depressed for nearly 4 months, and the depression appeared to be precipitated by two events: the death of his grandfather and failure to make the junior varsity basketball team. The course of treatment focused on two primary areas: getting Casey involved in positive or enjoyable activities again and helping him to change the way he was thinking about things. Casey reported that he seldom did things with friends anymore and that when he was around people, he often avoided conversation and usually failed to make eye contact in his reply when spoken to.

These three cases appear to have little in common, but they share a collective thread: Brandon, Sarah, and Casey all exhibited deficits in basic social skills, and as a result they all are suffering. These cases also serve as a starting point for this introductory chapter aimed at providing a basic definition and understanding of social skills, showing why they are important, and explaining how their presence, absence, or adequacy during childhood and adolescence may have powerful and far-reaching implications, not only during the formative years but throughout the course of the life span.

DEFINING SOCIAL SKILLS

Like many psychological or behavioral constructs, *social skills* has been defined in numerous ways. No single definition appears to enjoy widespread acceptance in the professional literature. Social skills is among the most widely misunderstood and ill-defined of all psychological constructs. Even the construct of human intelligence, which is notorious for lacking a unitary definition and understanding in the professional literature, appears to have a more cohesive and interrelated set of definitions and general agreement.

The difficulty in providing an adequate definition of social skills is partly because the construct is deceptively simple, yet relies heavily on a number of other psychological constructs and basic human traits such as personality, intelligence, language, perception, appraisal, attitude, and behavior–environment interaction. The diversity of related traits, abilities, and behaviors that constitute social skills, along with the complexity of the behavior–environment interaction necessary for their acquisition and performance, has resulted in numerous definitions.

Another definitional problem to consider is that professionals from a very broad group of disciplines including social work, education, psychology, psychiatry, special education, and psychiatric nursing have been interested in the construct of social skills. Each discipline has its unique perspective or way of looking at the construct, so it is not surprising that many different definitions of social skills exist. Table 1.1 lists the key elements of 16 relatively recent and influential definitions of social skills. Although this listing is certainly not exhaustive, it provides a solid general appraisal of current thinking regarding the essential elements of the social skills construct.

In comparing these 16 different definitions of social skills, it becomes obvious that although each is unique, there is a general familiarity or commonality among them. In other words, the definitions of *social skills* may differ somewhat, but the similarity among them is probably greater than any differences. Thus, recognizing that wording or terminology may vary among different definitions, Michelson, Sugai, Wood, and Kazdin (1983) proposed an integrated definition of social skills that includes the following seven components:

1. Social skills are primarily acquired through learning (especially social learning, including observation, modeling, rehearsal, and feedback).
2. Social skills contain specific and distinct verbal and nonverbal behaviors.
3. Social skills include both effective and appropriate initiations and responses.
4. Social skills optimize social reinforcement (e.g., beneficial responses from the social environment).
5. Social skills are interactive by nature and include both effective and appropriate responses (e.g., reciprocity and timing of specific behaviors).
6. Social skill performance is influenced by the attributes of the participants and the environments in which it occurs (i.e., situational specificity). Influences such as age, gender, and prestige status of the recipient affects one's social performance.

TABLE 1.1

Key Elements of Modern Influential Definitions of Social Skills

Authors or Source	Definitions
Argyle, 1981	Social behavior that is effective in realizing the goals of the interactors
Combs & Slaby, 1977	The ability to interact with others in a given social context in specific ways that are socially acceptable or valued and at the same time personally or mutually beneficial
Foster & Ritchey, 1979	Those responses that within a given situation maximize the probability of maintaining or enhancing positive effects for the interactor
Gresham, 1981	Behaviors that maximize the probability of reinforcement and decrease the likelihood of punishment contingent on one's social behavior
Gresham & Elliott, 1987	Behaviors that in given situations predict important social outcomes
Hargie, Saunders, & Dickson, 1987	The skills employed when interacting at an interpersonal level with other people, which are goal-directed, interrelated, appropriate to the situation, identifiable units of behavior, and learned behaviors
Kelly, 1982	Identifiable learned behaviors that individuals use in interpersonal situations to obtain maximum reinforcement from their environment
Libet & Lewinsohn, 1973	The complex ability to emit behaviors that are positively or negatively reinforced and not to emit behaviors that are punished or extinguished by others
Matson, 1988	A socially skilled person, who is much more likely to receive the types of reinforcers generally considered to be socially acceptable or desirable
Mcguire & Priestley, 1981	Those kinds of behavior that are basic to effective face-to-face communication between individuals
Shepherd, 1983	An individual's observed behavior during a social interaction, characterized by the ability to sustain social roles and relationships
Schlundt & McFall, 1985	The specific component processes that enable an individual to behave in a manner that will be judged as competent
Schneider, Rubin, & Ledingham, 1985	The nexus between the individual and the environment; the tools used to initiate and sustain the peer relations that are a vital part of psychological well-being
Trower, 1979	Individual targets or goals sought to obtain rewards, and goal attainment dependent on skilled behavior
Young & West, 1984	Specific positive interpersonal behaviors that lead to desirable social outcomes

7. Deficits and excesses in social performance can be designated and marked for intervention.

Thus, given these common core elements, it may be said that social skills are learned, composed of specific behaviors, include initiations and responses, maximize social reinforcement, are interactive and situation-specific, and can be specified as targets for intervention.

Aside from the specific similarities among definitions of social skills, it is both interesting and useful to analyze the content of different definitions in order to delineate major typologies. Gresham (1986) noted that the numerous definitions of social skills can be divided into three general types: a peer-acceptance, behavioral, and social validity.

Peer-acceptance definitions tend to rely heavily on peer acceptance or popularity indices (usually measured through sociometric assessment techniques) in defining social skill. Thus using this definition, one might say that a child who is well-liked by and has good relationships with other children is socially skilled.

Behavioral definitions tend to explain social skills as situation-specific behaviors that maximize the chances of reinforcement and minimize the chances of punishment based on one's social behavior. Many (if not most) of the definitions of social skills found in Table 1.1 use a behavioral definition framework, thereby showing the popularity of this approach. This popularity is probably because it is useful in specifying antecedents and consequences of social behaviors that can easily be operationalized for assessment and intervention purposes.

Social validity definitions depict social skills as behaviors that predict important social outcomes (such as good peer relations or positive social judgments by others. Gresham (1986) noted that the social validity definition is a kind of hybrid between the peer acceptance and behavioral definitions, is criterion referenced, and has received increasing empirical support. Social validity definitions historically have been used with less frequency than the other types, but have gained popularity in recent years.

EXAMPLES OF SOCIAL SKILLS

Regardless of how social skills are defined, a working definition of the construct is only one aspect necessary for understanding. To get a better idea of the tangible or practical aspects of social skills, it is important to look at the concrete examples in this chapter, which provide tangible frameworks for viewing social skills.

A good general framework of basic social skills categories and subcategories was developed for a social skills training program produced by Stephens (1978) and later detailed by Cartledge and Milburn (1986). By the

TABLE 1.2
Four General Categories and 30 Subcategories of
Social Skills*

Self-Related Behaviors	Environmental Behaviors
Accepting consequences	Care for the environment
Ethical behavior	Dealing with emergencies
Expressing feelings	Lunchroom behavior
Positive attitude toward self	Movement around environment
Responsible behavior	
Self-care	

Task-Related Behaviors	Interpersonal Behaviors
Asking and answering questions	Accepting authority
Attending behavior	Coping with conflict
Classroom discussion	Gaining attention
Completing tasks	Greeting others
Following directions	Helping others
Group activities	Making conversation
Independent work	Organized play
On-task behavior	Positive attitude toward others
Performing before others	Playing informally
Quality of work	Property: own and others

* Identified in a social skills training program developed by
Stephens (1978).

use of a task analysis method, social skills were grouped into four major categories and further analyzed into 30 subcategories. These general categories and subcategories are detailed in Table 1.2.

Obviously, even the 30 subcategories in this social skills breakdown could be divided and broken down even further. Stephens (1978) actually identified 136 specific social skills that fit into these general categories and subcategories. Using the major category of *interpersonal behaviors* and the subcategory of *coping with conflict* as an example, we see that six specific social skills can be identified:

1. Responds to teasing or name calling by ignoring, changing the subject, or using some other constructive means
2. Responds to physical assault by leaving the situation, calling for help, or using some other constructive means
3. Walks away from peer when angry to avoid hitting
4. Refuses the request of another politely
5. Expresses anger with nonaggressive words rather than physical action or aggressive words
6. Constructively handles criticism or punishment perceived as undeserved.

Of course, these six specific social skills do not exhaust the behaviors involved in the skill of being able to cope with conflict in an appropriate manner, but they serve to provide a good example of how social skills can be conceptualized at different levels ranging from the macro- (wide) to the micro- (narrow) spectrum.

The most likely places to find breakdowns of social skills categories and their specific behaviors are in social skills training curriculums, which are typically developed through task analysis procedures. Later chapters on social skills training in this volume provide more specific concrete examples of these sorts of task-specific social skills. Another way of identifying specific component behaviors or tasks within categories of social skills is through the use of multivariate statistical techniques such as factor analysis, a procedure employed more often in developing social skills assessment instruments than in the development of social skills training programs. More detail on the behavioral dimensions approach to identification of social skills clusters or dimensions is presented in later in this chapter.

HISTORICAL DEVELOPMENTS

To understand modern conceptualizations of social skills, it is important to examine historical developments in this area. Although the years since the early 1970s have witnessed a tremendous proliferation of scholarly and practical work related to children's social skills, interest in children's social skills, peer relations, and social adjustment is really nothing new. In 1917, Beery, a prominent educator of that time, published a series of books entitled *Practical Child Training,* wherein he offered parental advice on childrearing. One of his specific suggestions was directed to mothers of children who had few friends and who experienced difficulties in approaching peers. Beery suggested that mothers could help these children by creating opportunities for peer interaction, such as picnics, that would include their children's classmates. He noted that activities such as these would help children to "have a royal good time," and he also suggested that if a child showed fear in approaching other children, the mother should "not scold or make any scene, but simply appear to pay no attention to him" (cited in Asher & Parker, 1989, p. 5).

This anecdote and early attempt at extinction training shows that for many years adults have had a strong interest in understanding and facilitating children's social adjustment. However, it is important to recognize that the concept of childhood as a unique developmental period and related ideas regarding the distinctiveness of child psychopathology are relatively new notions in the history of psychological theory. As recently as the 17th century, prevailing Western views tended to consider children as "miniature adults": property of their parents and not differing from adults in terms of thought processes and mental development. In the Western world, it was not until the late 18th and early 19th centuries that childhood was viewed as a unique developmental period and that individuals with severe behavioral and emotional problems were given treatment that we would consider humane or even marginally effective.

In detailing some of the historical antecedents in the area of children's social skills, Rubin and Ross (1982) noted that the 1930s was a period of extensive activity in the area of developmental psychology, and that much of this activity was focused on children's social behavior. Important historical figures such as Mead, Piaget, Parten, and Moreno all made important contributions to the study of children's social behavior, and some of this work resulted in practical efforts to implement assessment and intervention systems for child social behavior. For example, Moreno's influential (and ominously titled) book *Who Shall Survive?* (1934) is generally credited as the first systematic published work on the use of sociometric assessment, and the journal *Sociometry* was first published in the 1930s.

It appears that the 1940s and 1950s were a period of retrenchment or hibernation in this area. The pressures of World War II no doubt contributed to the decline of work in the area of children's social behavior during the 1940s, and the political climate of the Cold War and Sputnik era of the 1950s probably added further to this decline. A strong academic emphasis on the biologic and physical sciences were the norm during this period.

The 1960s saw a resurgence of interest in children's social behavior, led in part by the rediscovery of Piaget's work and spurred on by such sociopolitical developments as the "War on Poverty," that resulted in the implementation of the Head Start program. However, the focus of interest during this period was most prominently on children's cognitive behavior. According to Rubin and Ross (1982), it was not until the early 1970s that children's social behavior again took the forefront in education and psychology. The publication of the third edition of *Carmichael's Manual of Child Psychology* (Mussen, 1970) and the appearance of highly influential research reports on the long-term effects of children's social skills and peer relations (Cowen, Pederson, Babigan, Izzo, & Trost, 1973; Roff, Sells, & Golden, 1972) were watershed events in this area.

Since the 1980s, high-quality research on children's social behavior has continued, but the most significant developments in this area may be the practical implementation or translation of this body of work into screening, assessment, and intervention programs for use in the classroom and clinic. It is unusual to attend large professional conferences in child/school psychology or special education in which social skills assessment and training are not prominently featured among conference topics. Any survey of professional materials catalogs also reveals the prominent applied place that children's social behavior now occupies in the fields of education and psychology. We are currently in a period of rapid growth in this field. Among the issues yet to be resolved and that still need attention are the development of a sound classification taxonomy for children's social skills, the development of ecologically valid assessment tools directly linked to intervention, and an increase in our ability to conduct social skills training in an effective and generalizable manner. These current issues are all specifically addressed in subsequent chapters of this volume.

SOCIAL SKILLS AND SOCIAL COMPETENCE

Our discussion so far has provided some basic definitions of social skills, outlined some examples of specific social skills categories and tasks, and looked at the historical antecedents of this field. We now move on to analyze the relationship between social skills and a closely related construct: social competence. Although the terms *social skills* and *social competence* are often used interchangeably, most experts in the field agree that they are independent, albeit related, constructs. The key differences between social skills and social competence and how the two constructs are thought to be related has been articulated in a frequently cited article by McFall (1982). According to McFall, *social skills* are the specific behaviors that an individual must exhibit to perform competently on a given task. On the other hand, *social competence* is an evaluative or summary term based on conclusions or judgments that the person has performed the task adequately. These judgments are typically based on the opinions of others (e.g., peers, parents, and teachers) or comparisons to some explicit criteria or some normative group (Gresham, 1986). As McFall explained, the presence of social competence does not necessarily imply that there has been exceptional performance of social skills; it merely indicates that social skills performance has been adequate. The evaluative or summary aspect of social competence has also been supported by Hops (1983), who defined the construct as "a summary term which reflects social judgment about the general quality of an individual's performance in a given situation" (p. 3).

Hops and Finch (1985) also wrote on the distinction between social skill and social competence, producing an analysis that generally concurs with McFall's (1982) conceptualization. They also pointed out that social competence consists of both nonsocial and social skills. For example, motor skills behaviors (nonsocial skills) are generally not thought of as being within the domain of social competence, yet they tend to be positively related to children's social competence as measured by peer sociometric assessments. One study cited to support this notion is that conducted by Broekhoff (1977), who demonstrated that ball-throwing distance was the best predictor of social status in elementary-age boys, and that this relationship remained quite stable over time.

A more recent study provided results indicating a similar conclusion: Motor skills subscales on some adaptive behavior measures may actually correlate with total scores on social competence measures to a greater degree than do adaptive subscales that appear to measure social skills (Jentzsch, 1993). In addition to motor skills, another nonsocial skill obviously important to social competence is language ability, perhaps the main vehicle we use to interact socially (Hops & Finch, 1985). To this list of nonsocial skills important to social competence, we could also add perceptual skills, particularly as they relate to the ability to perceive social situations. Cognitive skills must also be considered, because decisions regarding when and how to engage in various motor and language behaviors that may have social repercussions or how a particular social situation should be appraised are obviously made as part of a complex cognitive decision-making process (Meichenbaum, Butler, & Gruson, 1981).

In summary, there seems to be widespread professional agreement that both social competence and social skills are multidimensional constructs, and that social competence should be considered the superordinate of the two concepts; it is a summary or evaluative term that reflects the notion of judgment of one's social behaviors and adjustment by outside observers. At this point, however, the widespread professional agreement regarding social competence and social skills ends. Although the general definitions of these terms are not really controversial, there is considerable variation in working models or theories of these two constructs.

CLASSIFICATION OF SOCIAL SKILLS:
A BEHAVIORAL DIMENSIONS APPROACH

With so many historical developments and recent advances in our understanding of social skills, as well as their documented importance to a wide variety of critical social and emotional outcomes for children and adolescents, it might be expected that a valid, agreed-upon taxonomy for classifying social skills would be available. However, such is not the case. Although many measures have been developed to measure social skills, relatively few have empirically validated their classification system to arrive at a taxonomy of social skills. It is also important to recognize that the most widely used classification system in psychiatry and psychology, the *Diagnostic and Statistical Manual of Mental Disorders* (4th ed.; *DSM–IV;* American Psychiatric Association, 1994), is built around the concept of classifying and taxonimizing psychopathology. In this system the classification of adaptive functioning, which includes social skills, is largely ignored.

One solution to this classification problem may lie in a behavioral dimensions approach, which involves the use of multivariate techniques such as factor analysis to derive empirically based clusters of highly intercorrelated behaviors. These clusters are then labeled by the researcher, based on the types of specific behaviors in the cluster, to identify the underlying behavioral dimension. Whereas a relatively large body of research has been conducted using a dimensional approach to classify childhood problem behaviors, relatively few studies have used such an approach to classify child or adolescent social skills (Merrell, 1994a).

Quay (1986) reviewed 61 studies, all of which used factor analysis to derive empirically based dimensions of children's problem behavior. Quay matched the results of these studies by examining both the factor labels and the actual behaviors subsumed by the factors to develop a classification system of children's problem behavior. Quay noted that this approach has some distinct advantages over other methods of classification: "First, empirical evidence is obtained showing that the dimension in fact exists as an observable constellation of behavior. Second . . . the relatively objective nature of most of the constituent behaviors utilized in the statistical analyses permits reliable measurement of the degree to which a child manifests the dimension" (p. 10).

As an attempt both to account for the wide variety of social skill dimensions reported in the literature and to collect data from these studies to derive an empirically based taxonomy of childhood and adolescent positive social behaviors, the first author of this volume coauthored an investigation that sought to replicate Quay's (1986) methodology on the construct of social skills. A brief overview of this social skills meta-analysis review is presented in this section. For more detail on the methodology or results of this investigation, the reader is referred to the full report (Caldarella & Merrell, 1997).

After an exhaustive literature search and study elimination process, a total of 21 studies were included that involved multivariate approaches to classifying social skills with over 22,000 children and adolescents. The review and synthesis of these studies was accomplished by examining both the name of each social skill factor derived in the studies and the underlying behaviors subsumed by the factor (the approach used by Quay, 1986). For example, items comprising a factor labeled *Peer Interaction* were examined to ensure that the majority of the items (at least 50%) were directly related to peers. If so, that factor would be grouped with other peer-related factors under a common dimension. The most common social skill dimensions, those occurring in one third or more of the studies reviewed, were then identified. This method was used to eliminate outliers as well as study-specific findings. The one third cutoff is the same as that used by Quay (1986) in his landmark meta-analysis of problem behaviors. Using this methodology, five primary dimensions of child and adolescent social skills were identified (Table 1.3).

After the identification phase, the five dimensions presented in Table 1.3 were more closely examined to determine the most common social skills associated with each. First, the specific social skill components constituting each of the factors that comprised the dimension were listed (e.g., all of the items comprising the first Peer Relations factor). Second, individual items of the next Peer Relations factor were listed, with similar items grouped together. This process was carried out for all five of the most common dimensions. Third, similar social skills were grouped together to determine the principal behavioral characteristics (those occurring in one third or more of the studies) associated with each dimension. Finally, these principal social skills were rank ordered (based on frequency) as they appear in Table 1.3.

The peer relations dimension occurred in 11 (52.38%) of the studies. This dimension appears to be dominated by social skills that reflect a child or youth who is positive with his or her peers. Such skills as complimenting or praising others, offering help or assistance, and inviting others to play or interact appear to describe this dimension well.

The self-management dimension also occurred in 11 studies. This dimension reflects a child or youth who might be labeled by others as emotionally well adjusted and able to control his or her temper, follow rules and limits, compromise with others, and receive criticism well.

The academic skills dimension occurred in 10 (47.62%) of the studies. This dimension is dominated by social skills seen in a child or youth who might be called an independent and productive worker by a teacher. Such skills as accomplishing tasks or assignments independently, completing individual as-

TABLE 1.3
The Five Most Common Dimensions of Social Skills*

Names of the Most Common Social Skill Dimensions (in descending order of frequency)	Frequency (Individual studies)	Percentage
Peer relations (social interaction, prosocial, interpersonal, peer preferred social behavior, empathy, social participation, sociability-leadership, peer reinforcement, general, peer sociability)	11 (1, 2, 4, 6, 7c, 9, 10, 12, 13, 17, 18)	52.38%
Self-management (self-control/social convention, social independence, social competence, social responsibility, rules, frustration tolerance)	11 (1, 2, 3, 6, 7a, 7b, 7c, 10, 11, 15, 18)	52.38%
Academic (school adjustment, respect for social rules at school, task orientation, academic responsibility, classroom compliance, good student)	10 (2, 6, 8, 9, 10, 11, 12, 15, 17, 18)	47.62%
Compliance (social cooperation, competence, cooperation-compliance)	8 (1, 5, 7a, 7b, 7c, 12, 15, 19)	38.09%
Assertion (assertive social skills, social initiation, social activator, gutsy)	7 (7a, 7b, 7c, 11, 12, 16, 18)	33.33%

* Developed from a review and analysis by Caldarella and Merrell (1997).

signments, and carrying out teacher directions all appear to describe this dimension well.

The compliance dimension occurred in 8 (38.09%) of the studies. Pictured here is a child who essentially gets along with others by following rules and expectations, appropriately using free time, and sharing things. Essentially, this dimension involves complying with appropriate requests made by others.

The assertion dimension occurred in 7 (33.33%) of the studies reviewed. This dimension is dominated by social skills evidenced by a child or youth who might be called outgoing or extroverted by others. Such skills as initiating conversations with others, acknowledging compliments, and inviting others to interact all appear to describe this dimension well.

These five most common dimensions of child and adolescent social skills have a strong base of empirical support, being derived in more than one third of the studies reviewed, with two derived in more than half of the studies. No other known research has done such an extensive review of empirically derived social skill dimensions of children and adolescents. Indeed, it could be said that this review is breaking new ground by applying the influential research method used by Quay (1986), which combines aspects of both meta-analysis and qualitative review to an area of critical importance: child and adolescent positive social behaviors.

Because these dimensions of social skills have been identified so frequently over the past 20 years of research, practitioners and researchers should consider focusing on these areas for assessment and intervention. Many of the social skills subsumed by these dimensions have already been incorporated into excellent, well-validated assessment (Merrell, 1994a; Walker, Colvin, & Ramsey, 1995) and intervention (McGinnis & Goldstein, 1984) strategies. What this study provides is further empirical support for the five essential social skills dimensions comprising the taxonomy. Gesten (1976) noted that competencies in clients must be identified and reinforced to maximize treatment and research outcomes. Perhaps this review and the resulting taxonomy can help to identify appropriate behaviors to reinforce and balance the scales between assessing for both positive and negative behaviors in children and adolescents.

THEORIES AND MODELS OF SOCIAL SKILLS AND SOCIAL COMPETENCE

As defined in this chapter, theories or models of social skills and social competence refer to how these concepts look or they way they are constructed. Theories and models of how social skills and competence develop and are demonstrated are discussed separately in chapter 2. For the purposes of this discussion, the term *model* is used, which can be thought of as a paradigm of

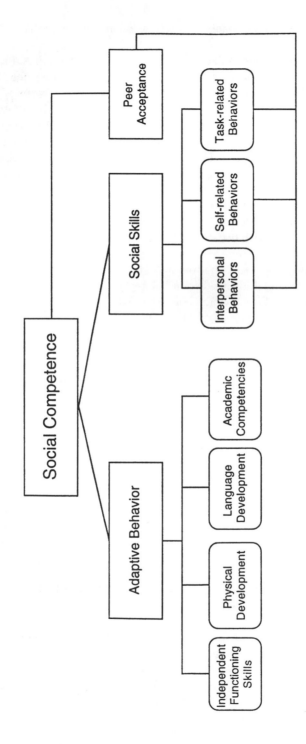

FIG. 1.1. A working model of social competence originally conceptualized by Reschly and Gresham (1981) and expanded by Gresham (1986) and by Gresham and Reschly (1987a).

how social skills and social competence appear and what constitutes their essential components. However, before exploring these ideas further, it is important to recognize that all the models we explore are hypothetical and thus somewhat speculative in nature. As already stated, psychological constructs are notoriously difficult demonstrate empirically. Thus, the ideas postulated herein must be considered as good working models based on the best evidence currently available, but not the definitive models hoped for in the future.

One of the most influential models of social competence in the school psychology, special education, and child development literature is that proposed by Reschly and Gresham (1981) and expanded further by Gresham (1986) and by Gresham and Reschly (1987a). According to the original model, social competence is considered to be the superordinate construct composed of two subordinate constructs: adaptive behavior and social skills. As the visual representation of this model indicates (Fig. 1.1), adaptive behavior for children is thought to consist of independent functioning skills, physical development, language development, and academic competencies. Social skills, however, are thought to consist of three major subcomponents: *interpersonal behaviors* (e.g., acceptance of authority, conversation skills, cooperative behaviors, and play behaviors), *self-related behaviors* (e.g., expression of feelings, ethical behavior, and a positive attitude toward self), and *task-related behaviors* (e.g., attending behaviors, completing tasks, following directions, and working independently). To the original model conceptualized by Reschly and Gresham (1981), Gresham (1986) added a third subordinate component of social competence: peer acceptance. As proposed in this model, the peer acceptance component is considered to be a part, but also an outcome or result, of socially competent behavior (Gresham & Elliott, 1987; Gresham & Reschly, 1987a). Thus, peer acceptance is seen as something separate from adaptive behavior and social skills under the broad model of social competence, but also as something that results from the adequate performance of these two other components.

Although this notion of social competence has been quite influential and appears to be based on a sound theoretical and empirical rationale, it is by no means definitive or universally accepted. Some potential problems inherent in the effort to identify the best model for a theory of social competence and social skills can be explored by looking at literature defining adaptive behavior, which already has been hypothesized as the second subordinate construct in the social competence model. Early in the 20th century, Edgar Doll (1935) discussed what we now refer to as the construct of adaptive behavior in widely influential writings that included references to factors known today as social competence and social skills. The construct of adaptive behavior eventually became a keystone in the definition of *mental retardation,* with the most widely accepted definitions considering deficits in adaptive behavior to be among its central defining components (American Association on Mental Retardation, 1992; Grossman, 1983).

As the interest in adaptive behavior grew, so did the technologies available for assessing this construct. Interestingly, most of the adaptive behavior scales currently in wide use, (e.g., *Scales of Independent Behavior* by Bruininks, Woodcock, Weatherman, & Hill, 1984, and the *AAMD Adaptive Behavior Scales, School Version* by Lambert & Windmiller, 1981) include subscales or components wherein the central behavioral constructs appear quite similar in name or content to social competence or social skills, thus raising the possibility that adaptive behavior actually may be the superordinate construct. The most recent definition of *mental retardation* (American Association on Mental Retardation, 1992) also seems to suggest this conclusion. However, empirical efforts to clearly define the essential components and hierarchical relationships of adaptive behavior have raised as many questions as they have answered (McCarver & Campbell, 1987).

Compounding this conceptual problem is the historic link between adaptive behavior and the human intelligence. Thorndike (1920) originally proposed that there were three types of intelligence, one of which was social intelligence or social competence. In summary, this excursion into the conceptual models relating to adaptive behavior, social competence, and social skills suggests that our best modern definitions lack the desired degree of perfect scientific precision.

In light of the complexities just discussed, the model of social competence articulated by Gresham and his colleagues and illustrated in Fig. 1.1 is accepted throughout this volume, but it also is acknowledged that there may be differing points of view in this area that are equally convincing. Furthermore, the term *social skills* is used primarily throughout this book, but in some cases it is used interchangeably with what has already been articulated as social competence (a summary judgment term) to facilitate simplicity of understanding.

OUTCOMES OF SOCIAL SKILLS

Now that we have looked at some definitional, classification, and conceptual issues relating to social skills, it is time to ask the following question: "What is so important about social skills?" In this section, we first look at the positive consequences known to stem from adequate social skills, then analyze the more disturbing consequences that seem to spring from inadequate social skills development and performance.

Positive Outcomes of Adequate Social Skills

A relatively large professional literature exists on the topic of social skills, but interestingly, most of the research and writing on outcomes of social skills are

focused on the negative consequences that arise from inadequate development and performance of these skills. By comparison, much less has been
documented on the positive outcomes of adequate social skills development
and performance. It seems as though researching the possible negative consequences of poor social skills is not only easier, but it also holds a greater degree of interest among professionals. The exceptional and abnormal arouses
more concern than the usual. Nonetheless, to fully understand abnormal performance, it is important at least to get some glimpse of what constitutes the
adequate, typical, or normal.

Like most other human traits, social skills can be viewed as existing along
a continuum within the population that probably represents a normal or bell-
shaped distribution. For the most part, people acquire and perform social
skills in a manner that serves them adequately. They have interpersonal successes and failures along the way, but can usually deal with the social situations and problems that face them.

A minority of individuals are exceptionally well-endowed in the interpersonal–social domain of life. Their outstanding social skills enable them to
develop and maintain friendships easily (thus providing them with a strong
network of social support), to resolve difficult social problems tactfully, and
essentially to breeze their way through the social thicket of life, gathering the
benefits that accrue to them along the way. A small percentage of persons are
so deficient in either the development or performance of social skills that they
are plagued throughout their lives with significant interpersonal, occupational, academic, and emotional–behavioral problems.

As indicated already, there is substantially more empirical evidence on the
results of social skills problems than on the outcomes of positive social skills.
However, there is also some pragmatic evidence to bolster these assertions. In
a frequently cited source on this topic, Hartup (1983) reviewed a plethora of
evidence suggesting that the ability to relate well to others is a critical con-
tributor to the positive growth and development of children. Walker and Hops
(1976) found that students who were more socially skilled had developed an
important foundation for achieving academic success in the classroom environment. Asher and Taylor (1981) showed that adequate social skills tended
to interpersonal successes and social acceptance with peers. Years ago, Wolpe
and Lazarus (1966) discussed clinical findings showing that individuals with
high levels of "commendatory skill" (being able to warmly and convincingly
compliment the positive attributes or actions of other people) tended to see a
reciprocation of their positive responses. In commenting on the relationship
between social skills and emotional or mental health, Kelly (1982) noted that
favorable global self-evaluation (such as selfesteem and self-confidence) usually was a result of a person's successful interpersonal repertoire of skills that
leads to outcomes the client deems reinforcing. Finally, social–psychodynamic
theorist Horney (1945), posited that interpersonal functioning (social skills)

was a central component of emotional adjustment and mental health and that
a child who developed the ability to interact successfully with others early in
life was likely to develop a personality style characterized by highly adaptive
and successful social behaviors. In summary, the amount of theoretical and
empirical work focusing on the positive outcomes of good social skills pales
beside the literature on deficits and problems, but it still lays an important
foundation of understanding.

Negative Outcomes of Inadequate Social Skills

After demonstrating that the adequate or successful development of social
skills is likely to lead to desirable outcomes, it is time to analyze the other side
of the coin: What happens when children fail to develop or perform social
skills adequately? In contrast to the relatively sparse amount of empirical evidence documented in the previous section, there has been substantially more
work done to show the negative effects of social skills problems. Most of this
research literature accrued during the last three decades of the 20th century.
After a general discussion of samples from this evidence, the following discussion turns to this body of work as a whole.

Social Skills and Psychiatric Disorders.   One of the most commonly
identified negative outcomes in the social skills literature is a link between
social skills problems or deficits and the broad category psychiatric disorders.
In our context psychiatric disorders comprise a broad general category that
reflects a variety of emotional and psychiatric problems ranging from major
mental illness (e.g., schizophrenia) to what once was called "neurotic" symptoms. It was established long ago that high rates of admission to psychiatric
facilities were strongly associated with social isolation and disintegration
(Bloom, 1968). Goldberg and Huxley (1980) identified a strong inverse relationship between the presence of positive social supports and various psychiatric symptoms. Bryant, Trower, Yardley, Urbieta, and Letemendia (1976)
showed that among a sample of persons receiving outpatient psychiatric treatment, those who were judged according to various independent criteria as being socially unskilled showed some distinct differences from other patients:
They tended to make poor eye contact, smile less, and use inappropriate
speech volume in comparison with their more socially skilled counterparts. In
a similar study, Rime, Bouvy, Leborgne, and Rouillon (1978) identified some
of the common core social skills problems of "psychopaths" as including behavioral intrusiveness (e.g., inappropriate assertive behaviors), lower rates of
smiling, and inappropriate eye contact. Wing (1978) identified some common social skills problems of individuals with schizophrenia as including
poverty of speech, poor eye contact, and a lack of appropriate verbal and nonverbal communication cues.

A most intriguing and widely cited study in this area was conducted by Cowen, Pederson, Babigan, Izzo, and Trost (1973). These researchers conducted an 11- to 13-year follow-up of Grade 3 children identified as "vulnerable" or at "clinical risk," based largely on peer problems, social isolation, and social rejection from peers. At follow-up, these children were found to have disproportionate rates of appearances in a community-wide psychiatric register (e.g., they were diagnosed and received services for psychiatric disorders at a substantially higher rate than their control peers who were not identified as vulnerable or at risk due to the social behavior criteria). Interestingly, the single best predictor of later psychiatric difficulty in this study was negative peer judgment using sociometric assessment techniques from a method referred to as the "class play" (discussed in detail in chapter 3). The assignment of negative roles in a hypothetical class play included such things as being nominated to play the role of someone who is too bossy, not liked by other people, in trouble, and so forth.

In summary, it has been well established that poor social adjustment and acceptance during childhood is a reasonably strong predictor of psychiatric or mental health problems later in life, and that individuals who exhibit psychiatric problems often are notably lacking or deficient in basic social skills. Although this link has been empirically established for some time, understanding the true nature or direction of this relationship is a somewhat more complex matter.

Social Skills and Externalizing Problems.   Perhaps the most strongly established link between social skills problems and poor outcomes has been found in the area of externalizing disorders, which by definition include a broad array of acting out and other-directed problems such as aggressive and antisocial behavior, hyperactivity, and the range of specific problems that are part of the conduct disorder syndrome (Quay, 1986). This syndrome and other externalizing disorders are worth a special note because of their immensity and expense. Matson and Ollendick (1988) cited a variety of evidence suggesting that externalizing conduct problems are the most common reason for behavior therapy referral, represent about one third to one half of all family and school referrals for mental health services, and probably cost society more than any other type of social–emotional problems.

Some of the most widely influential research on the link between social skills problems in childhood and later externalizing conduct problems was conducted by Roff (1961) and his colleagues during the 1960s and 1970s. These researchers found that high rates of delinquency during adolescence were strongly associated with social skills deficits and peer relationship problems, and that individuals discharged from military service because of bad conduct were likely to show a similar pattern of deficits and problems (Roff, Sells, & Golden, 1972). Ullman (1975) also demonstrated that teacher and peer ratings of social problems were a relatively strong predictor of school dropout, a common problem for adolescents who exhibit conduct disorders.

More recently, Wahler and colleagues (Wahler & Dumas, 1986; Wahler & Fox, 1982; Wahler, Hughey, & Gordon, 1981) have conducted research and written extensively on the development of antisocial behavior patterns in children and have developed a convincing theory of *coercion training*. This theory contends that patterns of antisocial and aggressive behavior tend to develop early in life, are learned within the family setting through various social learning processes, and have a cross-generational effect. As Wahler and Dumas (1986) stated, antisocial, aggressive children are usually "a chip off the old block" (p. 49). One interesting aspect of this theory relates specifically to social skills deficits in children: Individuals with stable antisocial and aggressive behavior patterns may not learn to achieve their social goals in positive ways (i.e., they lack certain positive social skills). Instead, they learn early in life to rely on painful, manipulative, and controlling behaviors to achieve their social goals, and the realization of these goals is often at the expense of other people.

Following up on this theory of how antisocial behavior develops, Wahler and Dumas (1986) reviewed a substantial body of evidence showing that delinquent youths tend to have a number of observable social skills deficits including deficiencies in eye contact, verbal acknowledgment of others' directives to them, use of questions, appropriate head nods, as well as deviant facial and body cues. These researchers also noted that antisocial and delinquent youths tend to have deviant patterns of interpreting social cues and the intentions of others, a finding that has been corroborated by Dodge and colleagues (Dodge, 1980, 1985; Dodge & Frame, 1982). In other words, antisocial, aggressive, and delinquent youths are not only likely to have basic deficits in social skills, they are also prone to inappropriately interpret hostile intent in routine social initiations made by others and follow these interpretations to further antisocial and aggressive acts.

The broad category of externalizing disorders not only includes conduct disorder and the patterns of antisocial and aggressive behavior that typically accompany it but a related disorder as well: attention-deficit hyperactivity disorder (ADHD). Although less attention has been paid to the social skills correlates of children with ADHD than to other externalizing problems, some compelling evidence has accrued suggesting that deficits in social performance may be a central characteristic of this disorder (Landau & Moore, 1991). Although the peers of children with ADHD may consider them to be deficient in social skills (Whalen, Henker, Collins, & Granger, 1987), it may be that many of these perceived deficits are performance deficits rather than skill deficits (a topic pursued later in this volume). For example, it has been demonstrated that children with ADHD may have an adequate knowledge of how to initiate and maintain friendships, but tend to exhibit behavioral responses perceived as unfriendly (Grenell, Glass, & Katz, 1987).

An interesting study in this area was conducted by Landau and Milich (1988), who developed a semistructured TV talk show game in which each child was given the opportunity to play the roles of both host and guest. In contrast to the non-ADHD children, those with ADHD were more likely to ask too many questions when they were in the role of the guest, and to ask too few questions when they were in the role of the host. In commenting on this study and similar studies, Landau and Moore (1991) suggested that youngsters with ADHD may be deficient in the skill of modulating their social communications and thus, may have production or performance deficiencies rather than skill deficits. In summary, youngsters with ADHD are also likely to have problems in performing appropriate social behaviors, but these problems may be more related to performance deficits than to social skill acquisition deficits.

Social Skills and Internalizing Problems.   By definition, the broad band of social–emotional problems referred to as internalizing disorders includes such syndromes as depression, anxiety, social withdrawal, and somatic (physical) problems which appear to have an emotional or psychological component. Although numerous researchers have hypothesized that internalizing problems are more transient and less costly to society than externalizing disorders (Merrell, 1994a), they still represent a tremendous burden to those who experience them. Not surprisingly, it has been found that deficits in social skills are a component of many internalizing problems.

One of the best established links between internalizing problems and social skills problems is the syndrome of depression, which can include severe cases of clinical depression as well as varieties and combinations of depressive symptomatology that do not involve full-blown clinical diagnoses. Many studies have documented that children who experience social relationship problems, such as rejection by peers, unpopularity, and social withdrawal, are more likely than their typical peers to experience depression and isolated loneliness (Asher & Wheeler, 1985; Cole & Carpentieri, 1990; Vosk, Forehand, Parker, & Rickard, 1982). These social skills deficits may take specific patterns when associated with depression. For example, Libet and Lewinsohn (1973) described the unusually low rates of verbal and nonverbal behavior among individuals with significant depressive disorders. This report was significant because it was one of the early major articles stemming from Lewinsohn's behavioral theory of depression, which was the first comprehensive theory of depression that postulated social skills deficits as a major component of depression. This theory led to the development of successful social skills-based behavioral interventions for treating depression and related internalizing problems (Lewinsohn, 1974).

A more recent study conducted by Bell-Dolan, Reaven, and Peterson (1993) illuminated some interesting new aspects of the relationship between depression and social functioning. Attempting to go beyond previous investigations that had identified simple negative correlations between measures of depression and social skills, these researchers examined the relationship between social functioning and depression from a multidimensional perspective.

Teacher, peer, and self-reports of both depression and social functioning for a large group of fourth- to sixth-grade students were obtained. The social functioning data were factor analyzed to reveal six different social functioning factors: negative social behavior, social withdrawal, other-rated social competence, self-rated social competence, social activity, and accuracy of self-evaluated social competence. These social functioning factors were then used to predict depression through a multiple regression analysis. Negative social behavior and the social competence measures were all predictive of depression. Social withdrawal predicted peer- and teacher-reported depression, and low social activity predicted self-rated depression. Composite depression scores (based on teacher, peer, and self-ratings), were all predicted by negative social behavior, social withdrawal, and low other-rated social competence. These findings are interesting in that they show specific relationship directions between components or dimensions of social functioning and different methods of gauging depressive symptomatology.

Although the internalizing disorders are often part of an overlapping syndrome of characteristics that exist simultaneously, most research exploring the link between social skills and internalizing problems have focused on depression (often with social withdrawal as part of the same syndrome). Less research emphasis has been placed on the relationship between social skills and anxiety or somatic problems, and most of the influential theories regarding these problems do not include social skills deficits as a major theoretical component. However, a few researchers have explored the link between anxiety and social skills in childhood. After analyzing some of the findings in this area, Kauffman (1989) hypothesized that children who are anxious and excessively shy may have some deficits in social skills, but they tend to distort their negative views of themselves, thinking that they have worse skills than they actually do, a cognitive distortion pattern that tends to further social isolation and loneliness. In another investigation of this topic, the first author of this volume (Merrell, 1995a) examined parent and teacher social skills ratings of children ages 3 to 6 who were rated as high for internalizing problems on various problem behavior measures. These internalizers were found to have significant social skills deficits in three different dimensions of social behavior: social cooperation, social interaction, and social independence. As a group, their social skills ratings ranged from more than one to nearly two standard deviations lower than those of a comparison group of noninternalizing children. Interestingly, a discriminant function analysis applied to the ratings of internalizing problems found that problem items indicative of depressive symptomatology were better able to predict social skills deficits than were problem items indicative of anxiety or somatic problems.

In summary, the relationship between internalizing problems and social skills has been explored less frequently than the role of externalizing problems, and the overall relationship appears to be somewhat weaker as well. However, the best evidence to date does suggest that social skills deficits are at least a moderate component of internalizing problems, particularly depression.

What Causes What? This section focused on the negative outcomes associated with inadequate social skills and placed a particular emphasis on psychiatric, externalizing, and internalizing disorders. With each of these problem areas it was demonstrated that social skills deficits are often a component of the syndrome. These findings lead to an unavoidable question: Do social skills deficits cause these various behavioral and emotional problems or are social skills deficits caused by these problems. Some theories (particularly the earlier and one-dimensional theories) postulate a definitive answer using either one of these two possible connections. For example, Lewinsohn's (1974) highly influential behavioral model of depression (particularly in its earlier forms) relies strongly on the notion that a disruption of pleasurable or positive events (i.e., a lack of social reinforcement due to a lack of or decrement in social skills) causes the syndrome of behaviors we refer to as depression.

The position most in favor currently, which the authors also advocate, is the notion that social skills deficits both cause and are caused by various behavioral and emotional problems. This notion is based on a model of mutual influence that is very consistent with Bandura's (1978) theory of reciprocal determinism. To visualize how this model of causation actually works, recall the case of Brandon, the 7-year-old boy with social skills deficits and significant antisocial and aggressive behaviors described at the beginning of this chapter. Brandon's early development may have been characterized by inadequate social skills acquisition coupled with his learning through coercive processes that aggressive behavior sometimes gets him what he wants. In the school setting, Brandon's inept attempts to approach peers and develop friendships results in some preliminary rejection from peers. Brandon responds to this preliminary rejection through a mechanism that in this case is maladaptive: aggressive and antisocial behavior directed toward his peers partially to get their attention and partially to punish them for rejecting him. These antisocial and aggressive behaviors lead to further alienation from the peer group, which in turn leads to an escalating pattern of hostility and aggression directed outward toward other children. The resulting isolation from peers, who might otherwise serve as positive social role models for Brandon, further inhibits his acquisition of social skills because he seldom observes positive social behavior directed toward him by his peers, who have learned to fear and avoid him.

Thus, the escalating and insidious cycle continues to perpetuate itself. Brandon's deficits in social skills, in a sense, have caused an increase in his externalizing problem behaviors, which also serve as a causal factor in Brandon's continuing pattern of social isolation and poor skills acquisition.

SOCIAL SKILLS AS A FORM
OF PRACTICAL INTELLIGENCE

This discussion would not be complete without a brief excursion into an area of current thought regarding social skills that has captured the imagination of the public in recent years, namely, the notion that social skills may reflect a specific type of practical human intelligence. For many years theoreticians, researchers, and clinicians working in the area of human intelligence have given at least peripheral attention to the idea that social–behavioral functioning may comprise a distinct form of what has been referred to as practical intelligence (Sternberg, 1986). For example, consider the administration of the Comprehension subtest on the various versions of the Wechsler Intelligence Scale for Children. A hallmark task on this subtest involves asking the child in effect: "What is the thing to do if someone who is younger than you wants to fight with you?" To receive full credit for answering this question, the child must in some way display self-restraint in his or her answer, recognizing the unfairness of a fight with a younger child. Obviously, the traits and skills involved in formulating such an answer (and in enacting it in the real world) are things already discussed as major features of social skills or social competence: interpersonal empathy, adequate self-control, and the ability to appraise a situation in terms of commonly accepted social mores and rules. In addition to this particular task, several other components of standardized IQ tests require the ability to make effective social judgments.

However, the inability to measure adequately the practical–social forms of intelligence has been one of the major criticisms of standardized IQ tests (Goleman, 1994), and most of the theorizing regarding social–behavioral skills as a form of practical intelligence has been proposed by those searching for better alternatives to standardized IQ tests, which tend to differentiate between academic and social forms of intelligence. This problem was summarized by Mercer, Gomez-Palacio, and Padilla (1986), who stated:

> We recognize that there is some overlap (between academic and social forms of intelligence), especially in infancy, when the two cannot be differentiated empirically. "Intelligence" tests for very young children contain many items relating to social behaviors, such as smiling, recognizing the mother's face, and recognizing a stranger. As the child develops, social–behavioral intelligence and academic intelligence gradually become differentiated, and traditional "intelligence" tests progressively eliminate items involving social competencies as the

age of the subject increases. By school age, traditional tests focus almost exclusively on academic intelligence." (p. 308)

As a response to critics who have contended that social–behavioral forms of intelligence cannot be reliably measured and are not related strongly to academic forms of intelligence, Mercer et al. (1986) presented some very impressive empirical evidence from a large cross-cultural data set in the United States and Mexico, in which both traditional IQ scores and adaptive social behavior scores were obtained. The adaptive social behavior scores were found to be highly reliable across cultural samples, and to comprise a stable underlying trait that the authors simultaneously referred to as *practical intelligence* and *social intelligence*.

Interestingly, some of the most influential recent work related to social skills as a practical form of human intelligence has been conducted by writers and researchers working outside the traditional areas of scholarly work in social skills and social competence. One of the best known recent popular books addressing this area has been Gardner's (1983) *Frames of Mind,* a book detailing his theory of multiple intelligences. Gardner is a Harvard University educator well known for his scholarly work related to creativity, art, and human development, and for his participation in The Project on Human Potential at Harvard. A more recent work in this general area is *New York Times* journalist and former *Psychology Today* editor Daniel Goleman's (1995) popular book *Emotional Intelligence*. This book deals with the problem that traditional notions of IQ fail to take into account some of the most important aspects of success: interpersonal relationships, altruism, compassion, and impulse control. Some of the main concepts from these two influential books are addressed in this section.

In *Frames of Mind,* Gardner (1983) contended that human intellectual functioning is best viewed in terms of multiple intelligences rather than as a single unidimensional construct. In Gardner's theory, there are seven distinct forms of human intelligence: linguistic, musical, logical–mathematical, spatial, bodily–kinesthetic, and two types of personal intelligence, interpersonal and intrapersonal. In this theory, it is the interpersonal form of intelligence that has a striking similarity to the definitions and conceptualizations of social skills presented earlier in this chapter:

> The core capacity (of interpersonal intelligence) is the ability to notice and make distinctions among individuals, and, in particular, among their moods, temperament, motivations, and intentions. Examined in its most elementary form, the interpersonal intelligence entails the capacity of the young child to discriminate among the individuals around him and to detect their various moods. In an advanced form, interpersonal knowledge permits a skilled adult to read the intentions and desires—even when these have been hidden—of many other individuals, and potentially to act upon this knowledge—for example, by

influencing a group of disparate individuals to act along desired lines. (Gardner, 1983, p. 239)

Although too comprehensive to fully detail in this book, Gardner's (1983) theory of multiple intelligences, and more particularly, his notions of interpersonal intelligence, are both convincing and compelling. There is no question that these notions share many important similarities with the constructs of social skills and interpersonal intelligence as they have been detailed in this volume. Perhaps interpersonal intelligence refers to specific areas or domains of social skills, most likely the areas of peer relationships, assertion, and empathy.

Like Gardner's theory of multiple intelligences including interpersonal intelligence, Goleman's (1994) popular book, *Emotional Intelligence,* created no small stir in circles where the relationship between social–emotional behavior and intelligence is considered. Unlike the construct of interpersonal intelligence, Goleman's conceptualization of emotional intelligence is not rooted in an overriding theory of human intelligence nor discussed in terms of statistical relationships with IQ tests, as in the work of Mercer and colleagues. Rather, the notion of emotional intelligence is developed and considered in terms of what maladaptive social–emotional functioning costs individuals, families, and society. The book's subtitle, *Why It Can Matter More Than IQ,* suggests one of the basic premises: When people of high IQ flounder in life while people of modest ability achieve great successes, the key variable is emotional intelligence. This concept is defined as comprised of self-awareness, impulse control, persistence, zeal and self-motivation, empathy, and social deftness. Like the idea of interpersonal intelligence, emotional intelligence is described in terms that bear a striking resemblance to many aspects of social skills and social competence discussed earlier in this chapter. In Goleman's (1994) own words:

> These are times when the fabric of society seems to unravel at ever-greater speed, when selfishness, violence, and a meanness of spirit seem to be rotting the goodness of our communal lives. Here the argument for the importance of emotional intelligence hinges on the link between sentiment, character, and moral instincts. There is growing evidence that fundamental ethical stances in life stem from underlying emotional capacities. For one, impulse is the medium of emotion; the seed of all impulse is a feeling bursting to express itself in action. Those who are at the mercy of impulse—who lack self-control—suffer a moral deficiency. The ability to control impulse is the base of will and character. By the same token, the root of altruism lies in empathy, the ability to read emotions in others; lacking a sense of another's need or despair, there is no caring. And if there are any two moral stances that our times call for, they are precisely these, self-restraint and compassion. (p. xii)

We can therefore relate the idea of emotional empathy directly to certain aspects of social skills: peer relationships, self-management, and empathy.

In summary, at the end of the 20th century there were several prominent attempts to publicly redefine the concept of intelligence or IQ to include and recognize the importance of social–emotional behavior. In this regard, social skills may be considered as either a key component or a major mediating variable in intelligence, but most experts in the area of human intelligence are now at least recognizing their critical importance.

SUMMARY

This chapter introduces the topic of child and adolescent social skills. Children and adolescents who have deficits in social skills tend to exhibit these deficits in differing ways, as is expressed by the three case studies that introduce this chapter.

Like a number of other behavioral or psychological constructs, social skills have been defined in the professional literature several different ways, and no single generally agreed upon definition of social skills exists. However, the current influential definitions of social skills seem to have some common core elements, and these definitions thus may be divided into three types: behavioral, peer acceptance, and social validity.

In the literature on assessment and treatment of social skills, specific categories and subcategories of social skills are identified, and each subcategory may contain numerous specific component behaviors. Specific examples of appropriate child and adolescent social skills are generally included in social skills training programs.

Although the study of children's social behavior has been prominent since at least the 1930s, only since the 1970s have the fields of psychology and education experienced that dramatic upsurge of interest in this area that exists today. Scholarly efforts in the area of child and adolescent social skills since the 1980s have been focused to a great extent on the development of clinically useful assessment instruments and intervention programs.

Social skills comprise part of a superordinate construct: social competence. Whereas social skills are generally viewed as being specific behaviors or activities that lead to desired social outcomes, social competence is a summary term based on judgment from others reflecting how a person's implementation of social skills is viewed in terms of adequacy.

A behavioral dimensions approach to classifying child and adolescent social skills was presented, wherein the same type of methodology used by Quay (1986) to develop his influential taxonomy of child and adolescent problem behaviors was utilized. A taxonomy of five dimensions of social skills resulted from this meta-analysis: peer relations, self-management, academic, compliance, and assertion skills. These dimensions may have important implications for future developments in a classification taxonomy for child and adolescent social skills.

Several models picturing the structure of social skills and social competence have been proposed, and although all of these models view both social skills and social competence as multidimensional constructs, there are some differences between these models that are both obvious and subtle. The model followed generally in this volume considers both social skills and adaptive behavior to be components of the superordinate construct of social competence.

Findings show that positive or adequate social skills development during childhood is an important foundation for good social, occupational, and personal adjustment throughout life. Conversely, it has been found that inadequate social skill development during childhood is associated with a number of negative outcomes including psychiatric problems; externalizing problems such as antisocial/aggressive behavior attention-deficit hyperactivity behaviors; and internalizing problems such as depression, social withdrawal, and anxiety. There have been differing perspectives on the causal relationship between social skills deficits and various social–emotional problems, but the position emphasized in this volume contends that this relationship is both mutual and reciprocal. In other words, social skills deficits may be caused by various social–emotional problems, and they may also serve as a causal factor in the development of such problems.

Several recent conceptualizations of human intelligence have directly or indirectly acknowledged the importance of social skills for adaptive goal-oriented behavior. Hence, the concepts of practical intelligence, social intelligence, and interpersonal intelligence have appeared within larger theories of human intelligence. Some recent widely read books in this area have placed the importance of social–emotional behavior in the public eye, and it seems likely that future research and public policy efforts concerning intelligence and its measurement may include social skills in some important way.

TWO

Developmental Issues
in the Acquisition and Performance
of Social Skills

Developmental considerations are often overlooked in the assessment and intervention of children's social skills, but they have obvious importance. Few people would argue that factors such as age, gender, ethnocultural background, and the presence of developmental disabilities are not potentially important considerations in the development of social skills. However, many otherwise careful professionals pay little attention to these influences in designing a social skills assessment or training program. In this chapter, various developmental aspects of social skills are discussed, for the purpose of providing the background necessary for designing developmentally sensitive assessment and intervention plans.

SOCIAL SKILLS ACQUISITION
AND CHILD DEVELOPMENT

In a review of social skills intervention techniques, Conger and Keane (1981) stated that among the various factors that may influence the development of social skills, "age is probably one of the most critical but severely neglected variables" (p. 479). Given the obvious link between developmental factors and social skills acquisition, and the rich breadth and depth of existing knowledge in the child development literature, it is indeed curious that relatively little attention has been given to the process of developmental social skills acquisition and performance. Thus, this section aims briefly to overview some

29

important developmental considerations and landmarks in social skills acquisition and performance. First, the process of social cognitive development is discussed. Next, some important developmental social skills issues are addressed as they relate to three specific stages of development: early childhood, middle childhood, and adolescence.

The Process of Social Cognitive Development

Of all the areas of child development, social cognitive development is perhaps the most directly linked and critical to the acquisition and performance of social skills. Stated simply, *social cognitive development* is the process whereby changes in cognitive functioning allow the developing child to engage in a hierarchy of increasingly complex and potentially meaningful interactions with other persons. The process of social cognitive development may be considered a specific application of the social cognitive theory proposed by Bandura (1986), as typified by his influential book, *Social Foundations of Thought and Action.* Bandura suggested that the nature of social cognitive development may be explained in terms of five basic human capabilities: symbolizing, forethought, vicarious, self-regulatory, and self-reflective capabilities.

Symbolizing capability involves the use of various symbols, including language, as a means of altering and adapting to different environments. The use of symbols allows communication with others, even at distant times or places. *Forethought capability* projects anticipation of likely consequences of behavior and is demonstrated by intentional and purposeful actions that are future-oriented. *Vicarious capability* allows that not all learning must result from direct experience, but can occur through the observation of other persons' behaviors and the consequences that follow them. *Self-regulatory capability* affects the development of our own internal standards and self-evaluative reactions to our behavior. Thus discrepancies between our internal standards and our actual behaviors serve to govern our future behavior. *Self-reflective capability* involves self-consciousness, or the uniquely human ability to think about and evaluate our own thought processes. Together, these five fundamental human capabilities form the basis for our vast human potential and help explain to the inner workings that result in our behavioral output.

In Bandura's view, observational learning is an essential part of social cognitive development. Its most elemental form is best understood as the process whereby we develop the capability to perform new behaviors through paying attention to models, retaining in memory what we observe, exercising the physical and cognitive ability to perform the new behavior, and having the motivation to do so. Another essential part of Bandura's social cognitive theory is the process of *triadic reciprocality,* which is best explained as a conception of human behavior development wherein the causes of behavior become influenced and shaped by the behavior itself (Bandura, 1978). As shown in Fig.

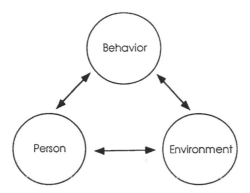

FIG. 2.1.   An outline of Bandura's Theory of Triadic Reciprocality.

2.1, three different influences or parts of the triad exist: the person, the behavior, and the environment. Each part makes a unique contribution to development, and the strength of each part may change over time. For example,
a child might be born with a biologically based, highly sensitive temperament
whereby unfamiliar stimuli are perceived as aversive (the person variable).
The child may then adopt a behavioral style of inhibition and avoidance to new
situations and persons (the behavior variable). The environment sought out
by the child selectively becomes one in which fewer opportunities for social
interaction exist, and other persons within the environment may then ignore
or avoid the child (the environment variable). As a result of these mutually influential processes, the child may develop a withdrawn and socially isolated
pattern of behavior and become deficient in basic social skills. Moreover, in a
sometimes insidious process, the three variables may continue to shape each
other and serve to strengthen the behavioral/personality style, even if it is
maladaptive.

In a more specific sense, social cognition or social cognitive development
may be viewed as consisting of various specific skills and processes that contribute in diverse ways to the development of social competence. Eisenberg
and Harris (1984) identified five aspects of social cognition considered to be
essential contributors to social competence: perspective taking, conceptions
of friendship, interpersonal problem-solving strategies, moral judgment, and
communication skills. *Perspective taking* (also referred to as *role taking*) involves the ability to understand another person's thoughts, intentions, and
feelings. *Conceptions of friendship* refer to what peer interactions mean to a
child, and as we shall see, these tend to change considerably during the developmental period. *Interpersonal problem-solving strategies* relate to the
capacity for solving relationship-based problems and the specific methods a
child uses to deal with these problem situations. *Moral judgment*, which

changes dramatically during the developmental period, involves the child's conception of rightness or wrongness, the developing value system, and tends to be related to the quality of social behaviors directed toward peers. *Communication skills* are the language and social strategies used to initiate interactions with others and to react to those initiated by others. Given the importance of the social cognitive developmental factors in children's social skills, the discussion must now focus on some very specific aspects of these factors as they relate to the acquisition and performance of social skills across three stages of development.

Social Skills Development During Early Childhood

For the purposes of this discussion, the early childhood developmental period can be seen to extend from about age 3 years to about the end of kindergarten or beginning of first grade, which is normally age 6 or 7. Cognitively, preschool and kindergarten age children are in what Piaget (1983) referred to as the *preoperational* stage. At this stage the child represents things with words and images but lacks logical reasoning ability. Preoperational children are easily confused by distinctions between reality and appearance and find it easier to follow positive instructions ("stay on the sidewalk") rather than negative instructions ("don't go in the street"). They tend to be *egocentric*, which means they may have difficulty understanding the perspective or experience of another person. Preoperational children often focus on just one aspect of a problem while neglecting other important aspects, a tendency Piaget referred to as *centration*. Memory retrieval strategies are typically not well developed during this stage. The child may have difficulty in some contexts understanding that actions can be reversed. Kohlberg (1969) suggested that the preconventional moral reasoning of children in this age range is characterized by considering actions right or wrong only in terms of the immediate consequences that such actions bring. During early childhood, a wide range of emotions may be experienced, but typically, these can be described by the child only along a limited number of dimensions (e.g., happy or sad, good or bad, mean or nice). In discussing psychosocial development during early childhood, Erik Erikson (1963) identified the development of autonomy or increasing independence from parents as a crucial factor, with maladaptive development resulting in guilt and shame.

In terms of specific social skills, it has been demonstrated that children increase rapidly in their ability to understand cognitions and emotions of others, even during the preschool years (Eisenberg & Harris, 1984), even though the preoperational nature of preschool cognitive development puts some natural limits on what is possible. By about age 4 or 5 years, the generation of alternative solutions is viewed by peers as a crucial skill, and ability to think in terms of consequences becomes increasingly important as well (Shure &

Spivack, 1980). Communication skills that become increasingly critical during early childhood include listener responsiveness, turn-taking, positive reinforcement, and the use of routines to maintain attention (Eisenberg & Harris, 1984).

In terms of friendship characteristics and activities during early childhood, there is a gradual shift from parallel play to coordinated play, which requires more skill but is also more satisfying socially. Gottman (1983) suggested that the highest level of coordinated play is nonstereotyped fantasy play, a level that provides a means for practicing social roles and a possible way to resolve some fears (Gottman, 1986). The theme of play in early childhood friendships can be summarized as the maximization of excitement, entertainment, and affect during play (Parker & Gottman, 1989). Finally, friendships during early childhood are mostly transitory. Young children tend to define friends on the basis of playing together, physical proximity, and common expectations, activities, and possessions.

Social Skills Development During Middle Childhood

The period of middle childhood begins about the time a child enters first grade and extends into early adolescence. Agewise, we consider this period to extend from about age 7 to 13 years. From a developmental theory framework, children at this age level are in the *concrete operations* stage of cognitive development (Piaget, 1983). This stage is characterized by the ability to use simple logic, but mental operations are performed only on images of tangible objects and actual events. In other words, the ability for abstract symbolic thinking is usually not yet developed.

During the concrete operations stage, many principles are mastered that were formerly elusive to the preschool-age child. *Reversibility* (observing that an action may be reversible), *decentration* (focusing on objects or tasks holistically rather than on one part only), and *conservation* (understanding that a change in appearance does not always constitute a change in quantity) are perhaps the best known of the concrete operational skills newly acquired at this stage.

Social development during middle childhood is characterized by learning to function beyond the family in a broader social context. Erikson (1963) referred to this developmental stage in psychosocial terms as *industry versus inferiority*, a stage that refers to development alternating between self-competence based on mastery of these new challenges and feelings of low self-esteem based on failure. Most elementary-age children make moral decisions with more complexity than they did during early childhood. Kohlberg (1969) suggested that these children reach a stage referred to as *conventional morality*, wherein rules and social conventions become more important in the decision-making process than just the immediate consequences of actions.

In terms of social skills, children become increasingly capable of affective and cognitive perspective-taking during the elementary school years. As they move from the early grades toward adolescence, most children become better able to understand that "people's personalities and identities are coherent and continuing and that others' inner states go beyond the immediate, observable situation" (Eisenberg & Harris, 1984, p. 269).

During middle childhood, the ability to generate alternative solutions to potential social problems becomes an increasingly important social skill. For example, one might expect that a young child would respond to teasing from peers with a limited range of options, but an older child who displays such limited solutions to social problems becomes increasingly at risk socially. Thus, means–ends thinking tends to emerge during this period as a critical interpersonal problem-solving skill (Pelligrini, 1980). In terms of communication-related social skills, mutual attention and providing feedback continue to be important skills during middle childhood, but the appropriate use of pauses in conversation also begins to emerge as important. By the later stages of middle childhood, the use of cooperative, helpful, and positive communications (as opposed to negative communications) becomes increasingly crucial to the quality of interpersonal communications and is often an expectation of peers (Keane & Conger, 1981).

By mid-elementary school, children tend to describe friends as people who help and support each other. With this increased emphasis on support, a major change in friendship values from those of early childhood has occurred. Specific traits become more important for friendships during this period, as do such variables as trust, loyalty, and admiration (Eisenberg & Harris, 1984). Goldstein and Gallagher (1992) summarized changes in friendship patterns during middle childhood by stating that the overall theme in the period revolves around inclusion by peers. Children tend to become increasingly concerned about self-presentation and the desire to avoid rejection.

Entrance into the elementary school opens up an increasingly complex social world. Children begin to form peer groups that differ in social status and power (Hartup, 1984). The use of humor, gossip, negative evaluation, and teasing increase. Although the increase in these social behaviors sometimes has negative social consequences, it also may serve the purpose of strengthening friendships and specific peer groups (Parker & Gottman, 1989). Obviously, as the use of specific forms of social communication increases, so must the complexity of a child's language and communication skills.

Social Skills Development During Adolescence

As typically defined, adolescence begins at about age 13 (12 to 14) years and ends at about the time that adult responsibilities are assumed. Obviously, great individual variation exists when the latter stages of adolescence are reached. Some individuals may assume many adult responsibilities and become relatively independent by age 17, whereas others may continue to be partially or fully dependent on their parents well into chronological adulthood. For purposes of this discussion, the adolescent developmental research reviewed in this section is limited to the upper teenage years.

According to Piaget (1983), the beginning of adolescence coincides with the *formal operations* stage of cognitive development. Youth in this stage characteristically develop the ability to use formal logic and to apply mental operations to abstract as well as concrete objects. Adolescents tend to become increasingly systematic in their problem-solving efforts, gradually reducing reliance on quick trial-and-error methods. It is important to recognize that not all persons reach this stage of cognitive development. Thus, persons with impaired cognitive functioning or related developmental disabilities may never acquire these higher level cognitive skills.

During adolescence, some persons reach what Kohlberg (1969) described as *postconventional moral reasoning*. This higher level of moral reasoning is characterized by making decisions about right or wrong based on abstract internalized values rather than relying solely on conventions, expectations, or external consequences as moral guides. As with the formal operations cognitive stage, some individuals may never reach this higher level of moral decision making.

Most of the Western industrialized world has adopted the notion that adolescence is a period of psychosocial storm and stress. Although there is considerable disagreement in the psychological literature on the universality of such adolescent turmoil (Merrell, 1994a), Erikson's (1963) widely influential work has suggested that the *identity versus confusion* crisis presents a major developmental task during this period. Although individuals solve this task in differing ways, and some put off the task until later in life, beginning to develop a sense of who they really are and what they are all about appears to be central to adolescent development.

Social skills development during adolescence is characterized by the increasing complexity of social expectations, demands, and abilities. As their cognitive and social capabilities mature, adolescents become capable of a higher level of cognitive and emotional perspective-taking. These advanced cognitive–emotional skills attained by many adolescents might be characterized as the formal development of empathy. Interestingly, in social skills assessment research conducted by Walker, Steiber, and Eisert (1991), a separate *empathy* factor of skills emerged through multivariate analysis on the adolescent version of the Walker–McConnell Scale of Social Competence and School Adjustment. This factor was not identified on the elementary-age version of the same scale, a finding that corroborates the notion that the advanced cognitive and affective skills needed for empathy do not tend to emerge until adolescence. The advanced language development that occurs by adolescence allows individuals to increase their complexity and number of supportive social communication statements (Eisenberg & Harris, 1984). Thus, the use of appropriate verbal comforting strategies becomes an important and expected social skill by the end of adolescence. As mentioned earlier, the generation of alternate solutions for solving social problems becomes an increasingly important social skill during middle childhood. During adolescence, the generation of alternate solutions to social problems becomes even more important, and advanced means–ends thinking becomes one of the most important interpersonal–cognitive problem-solving skills (Pelligrini, 1980).

Adolescent friendship patterns also are characterized by increasing complexity. By adolescence, *friends* become defined as individuals with close, mutual relationships who help each other with psychological problems, are open and sensitive, and do not cause problems for each other (Eisenberg & Harris, 1984). Being exclusive in a friendship arrangement and being "nice" become less important (Selman, 1981). Friendships seem to become more autonomous during this period, although increasing interdependence relating to psychological support tends to occur simultaneously. Gottman (1983, 1986) proposed that adolescent friendships are typified by the process of self-exploration and self-definition. According to Gottman, adolescents use friendships to explore who they are, what they believe, and what they will become through complex verbal interactions in a supportive environment. Thus, the adolescent quest for personal identity Erikson's (1969) seems to take place in the context of adolescent friendship patterns.

GENDER AND ETHNOCULTURAL FACTORS IN SOCIAL SKILLS DEVELOPMENT

In addition to age, a child's gender and cultural–ethnic background are variables that may have a substantial impact on social skills development. In this section, we give an overview of some evidence on what roles these variables may play in the acquisition and performance of social skills during childhood and adolescence. First, we explore the concept of gender as it relates to social skills development. Then, we explore culture and ethnicity as highly related factors in the social skills development process.

Gender and Social Skills Development

Ask a group of parents or teachers about the role of gender in the development of children's social skills and certain stereotypes will begin to emerge. Some stereotypes most likely to be heard include the following:

1. Boys are more likely to behave aggressively and competitively in social situations.

2. Girls are more likely to behave in a cooperative and helpful manner in social situations.

3. Girls prefer to interact socially through talking.

4. Boys prefer to interact socially through hands-on physical activities.

5. Girls are usually better than boys at adapting to structured social expectations of teachers in preschool and elementary settings, such as sitting still and listening during story time, complying with school rules, and cooperating with the teacher.

Of course, stereotypes, as everybody knows, are both intriguing and dangerous. They are intriguing because they often seem to be based on some common kernels of truth and are sometimes backed by evidence. They are dangerous because we strongly tend to overgeneralize our stereotypes to individuals and situations for which they do not apply, and because our tendency to use stereotypes often alters our expectations, limits the freedom individuals are given, and shapes our own behavior to ensure that these stereotypes are perpetuated over time. These stereotyped gender differences in social behavior also raise some poignant questions: Are any of them based on sound empirical evidence? If any of these stereotypes hold true, to what can the be attributed?

With the preceding caveat and questions in mind, the discussion now moves into the arena of gender as a factor in social skills of children and adolescents. This area is both fascinating and controversial. Because gender is important as a primary shaping force in human development, it would be careless to discuss the developmental factors in social skills without considering gender.

Environment and Biology: Influences in Social–Gender Development. At no time does the "nature versus nurture" argument generate more discussion than when it is applied to gender differences, whether real or imagined. To the modern behavioral scientist, this issue is not merely a question of whether nature (biology) or nurture (environment) is responsible for gender differences. Current thinking and evidence suggest that both biology and environment play important roles in social development. Given Bandura's (1978) theory of triadic reciprocality, it also may be assumed that these two factors may be interactive and mutually influential.

The evidence supporting environmental factors as an influence in gender differences in social behavior is compelling. In a review of the evidence in this area, Etaugh (1983) identified several empirically supportable environmental variables that are likely to influence gender-related social behavior development: adult behavior with infants labeled as girls or boys; the behavior of parents with their own infants; toys provided by parents; and differential reinforcement of sex-appropriate play by parents, teachers, and peers. In each of these areas, there is substantial evidence suggesting that strong environmental, gender-based factors are in place that shape our social behaviors and skills.

A most frequently researched area in this regard is the general category of adult behavior directed at children. Findings show that even when interacting with infants, adults are likely to treat them differentially according to gender. For example, adults of both sexes are likely to interact with infants using sex-typed toys based on the gender of the infant, not the adult (Bell & Carver, 1980). In their landmark review of gender differences, Maccoby and Jacklin (1974) summarized the evidence suggesting that parents of both sexes are likely to elicit more gross motor behavior from their sons, and more vocalized responses from their daughters.

Differential sex-typing of materials and behaviors seems to have tangible behavioral consequences. Several studies show that young children seem to "perform better and spend more time and effort on a variety of tasks labeled sex appropriate than on those labeled sex inappropriate" (Etaugh, 1983, p. 9). Adults (both parents and teachers) are also likely to reinforce "sex appropriate" play differentially and even to punish "sex inappropriate" play differentially as well (Fagot, 1974, 1981). Of course, adults are not the only actors in this process. Studies also show that peers are likely to engage in the same patterns of differential reinforcement and punishment for behaviors considered to be gender related (Fagot & Patterson, 1969).

Thus, a large variety of environmental influences most certainly plays an important role in the development of social behavior in general and social skills in particular. According to the five gender stereotypes of children's social behavior discussed earlier, it is clear that both environmental stimuli and social consequences are likely to differentially shape boys and girls into patterns consistent with these stereotypes.

Some evidence also supports the influences of biologic factors on gender differential social behavior development. However, the biologic evidence, in our view, is less compelling than the environmental evidence. The somewhat tenuous strength of evidence in this area is typified by a comment of Harway and Moss (1983), who reviewed a wide variety of evidence regarding biologic factors in sex differences in social behavior and concluded that "many of the areas that we have examined . . . do not suggest a clear-cut biological basis for sex differences in behavior. With the exception of research on sex hormones, there is no consistent evidence that nature causes sex differences" (p. 39).

Harway and Moss (1983) summarized their review of evidence on biologic factors by noting two major consistent findings:

1. Sex hormones seem to play a role in shaping sex differences in behavior in some areas, particularly as related to activity level and aggression. Early exposure to sex hormones may predispose individuals to engage in gender-

consistent behavior, and the interaction of sex hormones and brain cells at puberty may further guide these behavioral differences. However, the extent to which sex hormones dictate gender differences in behavior is unknown.

2. "It is also not clear to what extent actual permanent bodily changes (at the cell or organ level) can occur as a result of early life experiences combined with hormonal effects" (p. 40). Although we know that there are some sex differences in brain lateralization that may have implications for social behavior, and that these differences may be biologically caused, there is also some evidence that gender-related activity preferences (which may be socialized) can likewise shape and strengthen such differences.

Harway and Moss (1983) concluded their review by stating:

Sex differences (in social behavior) most consistently seem to be the result of social factors. This includes both the different socialization experiences that males and females have and the socially determined assumptions and viewpoints of the researchers studying this area. With the exception of findings on sex hormones, very few research directions convincingly demonstrate that sex differences come from sources other than societal. (p. 40)

In a related vein, Maccoby and Jacklin (1974) demonstrated that engagement in aggressive behavior was the most clear and consistent social behavioral difference between the sexes. Many other researchers have concluded that if there is a biologically caused sex difference in social behavior, aggressiveness is the most likely candidate, and hormonal influences are the most likely cause. But even here, caution in interpretation must be used because there is a strong body of evidence on environmental influences suggesting that gender differential tendencies in aggression are also socialized.

In summary, both environmental and biologic influences have been documented in the area of gender differences in social behavior. The evidence supporting environmental influences seems to be both larger and stronger, but it must be assumed that the two forces interact in a mutually influential or reciprocal manner. With an understanding of the possible causes of gender differences in social behavior during the developmental period, the discussion now turns to some specifics of what these behavioral differences are.

Social Skills and Gender During Childhood and Adolescence. Regardless of the reason for gender differences, a substantial body of evidence from the field of developmental psychology suggests that boys and girls are likely to have somewhat differing patterns of developing and displaying social skills and related social behaviors. As discussed already, patterns of gender differential social development have been observed to emerge even before the preschool years begin. Through a combination of influences (Eisenberg, 1983), toddlers develop sex role adoptions and preferences in toys and forms of play behavior (Eisenberg, Murray, & Hite, 1982). At an early age, boys as compared with girls are more likely to engage in play behaviors that involve higher motor activity levels, less verbal behavior, and higher levels of aggressiveness. Thus, even the earliest peer-related social interactions are often characterized by the somewhat differential use of social skills, with boys relying more on physical social activities and girls relying more on verbal interactions. As Eisenberg (1983) stated:

> Once a child has identified his or her own gender status, the child uses the label "boy" or "girl" to organize his or her own behavior. This occurs because, according to the cognitive development perspective, children value people and things like themselves. Thus a girls says to herself, "I am a girl; therefore I like to do girl things" (and vice versa for boys). To learn what are the appropriate sex-role behaviors, the child then looks for same-sex models and imitates their stereotyped behaviors. (p. 57)

By the preschool years, some social skill gender behavior patterns tend to emerge, some predictable and others not. In a review of literature on this topic, Johnson and Roopnarine (1983) noted that the typical preference of boys for highly active physical play continues, as does the likelihood that girls will engage in more passive and sedentary play activities. Social play behavior at this age is also more likely than not to occur in same-sex groupings. From here, though, the evidence on gender differences becomes more complex.

Johnson and Roopnarine (1983) contended that the "overwhelming weight of evidence suggests that preschool-aged girls exhibit a greater tendency to engage in constructive play behaviors than do boys and that boys are more disposed toward functional play" (p. 197). An example of functional play is the appropriate use of a toy (e.g., blowing bubbles or riding a big wheel), whereas constructive play involves using objects according to a plan that has some end result (e.g., completing a puzzle). Thus, preschool-age girls may be more likely to engage in social play behavior that is more goal directed and sequentially organized.

Some evidence suggests that girls are more likely than boys over time to engage in fantasy social play (Mathews, 1977; McLoyd, 1980). However, evidence is mixed concerning the level of social interaction during play. In their review, Johnson and Roopnarine (1983) pointed out contradictory findings with regard to gender differences in the amount of social play, parallel play, positive social interactions, or positive emotionality exhibited during play.

Although the evidence regarding gender and social skills at the preschool level is sometimes confusing, the majority of evidence suggests that teachers and parents of preschool-age children are more likely to rate girls as having higher overall levels of social skills than boys. For example, in the development of the Preschool and Kindergarten Behavior Scales, the first author of this volume found that the mean scores of girls on all three social skills subscales as well as their total social skills score were significantly higher than those for boys, whether the ratings were done by parents or teachers (Merrell, 1994b). This study was based on a large ($N = 2,855$) nationwide sample of subjects. This gender-related finding is relatively consistent across different assessment measures and studies, which tend to show that, as a group, girls receive higher global social skills ratings than do boys at the preschool level.

Gender differences in teacher and parent ratings of children's social skills tend to continue from preschool into the school-age years, and if anything, become more pronounced. For example, in the development of the School Social Behavior Scales (Merrell, 1993a, 1993b), a social skills and antisocial behavior rating scale targeted at students in the K–12 range, Merrell found that teacher ratings of girls' social skills and antisocial behavior were significantly more positive than those ratings for boys, based on a large ($N = 1,858$), nationwide sample of subjects. Interestingly, even though both were significant, the gender effect found with the normative group of the School Social Behavior Scales was even more substantial than that found with the normative group of the Preschool and Kindergarten Behavior Scales. If this trend is to be generalized, it suggests that some modest yet significant gender differences in social skills and antisocial behaviors begin to emerge during the preschool years and become even more pronounced during the elementary and secondary school years. The effect of this trend is that, as a group, girls are typically rated by independent raters as having higher levels of interpersonal and self-management skills and lower levels of antisocial, aggressive, and disruptive social behaviors than boys, a finding that has been documented by researchers using other nationwide samples and measures (Center & Wascom, 1986; Gresham, Elliott, & Black, 1987; Merrell, Merz, Johnson, & Ring, 1992).

In summary, the relationship between gender and social skills during the developmental period is complex. The most widely replicated findings show that (a) in early childhood boys tend to prefer social play that involves physical activity (including aggression), whereas girls are more likely to adopt social play styles that are more passive and sedentary; (b) the social play behaviors of young girls tend to be more goal-oriented or constructive than those of young boys, who are more likely to engage in functional social play behaviors; and (c) from early childhood through adolescence, girls are more likely to be rated as having higher levels of social skills and lower levels of antisocial behaviors than boys. The causes or influences of these gender differences appear to be complex and multidimensional. In this regard, there is some evidence for biological influences, but even more evidence for social learning influences. Finally, it would be remiss not to restate a simple truth: There tends to be more variation in social skills within rather than between gender groups. The findings of gender differences are important and interesting, but they are based on group rather than individual research. Thus, one must be careful not to generalize these findings to all individuals.

Ethnocultural Factors and Social Skills Development

The concept of *culture* is exceedingly broad. A *cultural group* is generally considered to be "any group of people who identify or associate with one another on the basis of some common purpose, need, or similarity of background" (Axelson, 1993, p. 3). Culture may include such diverse factors as social structure, kinship, ethnicity, and socioeconomic status. The concept of *ethnicity* is more specific than that of culture. Persons from a given ethnic group are those similar in national or ancestral origin. Both culture and ethnicity are likely to be related in a complex manner. For example, a child identified as White on census forms may be ethnically Italian, but the child may or may not have been raised in a cultural environment in which he or she identifies or associates with others on the basis of their ethnicity. In this section, the term *ethnocultural* is used, which refers to a diversity of cultural influences, but predominantly includes ethnicity or national origin as a cultural factor.

Like gender, ethnocultural influences appear to be important factors to study in the development and performance of children's social skills. Given the increasingly ethnoculturally diverse composition of the U.S. population and the strong emphasis placed on this variable in psychology and education in recent years, it would be expected that ethnocultural influences on children's social skills have been widely studied and discussed. Surprisingly, this assumption appears to be unfounded. In conducting a literature review of the PSYCHLIT and ERIC databases, using the keywords, *social skills, children,* and either *ethnicity* or *racial differences,* only a small handful of pertinent titles could be found. When the population for the literature search was expanded to include all ages, a few more titles appeared, although most were not relevant. Given this general lack of evidence on ethnocultural influences on children's social skills development, we must use caution in drawing conclusions.

The little evidence available in this area is complex and sometimes difficult to interpret. Most of this evidence can be divided into three types of findings. First, it is likely that the ethnocultural background of parents affects their valuing of various social skills, and thus how importantly they regard transmitting these skills to their children. Along these lines, O'Reilly, Tokuno, and Ebata (1986) found significant effects for ethnicity of the rater in comparing groups of Asian American and European American mothers who were asked to rank the importance of eight common social skills.

Second, it appears that there may be a complex interaction between race or ethnicity of raters and their objective evaluation of subjects' social skills. For example, Lethermon et al. (1984) found that similarity of race between evaluators and subjects appeared to affect raters' objectivity in evaluating children's social skills using a role-playing test: The most socially valid evaluations occurred when the evaluators were dissimilar in age and race from the subjects. In a related study, Lethermon, Williamson, Moody, and Wozniak (1986) found that Black and White raters provided significantly different ratings on some behavioral social skills categories, and that they differentially rated Black and White children in ratings of overall social skills and smiling. This finding of racial differences in rating social skill behaviors also has been corroborated with adult subjects in an inpatient setting (Turner, Beidel, Herson, & Bellack, 1984).

Third, in terms of large, nationwide datasets of child social skill behaviors, only minimal differences based on ethnocultural factors are usually found. For example, Achenbach and Edelbrock (1981) obtained social competency data by administering checklists to parents of 2,600 referred and nonreferred children, of whom half were White and Black. Only minimal differences were found when the data were examined using race as an independent variable, and these differences were even smaller when socioeconomic status was controlled in the analyses. In developing the School Social Behavior Scales and the Preschool and Kindergarten Behavior Scales, the first author of this volume obtained similar results: Extremely small correlations (generally in the range of about .08 to .15) were found between race or ethnicity of a rated child and his or her social skills or problem behavior ratings (Merrell, 1993b, 1994b). In summary, the relationship between ethnocultural factors and the development of social skills appears to be modest, but it is complicated by the finding that race or ethnicity of a rater or observer may be an important variable in how social skills are valued and assessed. Obviously, much more evidence is needed in this area before definitive conclusions are warranted.

Even though the little evidence available in this area is often complex and confusing, it must be assumed that ethnocultural factors are potentially strong forces in the development of children's social skills. Perhaps the best way to make this point is by an illustration of possible ethnocultural factors in interpersonal communication styles—a key element in social skills performance. Sue and Sue (1990) noted that in interpersonal communication, important differences may exist in how people are socialized based on ethnocultural factors. For example, the degree of eye contact and the desired amount of physical distance between the communicators may be issues in this regard. Sue and Sue noted that White U.S. Americans make eye contact with the speaker about 80% of the time, but tend to avoid eye contact about 50% of the time when speaking to others. This is in contrast to the eye contact patterns of many African Americans, who tend to make more eye contact when speaking and less frequent eye contact when listening. In contrast, American Indians are more likely to have indirect eye contact when speaking or listening, whereas Asian Americans and Hispanics are more likely to avoid eye contact altogether when speaking to persons they perceive to have high status. Because many social skills training programs include eye contact as an important skill in starting a conversion, the ethnocultural implications are obvious.

Sue and Sue (1990) noted that there are also cultural differences in terms of comfortable physical proximity or distance between persons. For Latin Americans, Africans, African Americans, Indonesians, South Americans, Arabs, and the French, a much closer physical stance between communicators is normal than most Anglos would comfortably allow. Although there is scant empirical research to support these generalities, they should not be discounted because they have obvious implications for the development of children's social skills based on their ethnocultural background. Some of the ethnoculturally based aspects of interpersonal communication styles among cultural groups in the United States are reflected in the information presented in Table 2.1.

It must be stressed again that variation within groups is almost always larger than variation between groups. The information presented in this section regarding possible group differences in social behaviors based on ethnocultural factors is used to heighten sensitivity rather than to cause inaccurate generalities.

TABLE 2.1
Generalized Communication Style Differences
Between Major Cultural Groups in the United States:
Overt Activity Dimension, Nonverbal and Verbal Communication

American Indians	Asian Americans and Hispanics	Whites	African Americans
1. Speak softly/slower	1. Speak softly	1. Speak loud/fast to control	1. Speak with affect
2. Indirect gaze when listening or speaking	2. Avoidance of eye contact when listening or speaking to high-status persons	2. Greater eye contact when listening	2. Direct eye contact (prolonged) when speaking, but less when listening
3. Interject less, seldom offer encouraging communication	3. Similar rules	3. Head nods, nonverbal markers	3. Interrupt (turn-taking) when can
4. Delayed auditory (silence)	4. Mild delay	4. Quick responding	4. Quicker responding
5. Manner of expression low-key, indirect	5. Low-keyed, indirect	5. Objective, task-oriented	5. Affective, emotional, interpersonal

From *Counseling the Culturally Different* (2nd ed.), by D. W. Sue and D. Sue copyright © 1990, John Wiley & Sons, Inc. Reprinted by Permission of John Wiley & Sons, Inc.

SPECIAL EDUCATION
DISABILITY CATEGORIES AND
SOCIAL SKILLS DEVELOPMENT

The discussion in chapter 1 demonstrated the strong link that exists between various forms of child psychopathology and deficits in social skills acquisition or performance. This chapter concludes with a similar exploration into the link between social skills development and some of the most common educational disability categories under which children receive special education services. Because about 12% of children in U.S. schools receive special education services, and because social skill and peer relationship problems are common in this population, it is essential to consider the developmental aspects of social skills deficits vis-à-vis the more prominent disability classification categories. Specifically, this chapter reviews and analyzes the body of evidence on children's social skills vis-à-vis four common special education service categories: learning disabled, seriously emotionally disturbed, mentally retarded, and speech–language disorders. These categories should be considered as developmental variables for a number of reasons, but perhaps the most prominent reason is that they are typically manifest during the developmental period and may adversely affect educational and social development.

Social Skills and Learning Disabilities

Even though most attention paid to conceptualizations of learning disabilities (LD) has focused on cognitive, academic, or neurological components of the disability, there is also a strong historic and empirical connection with LD and social skills problems. Learning disabilities in children have been conceptualized, assessed, and labeled a number of different ways over the years. During the 1950s and 1960s, practitioners and researchers relied on quasineurological explanations for LD and frequently identified the problem through observation of various neurological "soft signs" such as impulsivity, distractibility, staring blankly, and the like. The popularity of this quasineurological approach to LD led to the development of several perceptual processing type assessment instruments for detecting LD (e.g., the Illinois Test of Psycholinguistic Abilities). These tests tended to be based on the assumption that LD was caused by deficits in neurological–perceptual processes and that the successful treatment of LD would be found in identifying processing deficits and teaching compensatory strategies. During this era, the term *minimal brain damage* (MBD) was frequently used to describe the child with LD, which linked the learning problems to presumed underlying neurological dysfunction. Interestingly, even though most mid-1900s' conceptualizations of LD tended to focus on quasineurological factors, it was also apparent to many professionals and parents that deficits in social skills often were a key component of the disorder.

By the time the Education of All Handicapped Children Act (P.L. 94-142) was instituted by the U.S. Congress in the mid-1970s, emphasis on neurological soft signs was waning to some degree. Pragmatic educational outcome-based assessment procedures were adopted by most states by the late 1970s in response to the rather general language used to describe and define LD in the new federal law (Mercer, Hughes, & Mercer, 1985). However, the evidence for and interest in the connection between social behavior and LD continued to grow. Several federally funded research institutes for the study of LD flourished during the late 1970s and early 1980s. Two of these institutes emphasized the social behavior of children with LD as a major research strand.

Researchers at the University of Chicago Institute concluded that, compared with typical students, children with LD tend to experience greater peer rejection, to appear more hostile and defiant, and to engage in higher rates of off-task, distractible, and nonproductive behavior during instructional activities (Bryan, Pearl, Donahue, & Pflaum, 1983). At the University of Kansas Institute researchers focused on the social behavior of adolescents with LD. They concluded that as a group, adolescents with LD engage in fewer extracurricular activities, have fewer friends, and experience lower social status than their peers without LD (Schumaker, Deshler, Alley, & Warner, 1983).

By the mid- to late 1980s, the evidence and interest on the social–behavioral components of LD reached a zenith. The National Institutes of Health (NIH) established an Interagency Committee on Learning Disabilities (ICLD) to examine research priorities, projects, and findings related to LD. In its report to the U.S. Congress, the ICLD (1987) recommended a new federal definition of LD to be adopted. This proposed definition included social skills deficits as a major component of learning disabilities and even suggested that deficits in social skills alone could constitute a learning disability (LaGreca & Vaughn, 1992), even in the absence of some of the more traditionally used indicators of LD.

As the year 2000 approaches, the interest in social functioning and learning disabilities continues. This interest is typified by the popularity of social skills assessment and intervention techniques in special education programs for students with LD. Interestingly, the neurological approach to LD has made a strong comeback, although it now utilizes more sophisticated assessment and research technologies than were available during the 1950s and 1960s. This neuropsychological resurgence has resulted in some very interesting implications related to the psychosocial aspects of LD. For example, Rourke and Fuerst (1992) reviewed a series of studies conducted in their neuropsychological laboratory at the University of Windsor in Canada wherein neuropsychological subtypes of children with LD were identified. These researchers concluded that "social deficits . . . do not have a direct basis in central nervous system dysfunction; rather, these are the dependent variables that are thought to arise from basic neuropsychological deficits" (p. 361). Interestingly, children in the nonverbal learning disability subtype (NLD) seem to be particularly prone to developing social deficits and related emotional problems.

With all the interest and years of accumulated evidence concerning the social behavior of children with LD, just what is actually known? Perhaps the summary of the current state of knowledge in this area can be found in reviewing Swanson and Malone's (1992) meta-analysis of comparative studies investigating social skills and learning disabilities. This meta-analysis, perhaps the most comprehensive integrative study on social skills and LD to the present, utilized 39 studies published from 1974 to 1990 in which elementary-age children with LD were compared with children with LD along a number of social-behavioral dimensions. These 39 studies were selected from 117 studies initially identified; the remaining studies were excluded due to methodological problems. The most salient findings from this meta analysis include the followings:

1. As a group, children with LD are clearly deficient in age-appropriate social skills. In several of the studies, children with LD performed almost 1 standard deviation below their comparative peer group on measures of social skills.

2. Children with LD tend to be less well-liked and are more likely to be rejected by peers than children without LD. Social acceptance was the most frequently studied social skill variable in the meta-analysis. The average effect size difference for children with LD on measures of social acceptance was −0.79, indicating a negative difference of more than three quarters of a standard deviation from comparison peers.

3. Children with LD score consistently poorer on measures of social–emotional immaturity and personality problems than their non-LD peers.

4. Children with LD engage in a moderately higher rate of aggressive behaviors than their non-LD peers. Although the higher rate of aggression is worth noting, it was substantially less differentiating than the measures of social acceptance, general social skills, and immaturity or personality problems.

5. Children with LD engage in a moderately lower rate of on-task behaviors in academic settings than do their peers without LD.

6. Children with LD have a generally accurate perception of their social status within the classroom context. In other words, children with LD who are frequently rejected by their peers usually know that they have a low social status.

Swanson and Malone (1992) also noted that the available evidence suggests that although children with LD as a group exhibit various social–behavioral

TABLE 2.2
Average Effect-Size Estimates for Social Skills Deficits
of Students Who Are Academically at Risk or Have Disabilities

Low-Achieving	Learning Disabled	Mentally Retarded	Seriously Emotionally Disturbed
1.12	0.90	1.00	1.54

Results based on total social skills scores from teacher ratings on the Walker-McConnell Scale of Social Competence and School Adjustment and School Social Behavior Scales

Note. The effect size estimates are based on comparisons with regular education students, using data from Merrell, 1991; Merrell et al., 1992; and Merrell et al., 1993.

problems when compared with normal peers, they do not seem to differ substantially from most other groups of students with disabilities, or even from students with poor academic achievement who are not identified as having disabilities. This finding has been corroborated by research conducted by the first author of this book and his colleagues (Merrell, 1991; Merrell et al., 1992; Merrell et al., 1993) and is summarized by effect-size statistics in Table 2.2. It is important to recognize that these studies all utilized teacher ratings of social skills as the primary assessment methodology. Because social skills comprise a complex construct and because each method of behavioral assessment has certain limitations and types of error variance, the results from these studies may not generalize to situations in which other methods of assessment are used. In fact, a more recent study (Haager & Vaughn, 1995) that compared the social skills of LD students with average to high-achieving and low-achieving peers, but used a combination of assessment methods, yielded some interesting findings. These researchers found that parent ratings of social skills did not differ significantly among groups, but that teacher ratings indicated that LD and low-achieving students had poorer social skills than their peers. On social status measures, LD and low-achieving students were found to be less liked than their peers. The self-report measures indicated that LD and low achieving students rated themselves more poorly on the dimension of social cooperation than did their higher achieving peers. One of the interesting issues raised by this line of research is that both students with LD and low-achieving students without LD tend to have similarly low levels of social skills, regardless of the assessment source. Thus, it is quite possible that poor academic performance is the primary link to social skills deficits, and that the etiology or source of poor academic performance is not the primary concern.

In summary, the evidence regarding social–behavioral problems of children with LD is compelling, but does not support the notion that these problems are a primary component of LD (Swanson & Malone, 1992). The causal relationship between LD and social–behavioral problems is also still unclear at the present time.

Social Skills and Serious Emotional Disturbance

Like no other special education service classification category, the *seriously emotionally disturbed* (SED) category has social skills problems built directly into the federal definition. Section (i) of the original definition that was adopted into P.L. 94-142 by the U.S. Congress in 1975 was taken almost directly from Eli Bower's (1969) definition that sprang from his influential research on delinquent and disturbed youth in California. The first part of this definition, with italics added for emphasis by this author, reads as follows:

(i) The term means a condition exhibiting one or more of the following characteristics over a long period of time and to a marked degree, which adversely affects educational performance:

    (A) An inability to learn which cannot be explained by intellectual, sensory, or health factors;

    (B) *An inability to build or maintain satisfactory interpersonal relationships with peers and teachers;*

    (C) Inappropriate types of behavior or feelings under normal circumstances;

    (D) A general, pervasive mood of unhappiness or depression, or,

    (E) A tendency to develop physical symptoms or fears associated with school problems.

As part B of section (i) in the federal definition indicates, poor relationships with peers and teachers is a central defining component of this disability category. A child may qualify for special education services as SED solely through the demonstration of serious social skills deficits or peer relationship problems, assuming that these problems affect the child's educational performance. Although some states have slightly modified the federal definition or referred to it by another name (e.g., behavior disordered, severely behaviorally disabled), social skills and peer relationships are typically a central defining feature.

Not surprisingly, the empirical evidence describing the social–behavioral characteristics of children classified as SED and comparing them to children not so classified is compelling. Children with SED have been found to be differentiated easily from students without disabilities by their high rates of engagement in various maladaptive social–emotional behaviors (Stumme, Gresham, & Scott, 1982; Vaughn, 1987), and by their significant rates of social rejection from peers (Hollinger, 1987).

Although common sense and a fair amount of evidence suggest that children with SED have significant social skills deficits in comparison with typical children, much less is known about how children with SED fare when compared with children who have other types of disabilities. Although some policy advocates in the field of special education have argued for eliminating categorical service delivery breakdowns between SED, LD, and mild mental retardation because these groups are presumed to have more similarity than difference, some compelling evidence indicates otherwise. Research conducted by Merrell and his colleagues regarding the social skills patterns of SED students in comparison with regular education, low achieving, and other disability group students suggests that although low-achieving, learning disabled, and mildly mentally retarded students all exhibit social-skill deficits in comparison with students in regular education, the severity of SED students' deficits places them in their own pantheon of dysfunction.

In one study (Merrell et al., 1992) teacher ratings of social skills from the Walker–McConnell Scale of Social Competence and School Adjustment (Walker & McConnell, 1995) were utilized with 566 elementary-age students from different educational groups. As expected, students in regular education had significantly higher social skills ratings than any other student group. When the data were studied more closely, it was found that LD, low-achieving, and mildly mentally retarded student groups all had similar levels of moderate social skills deficits. The SED student group was significantly lower in social skills ratings than any of the other groups. They were nearly 2 standard deviations lower than the regular education students and nearly 1 standard deviation lower than the LD, low-achieving, and mentally retarded students on total social skills scores. The SED group was the only nonregular education group that could be correctly classified through a discriminant function analysis based on their social skills ratings with a high degree of accuracy. Interestingly, a particular cluster of social skills deficits emerged as the critical factor in isolating the SED students from the other groups: skill deficits relating to empathy, sensitivity to others, and self-restraint.

In another study (Merrell et al., 1993), teacher ratings of student social behavior were obtained from the *School Social Behavior Scales* (Merrell, 1993b) with LD, SED, and mildly mentally retarded students. All three groups of students with disabilities evidenced significant social–behavioral problems in comparison with regular education students. Again, the SED group emerged as having by far the most intensive social–behavioral problems, both in terms of social skills deficits and excesses in antisocial behavior. Interestingly, the social skills area that best separated the groups were skills related to self-management, whereas the antisocial behavior cluster that best separated the groups was a constellation of disruptive and demanding behaviors.

In summary, the evidence regarding social skills deficits of SED children is even more compelling than that for LD children. Social skills deficits, an essential feature of the federal SED definition, tend to be more pronounced with SED children than with any other educational group. These severe deficits in social skills of SED children tend also to be accompanied by significant excesses in antisocial behavior: violation of rules, intimidation of others, physical and verbal aggression, and destruction of property. We might say that, by definition, SED children are those whose maladaptive social behaviors set them distinctly apart from others in a very negative manner.

Social Skills and MR

The most recent definition of *mental retardation* (MR) from the American Association on Mental Retardation (AAMR, 1992) includes deficits in social skills as a potential primary definitional component of the disability. Like the SED definition, this definition of MR assumes that deficits in social skills may be a key component of the disability for some, but not necessarily for all individuals. The AAMR's brief definition is as follows:

> Mental retardation refers to substantial limitations in present functioning. It is characterized by significantly subaverage intellectual functioning, existing concurrently with related limitations in two or more of the following applicable adaptive skill areas: communication, self-care, home living, *social skills*, community use, self-direction, health and safety, functional academics, leisure, and work. Mental retardation manifests before age 18. (p. 5, emphasis added)

The AAMR also has provided an operational definition of what is meant by *adaptive social skills* in this definition. Their operationalization of social skills reads as follows:

> Skills related to social exchanges with other individuals, including initiating, interacting, and terminating interaction with others; receiving and responding to pertinent situational cues; recognizing feelings; providing positive and negative feedback; regulating one's own behavior; being aware of peers and peer acceptance; gauging the amount and type of interaction with others; assisting others; forming and fostering of friendships and love; coping with demands from others; making choices; sharing; understanding honesty and fairness; controlling impulses; conforming conduct to laws; violating rules and laws; and displaying appropriate socio-sexual behavior. (p. 40)

Therefore, assuming that the other definitional criteria are met, an individual would need to exhibit limitations in at least two out of nine adaptive skill areas, of which social skills is one, to be considered MR. If a functional limitation in adaptive social skills is just one of several potential areas to consider in MR, then just how prevalent and significant are social skills deficits in MR?

The evidence in this area is relatively clear, although we must remember that most of this evidence is based on group rather than individual research. By and large, individuals from essentially all age ranges (children, adolescents, and adults) who have MR tend to exhibit substantial limitations or deficits in social skills. In their review of issues surrounding the social skills of individuals with mild disabilities, Gresham and Reschly (1987b) suggested that deficits in social skills tend to be a key component in children with MR, and that these deficits must be an element of assessment, classification, and intervention planning. Gresham (1982) noted that children with MR tend to be rejected by peers to a greater degree than children without disabilities. Parke, Tappe, Carmeto, and Gaylord-Ross (1990) identified a lack of social support as a major problem for adolescents and adults with MR, and it is reasonable to assume that social skills deficits may play a critical role in this problem. Numerous other studies have demonstrated that groups of individuals with MR tend to show substantial deficits in adaptive social skills when compared with groups of individuals who do not have disabilities.

It is one thing to demonstrate that individuals with MR tend to have deficits in adaptive social skills in comparison with the normal population, but making sense of these deficits in comparison with other groups of individuals with mild to moderate disabilities is a more complex matter. The comparative social skills studies conducted by the first author and his colleagues have already been addressed in terms of children with LD and SED (Merrell, 1991; Merrell et al., 1992; Merrell et al., 1993). These latter two studies included children with MR in the multigroup social skills comparisons. These children, although rated as having substantial deficits in social skills generally, were at the same general level of social skills as low-achieving and LD students but showed higher levels of social skills than SED students. Thus, it can be said that social skills deficits are a typical complicating factor for students with mild MR, but these deficits appear to be no worse than those exhibited by students with LD, or even students without identified disabilities who are substantially low in their performance of academic skills. Moreover, the social skills deficits associated with MR, like those associated with LD and low academic achievement, tend to be less severe than the social skills associated with SED. Therefore, some caution is needed in interpreting social skills deficits of children and adolescents with MR. It is unclear where the causal link in these deficits exists, and it is possible that there is a stronger association between poor social skills performance and academic rather than intellectual deficiencies.

Social Skills and Speech–Language Disorders

Speech and language disorders include a somewhat diverse array of problems ranging from articulation and fluency difficulties to problems in comprehending spoken language. Next to LD, this group of disorders comprises one of the largest special education service categories, particularly in the primary and elementary grades. Most of the research on social skills problems and speech–language disorders has been with the category referred to as *specific language impairment* (SLI; as opposed to articulation disorders), a developmental language disability that is not attributable to any other type of disability condition. Children with SLI typically appear to have normal sensory, intellectual, neurological, emotional, and motor functioning. They generally test within normal limits on measures of visual and hearing acuity. A number of other terms have been used to describe this problem, including these: developmental aphasia, childhood aphasia, congenital aphasia, language delay, and specific developmental language disorder. The Individuals with Disabilities Act recognizes SLI as an appropriate special education service category, and the various states have operationalized this category using a number of different terms. Although the terminology used to categorize and describe the symptoms of SLI has been variable, the term *SLI* is currently most widely used (National Institutes of Health, 1990). Fewer than 1% of children nationwide are thought to have SLI. Many children identified as having SLI during their preschool years develop academic learning problems and may be incorrectly identified as learning disabled (Goldstein & Gallagher, 1992).

Although the social–behavioral aspects of SLI have not been studied nearly as extensively as they have with LD, SED, and MR, evidence is mounting that social and peer difficulties are a common component of this disability. Goldstein and Gallagher (1992) noted that social–peer problems stemming from SLI are a direct result of the consequences of limited peer access. In other words, the communication difficulties inherent in SLI isolate children from their peers. This isolation then stands as a barrier to the critical communication-based social development tasks that are normally part of childhood: effective interpersonal perspective-taking, code switching, communicative appropriateness and politeness, and the general role of communication in daily social life. Thus, the SLI child may not obtain a sense of social support and self-esteem from peer relationships. It is difficult to overestimate the critical importance that communication in peer relationships has in the overall social–emotional development of a child. For example, Bruner (1977) suggested that communicative interactions with peers during childhood are analogous to mother–child communicative interactions during early development. From preschool age on, peer relationships play an increasingly important role in social development. If there are substantial barriers to peer interaction such as those that may result from SLI, it is obvious that the affected child is increasingly at risk for developing social skills deficits.

The social skills deficits commonly seen in children with SLI are essentially language based. Research in this area has shown that such children are more likely than typical peers to experience difficulty taking turns in conversation (Craig & Evans, 1989), exhibit impaired commenting and requesting (Gallagher & Craig, 1984), respond poorly or inappropriately to requests from others (Brinton & Fujiki, 1982), and fail to make appropriate acknowledgements of comments by other children (Craig & Gallagher, 1986). A perusal of Table 1.2 in chapter 1 clearly shows how these types of language problems could impair social interactions. The social skills categories of self-related behaviors (e.g., expressing feelings), task-related behaviors (e.g., asking and answering questions, classroom discussions) and interpersonal behaviors (e.g., greeting others, making conversation, gaining attention) stand out as obvious potential problem areas for children with SLI.

In summary, children with SLI constitute a group that is at risk for developing social skills deficits and related peer problems. Although less is known about the specific and comparative aspects of social skills of SLI as compared with the other disability categories that have been discussed (LD, SED, MR), substantial evidence shows that this language-based disability results in potential impairment of virtually any language-based social skill, of which there are many.

Social Skills and Full Inclusion of Students With Disabilities

Having demonstrated that children and adolescents who receive special education services because of various mild to moderate disabilities are at heightened risk for exhibiting social skills deficits, it is appropriate to conclude with a discussion of some of the practical challenges presented by this disability–deficit link.

When the original federal special education law was passed by the U.S. Congress in 1975, it contained an important provision that students with disabilities should receive special education services in the least restrictive environment. The presumed meaning of this concept was that students with disabilities should be educated to the greatest extent possible in settings where they would otherwise be served if they did not have a disability. From the enactment of this law in 1977 until about the mid-1980s, the concept of *mainstreaming* such students in regular education settings was widely used to ensure that the requirements of this law were met. By the mid-1980s, the so-called *Regular Education Initiative* was advocated by the U.S. Department of Education as an effort to expand the concept of the least restrictive environment and to increase the percentage of time that students with disabilities were educated in regular educational settings. Since the mid-1980s, efforts and advocacy in this vein have taken the form of the full-inclusion movement (Stainback & Stainback, 1984, 1992). The rationale behind full inclusion is that special education and regular education should be merged into one seamless system, and that students with disabilities of virtually any type or severity should be educated in regular education settings.

Before discussing the implications of social skills deficits of students with disabilities vis-à-vis the concept of full inclusion, it is important to recognize that the concept of full inclusion is controversial and that there is no widespread professional agreement behind it. Strong advocates of the full inclusion concept (e.g., the Stainbacks) have been challenged by a number of other researchers, writers, and policymakers within the field who contend that the full-inclusion movement is logically flawed (MacMillan, Gresham, & Forness, 1996), has little or no empirical support (Fuchs & Fuchs, 1994), and may damage efforts to provide optimal services to students with disabilities (Kauffman, 1993, 1995). Therefore, when social skills deficits and training as related to full inclusion are considered, it is important to recognize that the concept may be in a state of flux.

Notwithstanding some professional disagreement about full inclusion, two important issues regarding social skills and full inclusion of students with disabilities are pertinent for discussion. First, there is substantial evidence that the significant deficits in social skills exhibited by many students with disabilities acts as a formidable barrier and obstacle to their successful placement in mainstream educational settings. One of the major premises of the full-inclusion concept is that placement in regular classrooms will provide socially deficient students with better models of behavior and allow them, through the observational learning process, naturally to acquire more adaptive social behaviors and thus increase their social acceptance by peers (Snell, 1991). But empirical evidence in this area indicates something quite different from this desired result. In a review of the literature on mainstreaming, Gresham (1982) found that mainstreamed students with disabilities are less accepted and more socially rejected by their peers, that social interactions between students with and without disabilities occurred with relatively low frequency and tended to be negative in quality, and that there is little or no evidence indicating that placement in regular education environments alone provides positive social modeling effects. Furthermore, Gottlieb (1975, 1981) concluded that when placed in classroom environments with socially skilled and typical students, those with social deficiencies tend to be poorly received and liked less over time. This and other such evidence points to the troubling proposition that mere placement in regular educational environments will not help children and adolescents with social skill deficits to improve their skills and receive better social acceptance (Gresham & MacMillan, in press; Kauffman, 1995).

On a more optimistic note, ample evidence indicates that well designed and executed social skills training interventions may help to overcome some of these social obstacles and increase the probabilities that students with disabilities and significant social deficits may be successfully included in regular education settings. Gresham (1981) reviewed the research in this area prior to 1980 and concluded that social skills training represented a potentially effective approach to successful mainstreaming (or inclusion) of students with disabilities.

Interestingly, most of the identified research indicating that students with disabilities and social skills deficits can be trained to increase their positive social behaviors in mainstream settings and thus enjoy better peer acceptance has come from the literature concerning severe disabilities such as autism and moderate to severe mental retardation. For example, Nientimp and Cole (1992) demonstrated a training procedure wherein two adolescents with severe disabilities increased their positive social behavior in an integrated setting, and treatment generalization was found to occur as well in students without disabilities. Similar results were demonstrated by Chin-Perez, Hartman, Park, and Sacks (1986), and these positive effects also have been demonstrated for social skills training programs with elementary-age students (Kamps, Leonard, Vernon, & Dugan, 1992). In addition, it has been shown that social skills training for preschool-age children with severe disabilities may result in increased social skills and peer acceptance (Hundert & Houghton, 1992; Rule, Stowitschek, Innocenti, & Striefel, 1987; Strain, 1983).

It seems that less research is available concerning the effects of social skills training on ability of children and adolescents with mild disabilities to be effectively served in mainstream educational settings. However, the existing evidence does indicate that effectively designed and implemented social skills training interventions may be critical variables in successfully integrating children and adolescents with social deficits into mainstream educational settings. For example, a study conducted by McMahon, Wacker, Sasso, and Melloy (1994) showed some very complicated beneficial effects of social skills training on elementary-age students with learning and behavioral disorders. In this study, not only were targeted behaviors of the subjects improved, but some nontargeted behaviors showed improvement as well. Additionally, some important positive changes in peer and teacher responses to the targeted students appeared as a result of the training program. In the light of what we know about negative teacher and peer perceptions toward students with social deficits, these findings are encouraging.

In summary, one barrier to successful integration or inclusion of students with disabilities into mainstream or regular education settings are the substantial social-skills deficits that many of these students exhibit. Although the evidence is not entirely conclusive in this area, numerous empirical efforts demonstrat that social skills training may be an effective, if not a critical ingredient, in promoting social acceptance and successful social interaction for these children and adolescents. Furthermore, it appears that without carefully designed and implemented social skills training programs, students with severe social deficiencies are likely to experience social rejection and fail to improve their social skills deficits when placed in fully integrated mainstream educational settings.

SUMMARY

Developmental issues often are overlooked in the design of social skills assessment and intervention programs for children and adolescents. Age is a particularly critical but often overlooked variable in this regard. The area of social cognitive development is directly linked to the capacity for developing social skills. Bandura's social cognitive development theory, which includes basic human capabilities, observational learning, and triadic reciprocality, provides an excellent framework for understanding social skills within a social cognitive development framework.

Six aspects of social cognitive theory that seem crucial in the development of social skills include perspective taking, conceptions of friendship, interpersonal problem-solving strategies, moral judgment, and communication skills. The three preadult developmental stages discussed in this chapter (early childhood, middle childhood, adolescence), each are accompanied by important developmental changes and expectations that have important ramifications for social skills. Social cognitive development, social–emotional development, and changes in friendship patterns and expectations across these three stages are particularly important for social skills.

Gender and ethnocultural factors also are important to consider in the development of social skills. Research on gender differences in social behavior has been fairly consistent with respect to three main findings. First, boys in early childhood tend to prefer social play that involves physical activity (including aggression), whereas girls are disposed to adopt social play styles that are more passive and sedentary. Second, the social play behaviors of young girls tend to be more goal-oriented or constructive than those of young boys, who are more likely to engage in functional social play behaviors. Finally, from early childhood through adolescence, girls are more likely to be rated as having higher levels of social skills and lower levels of antisocial behaviors than boys. The causes of these gender differences in social skills behavior are complex and thought to involve both environmental and biologic variables. Although evidence for both of these causal variables exists, it appears that support for environmental influences in gender-related social skill behavior is larger and stronger than the evidence supporting biological influences.

The term *ethnocultural factors* is a broad term that includes a variety of cultural, social, and economic variables, but has a specific focus on ethnicity or national origin. Ethnocultural factors appear to have some obvious and strong implications for social skills assessment and training, but surprisingly, the empirical evidence in this area is extremely small. There may be ethnocultural differences in the valuing of various social skills. Ethnocultural-based communication style differences also may have implications for social skills training and the interpretation of assessment data, particularly relating to degree of eye contact, physical proximity in interpersonal communication, and manner of expression or affectivity. Finally, there may be a complex interaction between the ethnocultural background of social skills raters/observers and subjects, which in some cases may affect the objectivity of obtained social skills information. Although there are perhaps more questions than answers about ethnocultural influences on social skills, to avoid bias, professionals should maintain heightened sensitivity and awareness in this area.

Children and adolescents receiving special education services because of various developmental disabilities are at substantially heightened risk for developing social skills deficits. Research has shown that students with the three most common special education disability conditions (LD, serious emotional disturbance, mental retardation) are likely to exhibit substantial social skills deficits in comparison with normal students. Of these three, students with serious emotional disturbance seem to suffer the most severe social skills deficits.

Social skills problems constitute an explicit part of the federal definition for serious emotional disturbance and a smaller part of the most recent AAMR definition of mental retardation. Some conceptualizations of learning disabilities have also included social skills deficits as a defining feature. Another disability condition, specific language impairment, is also likely to be accompanied by deficits in social skills, particularly communication-based social skill behaviors. Obviously, the social skill deficits exhibited by many children and adolescents with disabilities presents a substantial obstacle to their acceptance by peers and teachers, as well as their ability to serve effectively or enter mainstream or regular educational settings. Although the concept of full inclusion is controversial in some professional circles, there is emerging evidence that social skills training may be an effective tool, if not a crucial element, in the successful mainstreaming or full inclusion of students with disabilities who also exhibit substantial social skill deficits.

THREE

Assessment of Social Skills:
Best Practices and New Directions

Few professionals would argue against the importance of providing strong and effective training interventions for children and adolescents with significant deficits in social skills. Thus, social skills training interventions hold a place of prominence in this volume. The screening and assessment process is an important link between identifying a child who may have serious social skills deficits and establishing a suitable intervention plan for remediation. This chapter covers various aspects of social skills assessment, including the purposes of assessment, a comprehensive overview of four direct and objective methods of assessment, a comprehensive multifactored assessment model, and the use of assessment data as a link to intervention.

IMPORTANCE AND PURPOSES
OF SOCIAL SKILLS ASSESSMENT

Screening Versus Assessment

As already intimated, screening and assessment are critically important in the process of identifying and remediating social skills deficits and related problems. Often used interchangeably, the terms *screening* and *assessment* reflect differing purposes, even when similar procedures are used.

Screening has been referred to as the process for narrowing down a good suspicion (Kauffman, 1989). Screening serves the purpose of selecting cases from a general population that have a reasonably high probability of meeting our criteria for assessment, in this case, significant social skills problems.

A good screening procedure requires a minimum amount of time. Because they often use a broad-spectrum "shotgun" approach, good screening procedures often result in some *false-positive* errors (identifying some cases in which social skills problems really are not a serious concern), but seldom result in *false-negative* errors (failure to identify cases that meet the serious social skills problems criterion) (Merrell, 1994a). Screening procedures are intended to identify specific cases of concern, but typically do not identify the subtle nuances of the problems.

In contrast, formal assessment procedures are used to identify specific aspects of a problem in useful detail. Whereas good screening practices often involve the use of a single time-limited procedure, good assessment practices tend to involve substantially more time per case and hopefully include several difference assessment methods or procedures. The design of comprehensive multifactored assessments is discussed later in this chapter.

Purposes of Assessment

Social skills assessment procedures typically serve several important purposes. Assessment procedures are used to describe and identify the specific aspects of an existing problem in detailed ways that may be useful to other professionals and, ultimately, to the child or adolescent who is being assessed. It is one thing to state that a child has serious deficits in social skills (a parent or teacher can usually tell you this without a formal assessment) but quite another matter to clearly identify the dimensions, specific behaviors, and environmental constraints involved in the problem. Assessment procedures often are used to classify a client according to some diagnostic framework (e.g., the DSM–IV, special education classification guidelines, etc.). Although some individuals question the value of assessment for purposes of classification (the "label jars not people" school of thought), it is important to remember that classification often provides a gateway for obtaining needed intervention services for the client, supplies a common nomenclature or framework by which other professionals may identify and understand the specifics of the problem and, in some cases, serves as a means of obtaining financial remuneration for the client or their service providers (the proverbial "Blue Cross" form of validity). Ultimately, however, the most important purpose of assessment is to provide data that are useful in designing, implementing, and evaluating treatment or intervention procedures to remediate the identified problem. More discussion on linking assessment to intervention is provided later in this chapter.

The Direct and Objective Approach to Assessment

Although approaches to assessment of child and adolescent social behavior are possible, a specific approach is preferred and advocated in this chapter and throughout this book. This approach was defined previously as direct and objective assessment (Merrell, 1994a). Such approaches deemphasize mediating steps between obtaining and interpreting assessment data and the need for making qualitative inferences. Direct and objective assessment approaches have much more in common with empirical rather than clinical assessment (Meehl, 1954) and with nomothetic rather than idiographic assessment (Barnett & Zucker, 1990). This approach to behavioral, social, and emotional assessment tends to be more in line with psychometric standards for testing integrity, and tends to be more replicable than non-objective, nondirect methods.

Four specific types of assessment procedures that are useful for measuring child and adolescent social skills may be considered direct and objective in nature: direct behavioral observation, behavior rating scales, sociometric techniques, and objective self-report methods (including behavioral and structured interviewing techniques and objective self-report tests). These assessment methods are discussed in detail, particularly as they relate to social skills assessment, in the following four major sections of this chapter.

DIRECT OBSERVATION OF SOCIAL SKILLS

Essential Characteristics of Behavioral Observation

Perhaps the most direct and objective method of assessing social skills is direct behavioral observation, which by definition is a procedure in which the observers develop operational definitions of the targeted behaviors of interest, observe the subjects, and systematically record their behaviors. Most behavioral observation assessment techniques for children and adolescents are considered *naturalistic* methods in that they usually are conducted by a trained and impartial observer in the subject's normal environment (i.e., the classroom, playground, etc.). However, two other general methods of observation also exist: *analog*, which involves conducting the observation in a contrived situation (i.e., a lab or clinic) developed to simulate the natural environment, or *self-monitoring*, in which subjects are taught to observe and record their own behavior as it occurs. Naturalistic observation is the general focus of this chapter because it has been the most widely used and validated observational method in social skills assessment.

Rooted in behavioral theory and applied behavior analysis, direct observation techniques are considered by many behaviorally oriented practitioners and researchers as the assessment method of choice. Keller (1986) noted that the unifying factor of different behavioral approaches appears to be "their derivation from experimentally established procedures and principles" (p. 355). As such, most methods of behavioral observation, and specifically those methods and techniques covered in this chapter, have a strong emphasis on sound empirical methodology and a high degree of treatment validity. Alessi (1988) observed that one critical characteristic of observation methods for social behavior problems is that they permit a functional analysis of behavior and, as such, are intrinsically linked to valid interpretation of assessment data and the development of systematic intervention plans. Thus, direct behavioral observation of social skills appears to have the advantage of being more easily linked to social skills interventions than some other forms of assessment.

It must be recognized that like all assessment methods, direct behavioral observation has its problems and thus should be used in combination with other assessment methods within the context of a multifactored assessment design. Even strong proponents of this method admit that behavioral observation systems and technology are in need of further refinement, and that the accuracy, validity, and reliability of behavioral observation data often are not established adequately (Merrell, 1994a).

One issue in conducting direct behavioral observation is to define the observational domain adequately. The domain of child social behavior can be viewed as a continuum, with broadly defined behaviors on one end and narrowly defined behaviors on the other. Although defining each behavioral domain in a narrow manner may seem to make empirical sense, it may be impractical when the time comes to conduct the observation. For example, if the observational category, "does not respond to verbal initiations from peers," were used in a classroom setting during a 20-minute observation, it may be more restrictive and result in lower frequency than the more general category, "does not respond to peers."

Another issue in direct behavioral observation is the phenomenon of *observer drift,* the tendency of observers to depart gradually over time from originally agreed-on behavioral definitions or categories (Kazdin, 1981; Reid, 1982). For an observer working within a group of other professionals using the same system for social skills observational assessment, observer drift could indeed be a realistic concern. This problem may be curtailed through periodic reliability checks with other observers, occasional retraining, or simple consultation with peers regarding observational issues (Merrell, 1994a).

Use of *social comparison data* presents another potential issue in direct behavioral observation. When targeting a child or adolescent whose social behavior is to be observed, it makes good sense to compare the observational findings with those taken from comparison peers in the same environment. Otherwise, the obtained observational results may be difficult to anchor in a meaningful way. *Observer reactivity* occurs when the presence of the observer has the effect of altering or modifying the behavior of the subject(s). This problem may be curtailed if observers work carefully to be as unobtrusive as possible: by taking such precautions as entering a classroom between periods, sitting anonymously and quietly in the back of the room, and using other measures to minimize their presence. *Situational specificity of behavior* refers to the phenomenon that child and adolescent behavioral patterns may be very specific to the environment in which they were observed, but may not generalize to other environments (Kazdin, 1982). By conducting observations in several settings whenever possible (i.e., different classrooms, the playground, even the lunchroom), those behaviors that are primarily a function of a specific environment may be detected and the common or unifying social behavior problems for intervention more easily targeted.

Four Types of Observational Coding Procedures

Although an unlimited number of observational coding systems could potentially be developed for use in assessing child and adolescent social skills, all can be broken down into four general types of coding or recording procedures: event recording, interval recording, time-sample recording, and duration and latency recording.

Event Recording.   Event recording simply involves measuring or counting how many times target behaviors occur during the length of the observational period. Barton and Ascione (1984) suggested that event recording is best suited for use with behaviors that meet the following criteria: The behaviors should have a clear beginning and end; it should take approximately the same amount of time to complete each response every time the targeted behavior occurs; and the behaviors should not occur so frequently that it becomes difficult to separate each occurrence. In choosing specific social skill behaviors to observe, it should be relatively easy to identify targets that meet all three of these criteria. If the targets specified for the assessment do not meet these criteria, it would be wise to choose a different coding procedure.

Certain techniques can be used with event recording to maximize its usefulness as an observational recording procedure. To increase the utility of event recording, the events can be recorded sequentially or in the exact order of their occurrence. By developing a sequential analysis of observed events, social skill behaviors can be categorized according to antecedents and consequences, which may be helpful in fully understanding the behaviors and in developing intervention plans.

A useful way of transcribing event recording into an analysis of behavioral antecedents and consequences is through the use of an A–B–C (antecedent–behavior–consequence) evaluation, which follows these steps: (a) Divide a sheet of paper into three columns, one each for antecedents, behaviors, and consequences; (b) list the specific behaviors recorded in the middle column (behaviors); and (c) note what events or behaviors preceded the recorded behaviors (antecedents), and what events or behaviors followed the recorded behaviors (consequences).

Using this A–B–C procedure requires a bit more flexibility in the observation system. In some cases a targeted behavior recorded in the B column will also appear in the A column as an antecedent to another important behavior or event. However, the payoff of using this technique will come in the form of an ecologically sensitive observational recording system that has strong implications for treatment. Figure 3.1. shows how the A–B–C breakdown sheet can be used with event recording.

Interval Recording.   Interval recording involves selecting a time period for the observation, dividing this period into a number of equal intervals (e.g., a 30-minute observation period divided into 90 equal intervals of 20 seconds each), and recording whether the specified target behaviors occur during each interval. There are two basic types of interval recording: whole- and partial-interval procedures. *Whole-interval* recording requires that the behaviors being coded occur during the entire interval in order to be recorded and is a good choice if the targeted behaviors are continuous (such as playing with peers) and the intervals are short to medium in length (Shapiro & Skinner, 1990). *Partial-interval* recording requires that the observer code the target behavior if it occurs at any time during the interval and is a good choice for recording low-frequency behaviors (such as arguing or fighting with peers) observed over fairly long intervals of time (Shapiro & Skinner, 1990).

Interval recording is a good choice for social behaviors that occur at a moderate but steady rate, but is not as useful for behaviors that occur with low frequency. Rather than providing an exact count of behaviors, it estimates the relative prevalence of behaviors. This procedure requires the complete attention of the observer and the use of timing devices such as digital stopwatches. It can be difficult to implement if the intervals are too short or the number of behaviors targeted for observation are too great. Typically, interval recording is used with specific targeted behaviors, and a + or – is recorded in a box for each interval to indicate whether or not the targeted behavior occurred.

A number of useful and empirically validated interval recording procedures have been developed for observing child and adolescent social behavior. One excellent interval-based social behavior observation coding system is presented herein to give the reader an idea of what is possible: The Peer Social Behavior Code is the third stage of Walker and Severson's (1991) Systematic Screening for Behavior Disorders (SSBD), a multiple gating screening system for use with children in grades 1 to 6 that includes teacher screening at the first gate, teacher rating at the second gate, and direct behavioral observation at the final gate. The assessment method uses increasingly intensive procedures at each successive gate to narrow down the population. By the time the population has been narrowed after the direct observational process (the third gate), it should consist of children truly at risk for social behavior problems, including social skills deficits. The Peer Social Behavior Code observation system utilizes a series of 10-second intervals. The actual number of intervals used in an observation varies depending on the situation. Each record-

SUBJECT NAME:

AGE:

OBSERVATION DATE AND SETTING:

ANTECEDENTS	BEHAVIORS	CONSEQUENCES

FIG. 3.1. Social behavioral observation coding sheet using an event-recording procedure and the A–B–C technique.

ing form includes spaces for 40 different intervals. Observations are always conducted during free play situations (e.g., at recess), and a typical observation period might last 15 minutes.

Five different recording categories are included in the Peer Social Behavior Code: social engagement (SE), participation (P), parallel play (PLP), alone (A), and no codable response (N). Behavior in the first two categories may be coded as either positive (+) or negative (−). In the PLP and A categories behavior is coded by simply checking the appropriate box. A "no codable response" receives a check when the child is out of view and a dot when the child is interacting with an adult rather than a peer. After the observation, the data is transferred from the recording forms (Fig. 3.2) to an observational summary sheet (Fig. 3.3). The number of intervals recorded are entered for each category. Then the percentage of time spent for each category is calculated by dividing the total number of intervals in the session into the intervals recorded under different categories and multiplying by 100. The SSBD manual contains thorough directions for interpreting Peer Social Behavior Code observation data using the normative tables provided. Extensive research went into the development of the Peer Social Behavior Code, and the validity evidence and technical properties reported in the manual and other sources are impressive. An excellent observer training tape is provided as part of the SSBD kit, which also includes an audio timing tape for accurately using the 10-second intervals. The Peer Social Behavior Code is an exemplary interval-based coding procedure for direct observation of child social behavior and may also serve as a model for constructing similar coding systems for more specific purposes.

Time-Sample Recording.   Time-sampling recording is similar to interval recording in that the observation period is divided into intervals of time. The difference between the two procedures is that with time sampling, behavior is observed only momentarily at the prespecified intervals. Also, it is not unusual to have unequal units with time sampling, whereas interval recording usually involves equal units or time intervals. As with interval recording, time sampling is most useful for observing behaviors that occur at a moderate but steady rate.

Time-sample recording for child social behavior can be illustrated by observating the child playing with peers. The observation might occur during a 15-minute recess period at school that has been divided into 15 intervals of 1 minute each. As each minute ends, the observer records whether the subject was playing with a peer. In this example, the time units are divided into equal intervals, but the intervals do not need to be equal, and could even be generated randomly. If the time intervals used in time sampling are short, complex, or unequal, special electronic timing devices may be needed. Some innovative researchers and clinicians have even developed electronic timing devices that

Systematic Screening for Behavior Disorders
PEER SOCIAL BEHAVIOR RECORDING FORM[*]

Student Name _____ Teacher Name _____

School _____ Grade _____ Observer _____

Reliability Observer _____ Date _____ Time Start _____

Time Stop _____ Length of Session _____

Interval Number	+ - SE	+ - P	✓ PLP	✓ A	• ✓ N
0-1					
2					
3					
4					
5					
6					
7					
8					
9					
10					
11					
12					
13					
14					
15					
16					
17					
18					
19					
20					

Interval Number	+ - SE	+ - P	✓ PLP	✓ A	• ✓ N
21					
22					
23					
24					
25					
26					
27					
28					
29					
30					
31					
32					
33					
34					
35					
36					
37					
38					
39					
40					

FIG. 3.2.   Peer Social Behavior Code Recording Form. *Note.* From *Systematic Screening for Behavior Disorders* (rev. ed.), by H. M. Walker and H. H. Severson, 1992, Longmont, CO: Sopris West. Copyright © 1992 by Sopris West. Reprinted with permission.

Systematic Screening for Behavior Disorders
PEER SOCIAL BEHAVIOR
OBSERVATION SUMMARY SHEET[*]

Student Name _____

School _____ Grade _____

Dates Observed _____ and _____
                Session #1   Session #2

	Number of Intervals[*]	Observation #1[**]	Number of Intervals[*]	Observation #2[**]	Average of 1 and 2
1. Social Engagement (SE)	_____	_____%	_____	_____%	_____%
2. Participation (P)	_____	_____%	_____	_____%	_____%
3. Parallel Play (PLP)	_____	_____%	_____	_____%	_____%
4. Alone (A)	_____	_____%	_____	_____%	_____%
5. No Codeable Response (N)	_____	_____%	_____	_____%	_____%
6. Social Interaction (SI)	_____	_____%	_____	_____%	_____%
7. Negative Interaction (NI)	_____	_____%	_____	_____%	_____%
8. Positive Interaction (PI)	_____	_____%	_____	_____%	_____%
9. Total Positive Behavior	_____	_____%	_____	_____%	_____%
10. Total Negative Behavior	_____	_____%	_____	_____%	_____%

[*] Enter the number of intervals recorded for each category.

[**] Enter the percentage of time spent for each category by dividing the total number of intervals that you observed during the observation session into the intervals recorded under different categories and multiplying by 100.

FIG. 3.3.   The Peer Social Behavior Observation Summary Sheet from the Systematic Screening for Behavior Disorders. *Note.* From *Systematic Screening for Behavior Disorders* (rev. ed.), by H. M. Walker and H. H. Severson, 1992, Longmont, CO: Sopris West. Copyright © 1992 by Sopris West. Reprinted with permission.

randomly generate audible tones at varying time intervals within a given range. A simple alternative is making an audiocassette tape in which tones or other cues are recorded at prespecified random intervals. The observer may then use the tape (perhaps with an earphone) to guide the observational recording.

A major advantage of the time-sampling recording is that it requires only one observation per interval, and is thus less subject to the problems of getting off track that are readily encountered with interval recording. If the intervals are large enough, the time-sampling method may even free the observer to engage in other activities. For example, a teacher could direct an instructional activity while using a time sampling to conduct a social behavior observation, providing the intervals are large enough and the recording is simple. Interestingly, the major advantage of time sampling is closely related to its largest drawback. Because time sampling allows only for recording of behavior that occurs occasionally, an observer may miss recording many important behaviors and invalid conclusions may be reached. The longer the interval used with time sampling, the less accurate the data will be. As the interval increases, the sample of behavior decreases. Reaching an appropriate balance between the length of the interval needed and the necessity of freeing up the observer for other activities is the most reasonable way to use time sampling.

Duration and Latency Recording. Event recording, interval recording, and time-sample recording all have the similarity of focusing on exact or approximate counts of targeted behaviors that occur during a given time frame. Two related techniques, duration and latency recording, differ from the first three in that their focus is primarily on the temporal aspects of the targeted behaviors rather than on behavior frequency. Duration and latency recording are best used with behaviors that have a discrete beginning and end and that last for at least a few seconds each time they occur (Barton & Ascione, 1984).

In duration recording, the observer measures the amount of time a subject engages in a specific behavior. In other words, the most critical aspect of the observation is how long the behavior lasts. For school-based social behavior assessment, a good example of how duration recording might be used is provided by the observation of a child playing with peers on the playground. If the child has numerous opportunities to play with other children, but does it effectively only for a few seconds at a time, it may be useful to understand how long the playing-with-peers behavior is lasting. There is a big difference between a child who plays with one other child only during the recess period, but does it for 15 minutes, and a child who initiates play with four different peers, but the play lasts only a few seconds each. Duration recording might be useful in such a scenario, and a natural intervention goal would be increasing the absolute time that the child plays with peers during recess.

In latency recording, the observer attempts to gauge the amount of time from the end of one behavior to the beginning of another. In other words, the most critical aspect of the observation is how long it takes for the behavior to begin. A typical example of how latency recording could be used for observing social behavior comes from observation of a shy and socially unskilled child who does not respond immediately when peers or adults initiate conversation. The time between the end of the initiation ("Hey, what are you doing after school?") and the target child's response would be the duration, and reducing the duration of time in such situations would be a natural intervention goal.

BEHAVIOR RATING SCALES

Essential Characteristics of Behavior Rating Scales

Behavior rating scales utilize summative judgments or ratings by an informant who knows the child well, most often a teacher or parent. These judgments are made by using a standardized rating format that yields scores allowing comparison between the subject and a normative group.

Most rating scales now use an algebraic rating format by which the rater selects a number or other value that best represents the student's performance on the particular characteristic. For example, an algebraic response format for the item *is physically aggressive* might have the rater select the value 0 if the statement is *not true,* 1 if the statement is *sometimes true,* and 2 if the statement is *frequently true.* After the rating scale is completed, the numerical value of the ratings is added and compared in different configurations to those of a norm group.

The algebraic format is more sophisticated and sensitive to behavioral change or intensity than a checklist format, which is additive in nature, with the rater simply circling or checking items that seem to be true for the subject, and then adds the number of items checked. Rating scales have gained wide popularity in educational and clinical settings, particularly for behavioral assessment.

Rating scales have become used widely because they offer several advantages as assessment methods. Whereas direct behavioral observation is potentially an excellent method for assessing social competence, rating scales are less expensive in terms of professional time and training required, and are capable of providing data on low-frequency but important behaviors that might not be seen in a limited number of direct observation sessions (Sattler, 1988). When compared to other assessment methods (e.g., projective techniques and interviews), rating scales provide more objective and reliable data (Martin, Hooper, & Snow, 1986). Rating scales can be used to assess subjects who cannot readily provide information about themselves or be easily observed (e.g., very young children or adolescents in lock-up units in hospitals or juvenile detention centers). They can be developed with capabilities of capitalizing on observations from the student's normal environment (school and home) and the observations of expert informants (teachers and parents).

Notwithstanding the popularity and advantages of rating scales, some problems associated with their use need to be considered if they are to be used effectively. Two types of problems have been discussed by Martin, Hooper, and Snow (1986). The first type of problem is referred to as *bias of response,* meaning that the way informants complete rating scales may create additional error in the resulting scores. Three types of response bias are particularly problematic: *halo effects* (the tendency to rate a student's behavioral characteristics as good because that student does well on academic work or poor because that student's academic work is poor), *leniency or severity effects* (the tendency to be either excessively generous or critical in rating of all subjects), and *central tendency effects* (the tendency to select midrange rating points and to avoid extreme ratings such as *never* or *frequently*).

The second type of problem results from the fact that rating scale scores are subject to four different kinds of error variance: *source variance* (the way that ratings vary between different raters), *setting variance* (the way that ratings might differ across different classroom settings or between school and home), *temporal variance* (the way that behavior ratings change over time based on changes in the rater or the subject), and *instrument variance* (different results obtained by using different rating scales).

The recommended way of dealing with these two types of problems in rating scales is to use a multisource, multisetting, multiinstrument assessment design (referred to as a *multifactored design* in this chapter) that reduces the chance for bias and error by obtaining ratings of the subject from different informants, in different settings, and using different types of rating scales (Martin, 1988).

A Review of Six Selected Social Skills Rating Scales

Until the mid-1980s, there was a dearth of nationally standardized behavior rating scales for assessing social skills and peer relations. Most rating scales developed before this time were designed for the express purpose of assessing behavior problems, and there was a much smaller body of research on children's social competence (Achenbach & Edelbrock, 1983). However, during the past decade significantly increased interest and research in child and adolescent social competence has led to the development of several psychometrically sound standardized assessment instruments. This section provides an overview of six behavior rating systems that may be useful for assessing social competence and peer relations: the Behavioral Assessment System for Children, the Matson Evaluation of Social Skills with Youngsters, the Preschool and Kindergarten Behavior Scales, the School Social Behavior Scales, the Social Skills Rating System, and the Walker–McConnell Scales of Social Competence and School Adjustment. These six instruments do not represent all that is currently available in this area, but are included in this chapter because they all are: norm-referenced using nationwide standardization groups, psychometrically acceptable, designed to be useful for assessment of social skills and peer relations, and commercially published or otherwise easily available to practitioners and researchers. A brief overview of each of these instruments, in alphabetical order, follows.

Behavioral Assessment System for Children. The Behavioral Assessment System for Children (BASC; Reynolds & Kamphaus, 1992) is a sophisticated multimethod behavior rating system for use with children and adolescents. It includes a teacher rating scale, a parent rating scale, a self-report scale, a direct observation form for use in classrooms, and a developmental history questionnaire. Although most of the item content of the various rating forms is oriented toward problem behavior, there also are a number of items on the various report forms oriented toward adaptive social behavior or skills. Because they include several items and scales related to adaptive social behavior and social skills, the Parent Rating scales and the Teacher Rating scales of the BASC are reviewed and discussed here, particularly the items and scales oriented to these areas. However, it is must be noted that unlike most of the other parent and teacher rating scales reviewed in this chapter, assessment of adaptive social behavior does not appear to be the primary goal of the BASC, as demonstrated by the small percentage of items and subscales reflecting such content.

The Parent Rating scale and Teacher Rating scale of the BASC include between 109 and 148 total items, depending upon the specific form and the targeted age range (4–5, 6–11, or 12–18). The items in these scales comprise 14 subscales, and a T-score conversion is used to interpret the various subscale scores. Of the 14 BASC subscales on the Parent and the Teacher Rating scales, 4 subscales are referred to as Adaptive scales. Of these 4 Adaptive scales, 3 appear to be directly relevant to the domains of social skills or social competence.

The Adaptability subscale is said to assess the ability to adjust to changes in routine and environment, and includes from 0 to 8 items on the Teacher Rating Scale and from 0 to 10 items on the Parent Rating Scale depending on the age range of the targeted child or adolescent. The Leadership subscale is said to assess behaviors associated with leadership potential and directly related to social skills, and includes from 0 to 9 items on the Teacher Rating Scale and from 0 to 12 items on the Parent Rating Scale. The Social Skills subscale is said to assess peer relations and the interpersonal aspects of social adaptation, and includes from 10 to 12 items on the Parent Rating Scale and from 12 to 14 items on the Teacher Rating Scale. The fourth BASC adaptive scale, Study Skills, includes items more related to problem solving from a metacognitive perspective and is considered to be more strongly associated with the behavior problem domain than with social skills or social competence.

Impressive and highly detailed item and subscale development procedures were used in constructing the BASC, and the breadth and diversity of the national standardization sample for both the Parent Rating Scale ($N = 3,483$) and the Teacher Rating Scale ($N = 2,401$) is truly exemplary. A wide variety of psychometric evidence supporting the Parent and Teacher Rating scales is presented in the BASC manual. Both internal consistency and test–retest reliability of the scales is very strong, but like most other rating scales, the reported interrater reliability is moderate because various factors cause different raters in different settings to have differing perceptions of a child's behavior. The BASC manual also includes a number of other psychometric studies such as exploratory and confirmatory factor analyses, covariance structure analyses, convergent validity studies with several other instruments, and criterion validity studies with various clinical groups.

In summary, the BASC should be considered a highly sophisticated and potentially useful multimethod behavior rating system for use with children and adolescents. Several of the BASC items and 3 of the 14 subscales on the Parent and Teacher Rating scales appear to be specifically useful in the assessment of social skills and social competence, although these constructs are not the primary focus of the system.

Matson Evaluation of Social Skills With Youngsters. The Matson Evaluation of Social Skills with Youngsters (MESSY) is a 64-item behavior rating scale for teachers that measures both social skills and inappropriate behaviors that tend to interfere with the development of peer relationships. Unlike the other social skills rating scales reviewed in this chapter, the MESSY is not commercially published. Therefore, the information cited here regarding the development and psychometric properties of the MESSY comes from a variety of published sources rather than from a single test manual (e.g., Matson, 1984; Matson, Compton, & Sevin, 1991; Matson, Esveldt-Dawson, & Kazdin, 1983; Matson, Rotatori, & Helsel, 1983). Even though the MESSY is not easily available in a commercially packaged form, its impressive research base and validity evidence warrant its review and discussion in this section.

The 64 items of the MESSY teacher rating form scale are spread across two empirically derived (through factor analysis) domains: Inappropriate Assertiveness/Impulsivity and Appropriate Social Skills. The first domain includes items, such as "Brags too much when s/he wins" and "Acts like s/he is better than others," that tend to interfere with peer relationships and cause social rejection, whereas the second domain includes such traditional social skills and social competence items such as "Plays by the rules of the game" and "Looks at people when they are speaking."

The MESSY items have been field tested with children ranging in age from 4 to 18 years. Unlike the other rating scales reviewed here, the MESSY was not developed with a single large nationwide normative sample, but from studies of smaller groups in varying situations and settings. The psychometric properties of the MESSY are likewise identified through analyzing the various studies conducted with this rating scale over time rather than through consulting a single comprehensive source. However, the psychometric properties and other validity evidence on the MESSY appear to be solid. The most impressive evidence supporting the MESSY are various studies showing sensitivity to theorized group differences (e.g., depressed and nondepressed children, autistic and nonautistic children, hearing impaired or deaf children and nonhearing impaired children) and to treatment effects.

Percentile or standard score conversion charts are not available for comparing MESSY scores of individuals or groups with a normative population, so the practitioner or researcher will need to consult the basic descriptive statistics (means and standard deviations) available in the studies cited in this section. It certainly is a drawback that such a potentially useful measure as the MESSY is not available from a single source with consolidated evidence and user helps, but the extensive supporting evidence and thoughtful construction of this rating make it worth the extra trouble for those who desire to use it.

Preschool and Kindergarten Behavior Scales.   The Preschool and Kindergarten Behavior Scales (PKBS; Merrell, 1994b) is a 76-item behavior rating scale designed to measure both social skills and problem behaviors in the early childhood–preschool population (ages 3–6). This instrument may be completed by parents, teachers, day-care providers, or other behavioral informants who are familiar with a child's behavior. It was developed with a national standardization sample of 2,855 children generally comparable to the general U.S. population in terms of gender, ethnicity, and socioeconomic status. For example, 51% of the standardization sample were male and 49% were female; 80% of the sample were White and 20% were members of racial or ethnic minority groups (12.1% African American, 5.2% Hispanic; 1.5% Asian or Pacific Islander, 0.01% American Indian, and 1.2% other). Based on parent occupation of the participants, general similarity was found in occupational categories of this population compared with the most recent U.S. occupational breakdown statistics from the U.S. Department of the Census, indicating comparable socioeconomic status. The PKBS items were designed specifically with the unique social–emotional aspects of the early childhood–preschool developmental period in mind, and systematic item development and content validation procedures were employed.

Items on the PKBS are on two separate scales, each designed to measure a separate domain: a 34-item Social Skills scale, and a 42-item Problem Behavior scale. Each scale includes an empirically derived subscale structure.

The Social Skills scale includes three subscales: Social Cooperation (12 items describing cooperative and self-restraint behaviors), Social Interaction (11 items reflecting social initiation behaviors), and Social Independence (11 items portraying behaviors important for gaining independence within the peer group).

The Problem Behavior Scale includes two broad band subscales: Internalizing Problems and Externalizing Problems. Consistent with the theoretical and empirical breakdown of the internalizing–externalizing problem dichotomy (Cicchetti & Toth, 1991), the Internalizing Problems broadband scale includes 27 items describing undercontrolled behavioral problems such as overactivity, aggression, coercion, and antisocial behaviors, whereas the Externalizing Problems broadband scale includes 15 items describing overcontrolled behavioral–emotional problems such as social withdrawal, anxiety, somatic complaints, and behaviors reflecting depressive symptomatology. The Externalizing Problems broadband scale includes three narrowband scales: Self-Centered/Explosive, Attention Problems/Overactive, and Antisocial/Aggressive. The Internalizing Problems broadband scale includes two narrowband scales: Social Withdrawal and Anxiety/Somatic Problems.

Research findings presented in the PKBS test manual and in subsequent published research provide evidence for adequate to excellent psychometric properties. Respectively, internal consistency reliability estimates for the Social Skills and Problem Behavior total scores are 0.96 and 0.97; test–retest reliability estimates at 3-month intervals were found to be 0.69 and 0.78; and, interrater reliability between preschool teachers and teacher aides for the total scores were found to be 0.48 and 0.59 in one study. Validity of the PKBS has been shown through various psychometric procedures given detailed descriptions in the manual and in subsequent published studies. Content validity has been demonstrated through documentation of the item development procedures and by showing moderate to high correlations between individual items and total scores. Construct validity has been established through analysis of intrascale relationships; through factor analytic findings with structural equation modeling (Merrell, 1996); through documentation of sensitivity to gender differences (Merrell, 1994b), differences between behaviorally at-risk and normal children (Jentzsch & Merrell, 1996), and of differences between children with internalizing social–emotional problems and children without these problems (Merrell, 1995a); and through finding significant correlations with four other established behavior rating scales (Merrell, 1995b). In an independent review of several behavior rating scales designed for use with preschool-age children, the PKBS compared favorably in terms of several important criteria (Bracken, Keith, & Walker, 1994).

School Social Behavior Scales.   The School Social Behavior Scales (SSBS; Merrell, 1993b) was developed for use by teachers and other school personnel in assessing both social competence and antisocial problem behaviors of students in grades K–12. It includes two separate scales with a total of 65 items that describe both positive and negative social behaviors that commonly occur in educational settings. Items are rated with a 5-point scale ranging from 1 (*never*) to 5 (*frequently*). Each of the SSBS's two scales yields a total score using a raw to standard score conversion with a mean of 100 and a standard deviation of 15. Each of the two scales has three subscales, with scores reported as four different social functioning levels: *high functioning, average, moderate problem,* and *significant problem.*

Scale A, Social Competence, includes 32 items that describe adaptive, prosocial behavioral competencies as they commonly occur in educational settings. Subscale A1, Interpersonal Skills, includes 14 items measuring social skills that are important in establishing positive relationships with and gaining social acceptance from peers (e.g., "Offers help to other students when needed" and "Interacts with a wide variety of peers"). Subscale A2, Self-Management Skills, includes 10 items measuring social skills relating to self-restraint, cooperation, and compliance with the demands of school rules and expectations (e.g., "Responds appropriately when corrected by teacher" and "Shows self-restraint"). Subscale A3, Academic Skills, consists of 8 items relating to competent performance and engagement on academic tasks (e.g., "Completes individual seatwork without being prompted" and "Completes assigned activities on time").

Scale B, Antisocial Behavior, includes 33 negative behavior items describing problematic behaviors either other-directed in nature or likely to lead to negative social consequences such as peer rejection or strained relationships with the teacher. Subscale B1, Hostile–Irritable, consists of 14 items that describe behaviors considered to be self-centered, annoying, and likely to result in peer rejection (e.g., "Will not share with other students," and "Argues and quarrels with other students"). Subscale B2, Antisocial–Aggressive, consists of 10 behavioral descriptors relating to overt violation of school rules and intimidation or harm to others (e.g., "Gets into fights" and "Takes things that are not his/hers"). Subscale B3, Disruptive–Demanding, includes 9 items that reflect behaviors likely to disrupt ongoing school activities and place excessive and inappropriate demands on others (e.g., "Is overly demanding of teacher's attention" and "Is difficult to control").

A number of studies and procedures are reported in the SSBS manual and in subsequent journal articles concerning the psychometric properties and validity of the instrument. The scales were standardized with a group of more than 1900 K–12 students from all four U.S. geographic regions. In the standardization group the percentage of students with disabilities in various classification categories very closely approximates the national percentages of these figures. Various reliability procedures reported in the SSBS manual indicate the scales have good to excellent stability and consistency. Internal consistency and split-half reliability coefficients range from .91 to .98. Test–retest reliability at 3-week intervals is reported at .76 to .83 for the Social Competence scores and .60 to .73 for the Antisocial Behavior scores. Inter-rater reliability between resource room teachers and paraprofessional aides ranges from .72 to .83 for the Social Competence scores and .53 to .71 for the Antisocial Behavior scores.

Validity of the scales has been demonstrated in several ways. Moderate to high correlations were found between the SSBS and several other behavior rating scales: the Child Behavior Checklist and Teacher's Report Form (Emerson, Crowley, & Merrell, 1994); the 39-item version of the Conners Teacher Rating Scale, the Waksman Social Skills Rating Scale, and the adolescent version of the Walker–McConnell Scale of Social Competence and School Adjustment (Merrell, 1993a). These correlations with other instruments indicate that the SSBS has very strong convergent construct validity.

Other findings indicate that the scales can adequately discriminate between gifted and nongifted students (Merrell & Gill, 1994), students with disabilities and regular education students (Merrell, 1993a), and behavior disordered and other special education students (Merrell, Sanders, & Popinga, 1993). These findings of sensitivity to theorized group differences indicate that the SSBS has good construct validity. The factor structure of the two scales is very strong, with all items having a factor loading into their respective subscales of .50 or more, and with no items duplicated across subscales (Merrell, 1993a).

The SSBS appears to be useful as a school-based rating scale that provides norm-referenced data on both positive social skills and antisocial problem behavior. It has satisfactory to good psychometric properties, is easy to use, and contains items and structure that are highly relevant to the types of behavioral issues encountered by school-based professionals. It should be noted that the Antisocial Behavior scale is designed specifically to measure behavior problems that are directly social in nature, or that would have an immediate impact on strained relations with peers and teachers. The scale was not designed to measure overcontrolled or internalizing behavior problems such as those associated with depression and anxiety, nor was it designed to measure behavior problems associated with Attention Deficit Hyperactivity Disorder (ADHD). If problem behaviors of this type are a significant issue in a particular case, the assessment should be bolstered by the addition of an appropriate measure designed specifically for these behaviors. The Social Competence and the Antisocial Behavior scales of the SSBS are presented in Figs. 3.4 and 3.5, respectively.

Social Skills Rating System. The Social Skills Rating System (SSRS; Gresham & Elliott, 1990) is a multicomponent social skills rating system focused on behaviors that affect parent–child relationships, teacher–student relationships, and peer acceptance. The system includes separate rating scales for teachers and parents, as well as a self-report form for students. Each component of the system can be used alone or in conjunction with the other forms. Separate instruments and norms are provided for each of three developmental groups; preschool level (ages 3–5), elementary level (grades K–6), and secondary level (grades 7–12). Because there are considerable conceptual similarities between the different forms and age level versions in the system, the description here covers only the elementary teacher rating form, providing the reader with a general understanding of the SSRS that encompasses many aspects of the several different teacher and parent rating forms within the system.

The elementary level teacher rating form of the SSRS consists of 57 items divided over three scales: Social Skills, Problem Behaviors, and Academic Competence. For Social Skills and Problem Behaviors, teachers respond to

Scale A
Social Competence

	Never	Sometimes			Frequently		Scoring Key		
1. Cooperates with other students in a variety of situations	1	2	3	4	5				
2. Appropriately transitions between classroom activities	1	2	3	4	5				
3. Completes individual seatwork without being prompted	1	2	3	4	5				
4. Offers help to other students when needed	1	2	3	4	5				
5. Effectively participates in group discussions and activities	1	2	3	4	5				
6. Understands other students' problems and needs	1	2	3	4	5				
7. Remains calm when problems arise	1	2	3	4	5				
8. Listens to and carries out directions from teacher	1	2	3	4	5				
9. Invites other students to participate in activities	1	2	3	4	5				
10. Asks for clarification of instructions in an appropriate manner	1	2	3	4	5				
11. Has skills or abilities that are admired by peers	1	2	3	4	5				
12. Is accepting of other students	1	2	3	4	5				
13. Accomplishes assignments and other tasks independently	1	2	3	4	5				
14. Completes assigned activities on time	1	2	3	4	5				
15. Will compromise with peers when appropriate	1	2	3	4	5				
16. Follows classroom rules	1	2	3	4	5				
17. Behaves appropriately in a variety of school settings	1	2	3	4	5				
18. Appropriately asks for assistance as needed	1	2	3	4	5				
19. Interacts with a wide variety of peers	1	2	3	4	5				
20. Produces work of acceptable quality for his/her ability level	1	2	3	4	5				
21. Is skillful at initiating or joining conversations with peers	1	2	3	4	5				
22. Is sensitive to feelings of other students	1	2	3	4	5				
23. Responds appropriately when corrected by teacher	1	2	3	4	5				
24. Controls temper when angry	1	2	3	4	5				
25. Appropriately enters ongoing activities with peers	1	2	3	4	5				
26. Has good leadership skills	1	2	3	4	5				
27. Adjusts to different behavioral expectations across school settings	1	2	3	4	5				
28. Compliments others' attributes or accomplishments	1	2	3	4	5				
29. Is appropriately assertive when he/she needs to be	1	2	3	4	5				
30. Is sought out by peers to join activities	1	2	3	4	5				
31. Shows self-restraint	1	2	3	4	5				
32. Is "looked up to" or respected by peers	1	2	3	4	5				
						Totals			
							A1	A2	A3

FIG. 3.4. The Social Competence Scale of the School Social Behavior Scales. *Note.* From *School Social Behavior Scales,* by K. W. Merrell, 1993, Austin, TX: Pro-Ed. Copyright © 1993 by Pro-Ed. Reprinted with permission.

Scale B
Antisocial Behavior

		Never		Sometimes		Frequently	Scoring Key		
1.	Blames other students for problems	1	2	3	4	5			
2.	Takes things that are not his/hers	1	2	3	4	5			
3.	Defies teacher or other school personnel	1	2	3	4	5			
4.	Cheats on schoolwork or in games	1	2	3	4	5			
5.	Gets into fights	1	2	3	4	5			
6.	Lies to the teacher or other school personnel	1	2	3	4	5			
7.	Teases and makes fun of other students	1	2	3	4	5			
8.	Is disrespectful or "sassy"	1	2	3	4	5			
9.	Is easily provoked; has a short fuse	1	2	3	4	5			
10.	Ignores teacher or other school personnel	1	2	3	4	5			
11.	Acts as if he/she is better than others	1	2	3	4	5			
12.	Destroys or damages school property	1	2	3	4	5			
13.	Will not share with other students	1	2	3	4	5			
14.	Has temper outbursts or tantrums	1	2	3	4	5			
15.	Disregards feelings and needs of other students	1	2	3	4	5			
16.	Is overly demanding of teacher's attention	1	2	3	4	5			
17.	Threatens other students; is verbally aggressive	1	2	3	4	5			
18.	Swears or uses obscene language	1	2	3	4	5			
19.	Is physically aggressive	1	2	3	4	5			
20.	Insults peers	1	2	3	4	5			
21.	Whines and complains	1	2	3	4	5			
22.	Argues and quarrels with peers	1	2	3	4	5			
23.	Is difficult to control	1	2	3	4	5			
24.	Bothers and annoys other students	1	2	3	4	5			
25.	Gets in trouble at school	1	2	3	4	5			
26.	Disrupts ongoing activities	1	2	3	4	5			
27.	Is boastful; brags	1	2	3	4	5			
28.	Cannot be depended on	1	2	3	4	5			
29.	Is cruel to other students	1	2	3	4	5			
30.	Acts impulsively or without thinking	1	2	3	4	5			
31.	Unproductive; achieves very little	1	2	3	4	5			
32.	Is easily irritated	1	2	3	4	5			
33.	Demands help from other students	1	2	3	4	5			
						Totals	B1	B2	B3

FIG. 3.5. The Antisocial Behavior Scale of the School Social Behavior Scales. *Note.* From *School Social Behavior Scales,* by K. W. Merrell, 1993, Austin, TX: Pro-Ed. Copyright © 1993 by Pro-Ed. Reprinted with permission.

items using a 3-point response format based on how often a given behavior occurs: 0 (*never*), 1 (*sometimes*), and 2 (*very often*). On the Social Skills items, teachers also are asked to rate the importance of a skill (on a 3-point scale) to success in the classroom. The importance rating is not used to calculate ratings for each scale but for planning interventions. On the Academic Competence scale, teachers rate students as compared with other students on a 5-point scale. Scale raw scores are converted to standard scores ($M = 100$, $SD = 15$) and percentile ranks. Subscale raw scores are converted to estimates of functional ability called behavior levels.

The Social Skills scale consists of 30 items that rate social skills in the areas of teacher and peer relationships. This scale contains three subscales: Cooperation, Assertion, and Self-Control. The Cooperation subscale identifies compliance behaviors important for success in classrooms (e.g., "Finishes class assignments on time" and "Uses time appropriately while waiting for help"). The Assertion subscale includes initiating behaviors that involve making and maintaining friendships and responding to actions of others (e.g., "Invites others to join in activities" and "Appropriately questions rules that may be unfair"). The Self-Control subscale includes responses that occur in conflict situations such as turn-taking and peer criticism (e.g., "Cooperates with peers without prompting" and "Responds appropriately to teasing by peers").

The Problem Behaviors scale consists of 18 items reflecting behaviors that might interfere with social skills performance. The items are divided into three subscales: Externalizing Problems, Internalizing Problems, and Hyperactivity. The Externalizing Problems subscale items describe inappropriate behaviors that indicate verbal and physical aggression toward others and a lack of temper control (e.g., "Threatens or bullies others" and "Has temper tantrums"). The subscale Internalizing Problems includes behaviors that reveal anxiety, sadness, and poor self-esteem (e.g., "Shows anxiety about being with a group of children" and "Likes to be alone"). The Hyperactivity subscale includes activities that involve excessive movement and impulsive actions (e.g., "Disturbs ongoing activities" and "Acts impulsively").

The third scale, Academic Competence, has nine items that reflect academic functioning, such as performance in specific academic areas, student motivation level, general cognitive functioning, and parental support (e.g., "In terms of grade-level expectations, this child's skills in reading are . . ." and "The child's overall motivation to succeed academically is . . ."). Behavior is rated on a 5-point scale that corresponds to percentages ranging from 1 (*lowest 10%*) to 5 (*highest 10%*).

The entire SSRS rating system was standardized with a national sample of more than 4,000 children representing all four U.S. geographical regions. The manual states that overall psychometric properties obtained during scale development ranged from adequate to excellent. For the teacher scale, reliability was measured using internal consistency (i.e., alpha coefficients ranged from .74 to .95), interrater, and test–retest (i.e., correlations of .75 to .93 across the three scales). Criterion-related and construct validity were established by finding significant correlations between the SSRS and other rating scales. Subscale dimensions were determined through factor analyses of each scale. Items that met a criterion of a .30 or greater factor loading were considered to load on a given factor.

The SSRS's distinct strength is that its integrated system of instruments can be used by teachers, parents, and students. The manual is extremely well written, and the rating instruments have been designed to be easily usable and understandable. The sections of the instruments that measure social skills are very comprehensive and useful, and those sections assessing problem behaviors and academic competence are quite brief and should be considered as short screening sections to be used in conjunction with a social skills assessment.

Walker–McConnell Scales of Social Competence and School Adjustment. The Walker–McConnell Scales of Social Competence and School Adjustment (SSCSA; Walker & McConnell, 1995) are social skills rating scales for teachers and other school-based professionals. Two versions of the scale are available: an elementary version for students in grades K–6, and an adolescent version for students in grades 7–12.

The elementary version contains 43 positively worded items that reflect adaptive social–behavioral competencies within the school environment. The items are rated with a 5-point scale ranging from 1 (*never occurs*) to 5 (*frequently occurs*). The scale yields standard scores on three subscales ($M = 10$, $SD = 3$) as well as a total score ($M = 100$, $SD = 15$), which is a composite of the three subscales. Subscale 1, Teacher-Preferred Social Behavior, includes 16 items that measure peer-related social behaviors that are highly valued by teachers and reflect their concerns for empathy, sensitivity, self-restraint, and cooperative, socially mature peer relationships (e.g., "Is considerate of the feelings of others" and "Is sensitive to the needs of others"). Subscale 2, Peer-Preferred Social Behavior, includes 17 items that measure peer-related social behaviors that are highly valued by other children and reflect peer values involving social relationships, dynamics, and skills in free play settings (e.g., "Spends recess and free time interacting with peers" and "Invites peers to play or share activities"). Subscale 3, School Adjustment Behavior, includes 10 items reflecting social–behavior competencies that are especially important in academic instructional settings, such as having good work and study habits, following academic instructions, and behaving in ways conducive to classroom management (e.g., "Attends to assigned tasks" and "Displays independent study skills").

The adolescent version of the scale, designed as an upward extension of the elementary version, is very similar to it. The adolescent version includes the

43 items from the elementary version (with 9 of the scale items revised to better reflect adolescent behavioral content) plus an additional 10 items designed to measure self-related social adjustment based on content from an adolescent social skills training curriculum (Walker, Todis, Holmes, & Horton, 1988). The factor structure of the adolescent version includes the same three factors found on the elementary version plus a fourth subscale containing 6 items labeled as the Empathy subscale. This fourth factor includes items designed to measure sensitivity and awareness in peer relationships (e.g., "Listens while others are speaking" and "Is considerate of the feelings of others"). The adolescent version of the scale uses the same rating format and scoring system as the elementary version, and the four subscale scores are summed into a total score.

Extensive information on the standardization data and psychometric properties of the SSCSA's two versions are reported in the scale technical manuals. The scales were standardized on groups of approximately 2,000 students representing all four U.S. geographical regions. Studies undertaken during the development of the scales cited in the scale manual indicate adequate to excellent psychometric properties.

Reliability of the scales was established using test–retest (e.g., .88 to .92 correlations over a 3-week period with 323 subjects), internal consistency (e.g., alpha coefficients ranging from .95 to .97) and interrater (e.g., a .53 correlation between teachers and aides ratings on the total score in a day treatment facility) procedures. Validity of the scales was assessed by a variety of procedures. Discriminant validity was established in studies that found that the SSCSA differentiated among groups of students who would be expected to differ behaviorally (behavior disordered and normal, antisocial and normal, behaviorally at risk and normal, and those with and without learning problems). Criterion-related validity was demonstrated by finding significant correlations between the SSCSA and a number of criterion variables: other rating scales, sociometric ratings, academic achievement measures, and a systematic behavioral screening procedure. Construct validity of the scales was shown by such procedures as finding strong correlations between evaluative comments about subjects by their peers and teacher ratings on the scales, and finding low social skills ratings to be strongly associated with the emergence of antisocial behavior in a longitudinal study of elementary-age boys.

A number of other psychometric validation studies reported in the test manual substantiate the reliability and validity of the scale. Subsequent investigations have found the SSCSA to correlate highly with other behavioral rating scales (Merrell, 1989) and to accurately discriminate groups of students referred for learning problems from average students (Merrell et al., 1992; Merrell & Shinn, 1990). The six-item Empathy subscale from the adolescent version of the SSCSA has been found to discriminate between a group of antisocial subjects with a record of arrests and an at-risk control group

(Walker et al., 1991). The factor structure of the SSCSA scales has been shown to be strong and stable.

Both versions of the SSCSA are brief, easy to use, and contain items that are highly relevant for assessing social skills in educational settings. The research base behind the scales is truly exemplary, particularly when considering that the scales have been published only recently. Because neither version of the SSCSA was designed to measure problem behaviors, these instruments should be supplemented with an appropriate problem behavior assessment if warranted by the referral issues.

SOCIOMETRIC TECHNIQUES

Essential Characteristics of Sociometric Techniques

By definition, sociometric assessment techniques have one essential element: The obtain information from within a peer group (usually in a classroom setting) concerning the social dynamics of that group. The key feature of these techniques is that assessment data on various aspects of persons' social status within the peer group is obtained directly from its members rather than through teacher ratings or observations by an outside evaluator. These techniques allow the evaluator to tap directly into the ongoing social dynamics of a group, an obvious advantage because there may be many social skills issues within a classroom environment of which the students are more aware than the teacher (Worthen, Borg, & White, 1993). Sociometric procedures have a long history of use in psychology and education, and allow for assessment of such varied qualities as level of popularity, acceptance or rejection status, and attribution of specific positive and negative characteristics such as leadership ability, athletic or academic prowess, aggressiveness, and social awkwardness.

Recent efforts in the area of sociometric assessment have led investigators to conclude that the construct of social status is both complex and multidimensional. For example, Coie, Dodge, & Cappotelli (1982) used peer preference questions in a sociometric technique with several hundred elementary and middle school-age children and analyzed the obtained data to develop five different social status groups: popular, rejected, average, neglected, and controversial. An analysis of students' characteristics indicated that although there was some overlap between categories, each had some distinct features. Popular children were those rated by peers as being cooperative, having leadership ability, and exhibiting very few disruptive behaviors. Rejected children were rated as frequently fighting and being disruptive, being uncooperative, and having few leadership characteristics. Neglected children were those largely ignored by other children and seen as socially unresponsive. The fourth nonaverage group, controversial children, tended to exhibit features of both the popular and rejected groups, being considered as disruptive and starting fights, but at the same time perceived as assertive leaders. This conceptualization of social status ratings into five groups, validated by subsequent research, shows how complex social dynamics within peer groups can be and suggests that sociometric procedures can indeed provide complex and useful social skill assessment information.

Unlike some other social assessment methods, sociometric procedures usually are not norm-referenced or commercially published. Instead, they tend to comprise variations of a few relatively simple methods originally developed for research use but fully capable of transfer into school or clinical practice. The technical and psychometric aspects of these procedures have been investigated in a large number of studies that generally have produced favorable technical evidence.

Temporal stability of sociometric assessments has been shown to be relatively high, at both short- and long-term stability periods (Hartup, 1983; Roff et al., 1972). Landau and Milich (1990) reviewed several studies of interrater correspondence in sociometric procedures and noted that moderate to high levels of correspondence between raters are typical. However there is one interesting and peculiar finding regarding rater consistency—a gender difference on social convergence in ratings wherein both boys and girls tend to attribute more positive attributes to members of their own gender and more negative attributes to members of the opposite gender.

Validity of sociometric assessment procedures has been established in several classic studies (Cowen et al., 1973, and Roff et al., 1972) wherein social status ratings were predictive of various types of social adjustment and maladjustment later in life. In summary, although sociometric assessment procedures tend not to be standardized or commercially published like most other tests used by psychologists, their generally favorable technical properties nonetheless have been demonstrated, and these procedures should be viewed as a potentially useful method of assessing peer relationships and social skills.

Four Sociometric Techniques

It is difficult to divide sociometric techniques into distinct categories because they have considerable overlap. However, there are certain similarities and differences between varied techniques that make a general categorization possible. This section provides an overview of four general types of sociometric techniques: peer nomination, picture sociometrics, "guess who" techniques, and the class play. In some cases these categories involve general descriptions common to many methods within the category. In other cases, the categorical description is rather unique to a specific procedure that has been developed.

Peer Nomination.   The oldest, most widely used sociometric approach, and the basis for most other types of sociometric measures is the nomination method, originally introduced by Moreno (1934). The essence of the peer nomination technique is that students are asked to nominate or name classmates that they prefer according to specific positive criteria. This approach typically involves the student naming three classmates they would most like to study with, play with during free time, work with on a class project, or participate with in some other positive way. For children with sufficient reading and writing ability, peer nomination procedures can be administered by either an item-by-peer matrix or a questionnaire wherein they fill in names of classmates on blank lines after questions.

The item-by-peer matrix consists of having the names of all children in the class across the top of the page and the social interaction items listed vertically on the left side of the page. The students are instructed to put an "X" under the names of the other students to whom they think the item applies (e.g., "Which three students would you most like to have as your best friends?"). Use of a questionnaire format accomplishes essentially the same thing (e.g. "Write the names of three students in your class that you would most like to have as your best friends," followed by three numbered blank lines). Scoring of peer nominations typically is done by totaling the number of nominations that each child receives. Worthen et al. (1993) suggested that the results of positive peer nomination procedures can be classified and interpreted according to a frequently used set of criteria. *Stars* are individuals frequently chosen. *Isolates* are those never chosen in the process. *Neglectees* receive only a few nominations. The results also can be plotted on a sociogram that shows the patterns of choice for each student and is helpful in identifying not only frequently and never-nominated students, but cliques or small groups as well. A *mutual choice* occurs when an individual is chosen by the same student that he or she selected. A *cross-sex choice* occurs when a boy chooses a girl or a girl chooses a boy. A *clique* is identified when a small group of students choose each other and make few or no choices outside that group. *Cleavage* is said to occur when members of two or more groups within the class or social unit never choose someone from the other group(s). Using these scoring and classification criteria, one can easily see how a procedure as deceptively simple as the peer nomination method can yield information regarding student social behavior that is both striking and complex. An example of a sociogram depicting the results of a positive peer nomination procedure with a group of elementary-age girls, is presented in Fig. 3.6.

Although the peer nomination technique historically most often has involved the use of positive items that indicate high social status, many practitioners and researchers have used variations of this method by employing negative nominations and using items created to identify students who are socially rejected by peers (e.g., "Who would you least like to play with?" or "Who would you never want to be friends with?"), and thus likely to have poor social skills. The use of negative peer nomination procedures has proved to be controversial, with ethical questions being raised about the potential for negative

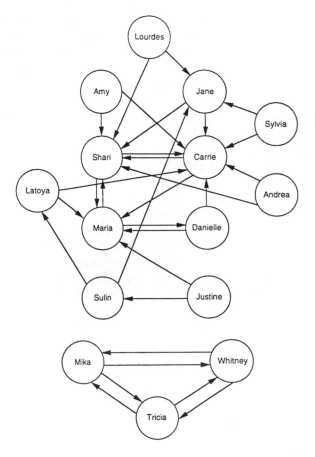

FIG. 3.6.   A sociogram based on the results of a positive peer
nomination procedure with a group of elementary-age girls.

effects. Although research indicates that sociometric assessment may have no
effect on peer interactions (Hayvren & Hymel, 1984), many educators, administrators, and parents disapprove of these procedures when negative nominations are used.

Picture Sociometrics.   Picture sociometric techniques involve placing ar-
bitrarily assorted photographs of all the children in a class before each child,
and then asking the child to answer a series of questions by pointing to or selecting a photograph of a peer. This method, an adaptation of other peer nomination methods, is useful for work with preliterate subjects. Landau and
Milich (1990) stated that it is the preferred method for preschool through second grade level subjects. Examples of questions that have been used with this

technique include "Who do you like to play with the most?" "Who is your best friend?" and "Who is the best student in your class?" As with most other sociometric techniques, specific questions can be developed for clinical or research questions, and these questions can be produced to indicate either social acceptance or social rejection.

The original picture sociometric technique and minor variations of it are scored by totaling the number of times each child was nominated by classmates based on questions indicating positive social status. Using this scoring scheme, rejected or neglected children would have significantly lower scores than accepted children with higher social status. Of course variations in scoring procedure would be needed if there were any significant deviations in administration method from the original study by McCandless and Marshall (1957). For example, questions that reflect both positive (e.g., "Who do you most like to do schoolwork with?") and negative (e.g., "Who are you afraid to be around on the playground?") social status could be mixed, and the scoring system could be divided into positive and negative status categories.

The use of picture sociometrics has subsequently been used in a number of other published studies. Studies have shown the psychometric properties of picture sociometric techniques to be quite good, with relatively high interrater reliability, very high short-term test–retest reliability, and adequate long term test–retest reliability (see Landau & Milich, 1990). Validity of the picture sociometric method has been demonstrated by producing significant discriminations between groups of aggressive, aggressive–withdrawn, and normal boys (Milich & Landau, 1984). Interestingly, this technique has been shown to produce more effective discriminations of social status than information provided by teachers.

"Guess Who" Measures. The "Guess Who" technique is a sociometric approach wherein brief descriptions are provided to students and they are asked to write down names of a few other students (usually three or fewer) that they think best fit the descriptions. For example, the students might be asked to respond to descriptions such as "Guess who fights with other children," "Guess who has many friends," "Guess who no one knows very well," or "Guess who is often angry at other children." The descriptions can be given to the students either verbally or in written format. The content of the "Guess Who" items can be decided by teachers, clinicians, or researchers based on specific characteristics they wish to identify. Scoring is done by making simple frequency counts of each question/description. More elaborate scoring methods are also possible, such as grouping descriptions into categories of similar social behavior (e.g., antisocial behaviors, helping characteristics, peer popularity, etc.) and obtaining frequency counts within each broader category.

A "Guess Who" measure used with a large number of students and carefully investigated is the Revised PRIME Guess Who Measure developed for use in Project PRIME, a large-scale investigation of students with mild disabilities who had been integrated into regular education classrooms for part of their instructional day (Kauffman, Semmell, & Agard, 1974). The original instrument consisted of 29 questions/descriptions, and was administered to over 13,000 students in grades 3–5. Factor analytic procedures conducted on the instrument divided the items into four major factors labeled *disruptive, bright, dull,* and *well-behaved.* A revised scale including 20 items (the 5 items contributing the most to each factor) was developed by Veldman and Sheffield (1979), who reported reliability coefficients ranging from .56 to .77 for each factor score and developed a satisfactory concurrent validity procedure for the instrument by correlating the instrument items with teacher ratings along similar dimensions.

In summary, the "Guess Who" technique is flexible and easy to administer and score. It has been used in a large number of studies and projects and found to have satisfactory technical properties. Clinicians and investigators desiring an adaptable, easily administered sociometric measure may find "Guess Who" techniques to be a useful choice in assessment instrumentation.

The Class Play.   The Class Play procedure was first developed by Bower (1969), and has been further revised by Masten, Morrison, and Pelligrini (1985). A frequently used sociometric technique, it has been employed in several large-scale investigations, including the classic 11- to 13-year follow-up study of elementary-age children by Cowen and his colleagues (Cowen et al., 1973). In this procedure children are asked to assign their peers to various roles (usually both positive and negative) in an imaginary play. The original Class Play described by Bower (1969) included both positive (e.g., "someone who will wait their turn") and negative (e.g., "someone who is too bossy") roles, but consisted of a scoring procedure wherein only a single score (negative peer reputation) was derived, which was done by calculating the number of negative roles given to a child and dividing that by the total number of roles given to that child. Large percentages are supposed to indicate a high degree of peer rejection (and presumably, poorer social skills), whereas low percentages are meant to indicate that the child has higher social status (and presumably, greater social skills). As is the case with most sociometric approaches, the specification of roles in the Class Play procedure (as well as the method of scoring) can be manipulated by clinicians or researchers to suit their goals.

The use of class play procedures in sociometric assessment is attractive for two reasons other than the measurement capabilities they may have: children (particularly younger children) usually enjoy casting their peers into the various roles in make-believe plays and teachers and administrators seem to view this procedure more positively than some other sociometric methods. Therefore, the Class Play is more likely to be supported and approved than some other approaches. Masten et al. (1985) suggested that the diversity of roles needed in a play would reduce the probability of disapproving labels on children with high negative scores by other children in the rating/casting process.

Some Final Comments on Sociometric Techniques

The sociometric assessment techniques described in this chapter, as well as other types of sociometric measures, have a great deal of appeal to clinicians and researchers and a long history of use in psychology and education. However, these approaches are not without controversy. As the discussion shows, many sociometric methods involve negative ranking or nomination procedures, or the use of negative characteristics to single out peers. Largely because of these negative nomination procedures, parents (and some teachers and administrators) are often hesitant (or outright angry) at the possibility of their children participating in sociometric assessments, for fear that as a result their child or other children will be singled out by peers and further ostracized. Although there is little empirical evidence to completely warrant this assertion, and some evidence to the contrary (Hayvren & Hymel, 1984), there seems to be a common concern that children will compare their responses after the assessment to find out which children were singled out for negative nominations, and that this process will end up causing increased isolation or social exile for the children commonly perceived in negative terms. Whether such concerns are founded or not, clinicians and researchers desiring to utilize sociometric approaches would do well to pick carefully the most appropriate method for their purposes, to communicate closely and carefully with their constituent groups, and to educate those involved on the purposes and procedures involved. In the meantime, additional research on any potential peer effects of sociometric measurement involving negative ranking or nomination would be very helpful.

SELF-REPORT ASSESSMENT METHODS

Self-report assessment obtains information directly from the subject rather than through informants, observers, or peers. Direct and objective self-report assessment eschews highly inferential techniques such as projective tests, fill-in-the-blanks tasks, and drawing exercises. Instead, the subject is asked directly to provide objective information to the examiner, usually through a semistructured interview or on a paper-and-pencil objective self-report test. Both of these self-report assessment forms are examined in this section to overview their usefulness in assessing child and adolescent social skills.

Interviewing

Interviewing techniques have long been a keystone of behavioral, social, and emotional assessment. In assessing child and adolescent social skills, interviewing has a potentially prominent position, whether it consists of identifying problems, conducting behavioral interviews with parents or teachers, or obtaining the self-report from the child or adolescent being assessed. This section focuses on the latter use of interviews in social skills assessment: Evaluating the child or adolescent client's own perception of his or her social skills and general social adjustment through interviewing. Also included in this section is additional information on using the interview process as a diagnostic tool for making important observations about social skills.

Before getting into the specifics of using interviews in the social skills assessment process, it is important to consider the dynamic aspects of child and adolescent development that may affect the quantity and quality of interview information obtained. In brief, each distinct stage of development carries with it certain characteristics that may affect the interview process. Preschool- and primary-age children frequently cannot describe their thoughts, experiences, and feelings through verbal mediation processes, have difficulty understanding events from any point of view but their own, and consider what is right or wrong only in terms of immediate consequences. Hughes and Baker (1990) observed that effective interviewing of very young children will require familiarity with the child and the child's experiences, reduced complexity of questions, and the use of physically manipulative objects (e.g., dolls, toys, clay) as a means of eliciting behavior and information.

By the time they have reached the elementary-age years, most children have increased their verbal skills dramatically, making clinical interviewing potentially more useful. However, most children at this age tend to think and communicate in concrete, nonabstract ways. Thus, interview techniques that rely on familiar settings and situations, provide contextual cues (i.e., specific examples), and avoid abstract or symbolic sorts of references are more likely to secure valid and useful information.

By midadolescence, most individuals are capable of thinking and communicating in more abstract and symbolic ways, and many young people begin to select values and judge the morality of actions according to self-selected principles rather than simple rules of behavior. Thus, many adolescents have the intellectual and social capabilities that make a high-quality interview more possible. However, some other developmental considerations about adolescents create unique challenges for interviewing, such as the intensity and variability of emotional experience and feelings that they may not be understood by adults. Therefore, adult interviewers should be careful not to apply adult normative standards to adolescent interview responses, or faulty conclusions may result. In summary, understanding and considerating the developmental processes and stages of child and adolescent subjects is a practice necessary for maximizing the usefulness of self-report interview data in assessing social skills. More detailed discussion on developmental considerations in the interviewing of children and adolescents can be found in previous work by Hughes and Baker (1990) and Merrell (1994a).

Because referred children and adolescents may have limited insight into their psychosocial functioning, and because many have adopted self-censoring rules (Boggs & Eyberg, 1990), open-ended clinical interviewing typically is a poor choice for assessment of social skills. Moreover, even though behaviorally focused interviews are one of the most commonly used ways of obtaining self-report information, they have not been systematically investigated as social skills assessment techniques. Furthermore, no systematic interview schedules or structured interview techniques have been developed and validated specifically for assessing social skills in children and adolescents. Thus, role-playing or behavioral role-play techniques are the interview methods most widely used and studied for obtaining social skills data.

Behavioral role-play techniques may be considered a merger between interviewing and direct observation because they use traditional components of each method. According to Gresham (1986), behavioral role-play techniques have been frequently used because of the following advantages: they can be used to assess important social behaviors that occur with low frequency in the natural environment; they assess actual behavior enactment rather than perceptions of behavior; the interview setting can be tightly controlled to simulate important natural environments; and they are less expensive than naturalistic observation.

There is no set format or step-by-step process that must be followed for assessing social skills via behavioral role-play interviews. Rather, interviews wherein social skills are assessed via role-play simply evolve into a situation in which social exchange roles are assigned, performances occur, and the interviewer takes special note of the child or adolescent's responses. The following instructions from an interviewer to an early adolescent-age client show how a role-play sequence may be set up during an interview:

> You've been explaining to me that it's hard for you to just go up to other kids at school and talk to them. I would like to be able to better understand what this is like for you. So, let's try something different. Let's do some "acting." I want you to just be yourself, and for you to pretend like I am a kid you would like to get to know at school. I'll try and act like that person, and let's practice having you come up to me and try to start a conversation.

Of course, the principles of behavioral generalization indicate that a role-play such as this one will more likely result in meaningful results if the role-play situation is constructed to parallel the real environment closely (Stokes & Baer, 1977). Therefore, the interviewer in this situation would do well to get from the adolescent client information that would allow the situation to be set up as closely as possible to the real thing. Little details such as the name and typical mannerisms of the other kid, the physical aspects of the setting, and a situation that is likely to happen will make the difference in this respect.

Gresham (1986) noted that social skills role-playing situations are more likely to inform us about social skill deficits rather than social performance deficits. In other words, if a child or adolescent cannot enact a specific social behavior during a role-play, that skill likely is not in his or her behavioral repertoire. In contrast to this situation, a child who can exhibit a specific social behavior during a role-play but does not do so in the naturalistic environment could be said to have a performance deficit, in that the child has demonstrated ability to perform the skill, but not across various settings or situations. Thus, according to Gresham, "role-play measures perhaps are better considered diagnostic measures of social skill difficulty than assessment measures for intervention or evaluation of outcomes of social skills training programs" (p. 162).

Gresham (1986) further noted that the research on social skills assessment via behavioral role-plays often has shown little correspondence of role-play behavior to social behavior in the natural environment. Therefore, social skills assessment through role-playing in interview and observation sessions may inform us regarding possible social skill deficits, but these techniques should always be used in conjunction with other methods of assessment for evaluation and intervention purposes.

Objective Self-Report Tests

Over a decade ago, Gresham (1986) made this observation regarding self-report tests and their utility in assessing children's social skills:

> It is not difficult to summarize the current status of self-report measures of social skills with children. In short children's self-report measures have not shown to be useful in predicting peer acceptance, peer popularity, teacher ratings of social skills, role-play performance, or social behavior in naturalistic settings. Given this abysmal validity evidence, self-report measures should not be used as either selection or outcome measures in social skills training research until and unless more convincing data can be accumulated to support their use. (p. 163)

Given such a bleak state of affairs, why should self-report social skills assessment be given any prominence in this chapter? There are two reasons. First, the 1980s and 1990s has seen a resurgence of interest in obtaining self-report information from children coupled with a number of advances on psychometric technology in this area (Harter, 1990). Second, it appears that the field is now reaching a point at which psychometrically acceptable self-report measures of child and adolescent social skills are being developed. Two relatively recent self-report measures of child and adolescent social behavior (including one developed by Gresham and his colleague Elliott) are briefly reviewed here. Both measures, the Assessment of Interpersonal Relations (Bracken, 1993), and the self-report forms of the SSRS (Gresham & Elliott, 1990), appear to be improvements over what was available in this area only a decade ago and stand out as the first self-report instruments for assessing child and adolescent social skills to utilize state-of-the-art modern development techniques, project reasonably acceptable psychometric characteristics, and supply norms based on large and representative nationwide samples.

Assessment of Interpersonal Relations. The Assessment of Interpersonal Relations (AIR; Bracken, 1993) is an instrument designed to assess the quality of interpersonal relationships from the child's perspective. Theoretically, the AIR is based on the same multidimensional model of psychosocial adjustment as the Multidimensional Self-Concept Scale (Bracken, 1992), and both instruments were normed with the same standardization population.

The AIR may be used with children and adolescents between the ages of 9 and 19 years. It includes a total of 105 self-report items on three separate 35-item scales that assess perceived quality of relationships with parents ("I like to spend time with my . . ."), peers ("I am treated fairly by my . . ."), and teachers ("I am really understood by my . . ."), respectively. Thus, the AIR appears to be not only a measure of peer-related social adjustment, but parent- and teacher-related forms of adjustment as well. Subjects respond to each item by indicating whether they *strongly agree (SA), agree (A), disagree (D)* or *strongly disagree (SD)*. According to the test author, the AIR takes about 20 minutes to complete. In the parent section, separate responses are recorded for perceptions regarding the subject's mother and father. In the peer rating section, separate responses are recorded for general perceptions regarding peers by gender. Raw scores in each area are converted to norm-referenced standard scores. Given the response breakdowns, the completed profile of scale scores includes separate scores for perceptions of interpersonal relationships in six domains, mother, father, male peers, female peers, teachers, and a Total Relationship Index.

The AIR manual provides ample details regarding scale construction methods, psychometric properties, and other relevant research findings. The AIR was standardized on a sample of 2,501 children in Grades 5 through 12 from various communities nationwide. Internal consistency and test–retest reliability (2-week intervals) of the AIR is exceptionally high, with coefficients in the .90s for all scaled scores. AIR scores have been shown to differentiate children based on age groupings, gender, and clinical status. Discriminant construct validity was established by finding weak to moderate correlations with the Multidimensional Self-Concept scale, an instrument purported to measure a somewhat different underlying construct, but perhaps weakly to moderately associated with interpersonal relationships.

In summary, the AIR seems to hold substantial promise as a self-report measure for assessing perceptions of interpersonal relationships, a key correlate of social skills in children and adolescents. The content validity and reported technical characteristics appear to be solid. However, some cautions and limitations are also apparent. Missing from the AIR manual are any convergent validity data regarding the correlation between AIR scores and other interpersonal relationships measures (i.e., parent or teacher report, direct observation, etc.). Demonstration of at least modest relationships between the AIR and other measures of interpersonal relationships/social skills is a crucial need that must be met before complete confidence in the AIR is warranted. Another limitation is that this instrument cannot be used with younger children (below Grade 5) because the reading level and standardization sample clearly were aimed at the intermediate to secondary school population. Despite these limitations and cautions, the AIR appears to be a substantial improvement in several respects over the earlier generation of self-report measures designed to assess children's perceptions of their own social skills. Future research with the AIR may provide answers to some of the questions that have been raised.

SSRS. The SSRS (Gresham & Elliott, 1990), referred to earlier in this chapter, is a comprehensive system for assessing child and adolescent social skills. Of particular interest for this section is the fact that the SSRS includes two student self-report forms: a 34-item elementary-age form (Grades 3–6), and a 39-item secondary-age form (Grades 7–12). Items from both forms fall into four social skills subscales: cooperation (e.g., "I do my homework on time"), assertion (e.g., "I start talks with my classmates"), empathy (e.g., "I feel sorry for others when bad things happen to them"), and self-control (e.g., "I politely question rules that may be unfair"). The items for the two grade levels reflect the same general content, but have slightly different wording to reflect language and reading ability changes, and in some cases, slightly differing social concerns. Unlike the parent and teacher versions of the SSRS, the student self-report forms focus exclusively on social skills and do not include problem behavior screening sections. Like the other SSRS forms, the student self-report forms convert raw scores to standard scores and descriptive behavior levels. Confidence bands and percentile scores are also available.

Systematic item development and content validation procedures were used to select the SSRS student form items. Diverse national normative standardization data was obtained from 1,980 cases for the elementary student form and 1,690 cases for the secondary student form. Internal consistency reliability for the student form scores reported in the SSRS manual is modest to reasonably strong, with coefficients ranging from .51 to .77 for the subscale scores, and a total score coefficients of .83 for both grade level versions. Test–retest reliability for the SSRS student forms at 4-week intervals was modest to adequate, averaging .56 for the subscale scores and .68 for the total scores. Discriminant construct validity evidence for the SSRS student forms was obtained by finding weak to modest correlations with the various self-report tests purported to measure constructs weakly to modestly associated with social skills. Correlations of common SSRS subscales between student–teacher and student–parent forms were reported to be modest to weak, averaging .17 and .09, respectively, for teacher–student and parent–student comparisons at the elementary level, and .32 for both sets of comparisons at the secondary level. SSRS scores have been shown to differentiate groups of students significantly according to gender and disability status.

In summary, the SSRS student self-report forms also appear to be considerable improvements over what was previously available in the area of self-report tests for child and adolescent social skills. Although some of the reliability data for these forms is somewhat troubling, and the strength of association between student reports and parent or teacher reports is somewhat disappointing (perhaps an artifact of source and setting variance rather than a weakness of the instrument), the student self-report forms have many strengths. State-of-the-art scale construction and standardization procedures were used in their development, and the student self-report forms have the distinct advantage of being part of the comprehensive SSRS system. Instead of dismissing student self-report scores on the SSRS because of the marginal reliability data, a better practice would be to use student reports in conjunction with parent and teacher ratings to obtain a comprehensive picture of child and adolescent social skills, and to overcome error variance based on one method of administration.

A MODEL FOR MULTIFACTORED ASSESSMENT PRACTICE

During the 1980s and 1990s significant advances were made in the research and technology base for assessing behavioral, social, and emotional problems of children and adolescents. One of the major developments was the articulation of a model for a broad-based assessment design. The essential feature of this model is that by using various assessment methods with different informants or sources and in several settings, the amount of error variance in the assessment is reduced, and the result is a comprehensive representation of the referred client's behavioral, social, and emotional functioning. This type of broad-based assessment design has been referred to by various names, including multifactored assessment (Barnett & Zucker, 1988), multisetting, multisource, multi-instrument assessment (Martin, 1988; Martin, Hooper, & Snow, 1986), and multiaxial empirically based assessment (Achenbach, McConaughy, & Howell, 1987). Although there are some differences between the

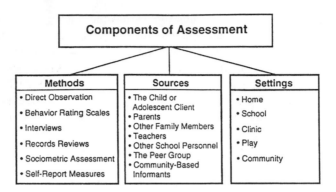

FIG. 3.7.   Graphic representation of various elements of a multimethod, multisource, multisetting assessment design.

way these various models have been articulated, the critical feature of obtaining assessment data on a client through a number of different instruments,
methods, sources, informants, and settings remains the same.

The term *multimethod, multisource, multisetting assessment* has been
chosen to represent the features of conducting broad-based, multifactored assessments that are most relevant to the topic of this chapter. In Fig. 3.7, a
graphic representation of the model is displayed.

To see how such a multifactored assessment would be conducted in actual
practice, it is useful to look at the hypothetical case of a child client referred
to a clinical setting for a variety of behavioral and emotional problems, including social deficits and peer interaction problems. In terms of method, it
probably would be desirable to include behavioral observation, interviews,
rating scales, and self-report instruments as part of the assessment from the
onset. Within each method, a variety of instruments or specific techniques
should be used when possible. Because this child is reportedly experiencing
social adjustment problems and there is potentially easy access to a social
group (i.e., classmates at school) for assessment, it also might be desirable under some circumstances to gather sociometric assessment data. In terms of
source, it would be necessary, at a minimum, to gather assessment data from
both the client and the parent(s) because this is a clinic-based referral. If possible, it would be desirable to include other relevant sources, who know the
child well, as informants. These other sources might include school personnel
(most importantly, the primary teacher of the child), other family members,
and in some circumstances, community-based individuals such as clergy,
youth group leaders, and the like. In terms of setting, clinic, home, and school
would be included in an optimum assessment, and when feasible, community-
based settings as well.

In reality, it is often difficult or impossible to include all of the possible relevant sources and settings, and it is sometimes a problem to even include more than a few methods. The main point to keep in mind here is that as the assessment becomes more diverse and broad-based, an aggregated picture of the child's behavioral, social, and emotional functioning is obtained. Such an assessment design is considered to be a best practice that has the possibility of reducing error variance and providing a more comprehensive picture of the child (Achenbach et al., 1987; Martin et al., 1986; Merrell, 1994a).

Some caution is warranted in considering the possibilities and advantages of an aggregated multimethod, multisource, multisetting. Although most current thinking suggests that such a design is indeed a best practice and the most sophisticated way of implementing the assessment, there is some divergence of professional opinion here. Some experts in the field of child and adolescent psychopathology (Arkes, 1981; Locber, Dishion, & Patterson, 1984; Reid, Baldwin, Patterson, & Dishion, 1988; Wiggins, 1981) have presented very persuasive arguments that aggregated multiple assessment data may actually increase error variance in some cases owing to covariation between different assessment sources and the inability of clinicians to effectively aggregate assessment data that is contradictory. Indeed, this is a compelling and interesting argument, and at least partly accounts for the impetus behind efforts that advocate sequential or multiple-gating approaches to assessment, which have already been alluded to in this chapter. Even some experts who advocate the aggregated multiple assessment model (Achenbach & Edelbrock, 1984) have acknowledged this possibility. In light of these somewhat contradictory arguments, then, what is the best practice? The position advocated here is that the informed and judicious use of an aggregated multiple assessment model is still the best practice for general referral and assessment cases, particularly when the assessment design is created sequentially based on the increasing availability of information. However, clinicians and researchers need to be informed of the potential liabilities of their assessment design. In the meantime, additional empirical evidence on this assessment issue would help those in the child and adolescent assessment field to articulate a better state-of-the-art assessment model for the next century. Because most of these contradictory arguments on assessment design are theory-based but not yet empirically validated, being aware of both positions and their possibilities seems to be a prudent step at the present time.

SUMMARY

Screening and assessment are both exceedingly important but sometimes overlooked or misunderstood aspects of identifying social skills deficits in children and adolescents, and of providing appropriate social skills interventions. The terms *screening* and *assessment* are sometimes used interchangeably but reflect differing uses of evaluation procedures.

Screening is a practice intended to narrow down a larger population to a smaller sample more likely to meet the criterion of interest. Appropriate screening procedures are those that have low cost in terms of time and that narrow down the population while making few false-negative errors.

Assessment, however, comprises of a variety of measurement and evaluation procedures designed for the purpose of describing and identifying given characteristics in detail. Formal assessment of social skills is used for purposes of classification, service eligibility, and intervention planning. In this chapter, a direct and objective approach to assessment is advocated, wherein the assessment results are more likely to be empirically defensible.

Four general methods for assessing social skills are outlined: direct behavioral observation, behavioral rating scales, sociometric techniques, and self-report assessment. Direct behavioral observation is perhaps the most empirically sound method of assessing social skills, but it requires a great deal of cost in terms of professional time and training. Several potential problems that may interfere with the validity of observational data are presented. The specifics of four different observational coding systems (event recording, interval recording, time-sample recording, duration and latency recording) are outlined in terms of their possible uses in social skills assessment. Behavior rating scales have become an increasingly popular and empirically sound method for assessing social skills. The advantages and problems of rating scale assessment are presented, and six rating scales for assessment of social skills are overviewed: The Behavioral Assessment System for Children (BASC), the Matson Evaluation of Social Skills With Youngsters (MESSY), the Preschool and Kindergarten Behavior Scales (PKBS), the School Social Behavior Scales (SSBS), the Walker–McConnell Scales of Social Competence and School Adjustment (SSCSA), and the Social Skills Rating System (SSRS).

Sociometric techniques were used less frequently in the 1980s and 1990s, but nevertheless appear to offer many advantages for social skills assessment. The basic principles and techniques of sociometric assessment are outlined, and four specific techniques are presented: peer nomination, picture sociometrics, "Guess Who" techniques, and the Class Play. Self-report assessment of child and adolescent social skills has been the focus of several technical advances in recent years, and appears to have some potential for social skills limitations in spite of some obvious problems and limitations. Informal analogue role-playing within interview situations is probably the most commonly used form of social skills self-report. However, in recent years there have been some technical advances in objective self-report assessment, and two potentially useful instruments have been developed: The AIR and the student report form of the SSRS.

A model for multifactored assessment of social skills is presented. This model is referred to as multimethod-multisource-multisetting assessment and appears to have broad applications across several different aspects of behavioral, social, and emotional assessment. Assessment of child and adolescent social skills through a well-planned design and including multiple assessment methods and multiple sources of information across several environmental settings is a practice with the potential to overcome error variance limitations and result in comprehensive and empirically sound assessment data. A multifactored assessment design such as the one advocated in this chapter may ultimately prove to be more defensible and useful if it is carried out sequentially, moving from less to more costly types of assessment as the assessment picture becomes more clear.

FOUR

Designing, Implementing, and Evaluating Social Skills Interventions

The first three chapters of this book lay a background foundation for conceptualizing and assessing child and adolescent social skills. The remaining chapters focus exclusively on various aspects of social skills intervention. This
chapter provides extensive background on the basics of conducting social
skills training interventions with children and adolescents in educational and
clinical settings. It really provides the "nuts and bolts" of social skill intervention. Some topics among others covered herein include instructional design
principles, group composition and structure questions, defining social skills
intervention targets more specifically, a basic technology for outlining and delivering social skills intervention modules, enhancing transfer of training, and
comprehensive evaluation of intervention

SOME BASIC ISSUES:
ACQUISITION AND PERFORMANCE

Prior to designing and implementing a social skills training intervention, it
may be important to consider some additional basic issues about how children
acquire and perform social skills. In chapter 2, we overviewed a number of developmental issues in the acquisition and performance of social skills. This
discussion covers some similar issues, but is less expansive and more oriented
toward the end result of designing social skills training interventions. It is im-

portant to consider acquisition and performance issues before training because the specific cause or etiology of the social skills problem or deficit may have some implications for the most appropriate way to initiate training.

Acquisition Versus Performance

Michelson et al. (1983) suggested that there are two general approaches to the treatment of socially incompetent children. According to this paradigm, the two approaches are based on either a skill deficit model or a competing emotions model. The *skill deficit model* is based on the idea that a specific social skills problem or deficit in a child is caused by the child's failure to learn that particular skill. In other words, the skill is not in the child's repertoire, and thus he or she cannot perform it. In contrast, the competing emotions model is based on the idea that the requisite social skill may be in the child's behavioral repertoire, but the child does not demonstrate it adequately because of competing emotional or cognitive states such as depression, anxiety, and automatic negative thought patterns (e.g., "I can't do this"). These two notions are not necessarily incompatible. It is easy enough to assume that in some cases, socially incompetent behavior may be caused by a failure to learn the requisite skills, whereas in other cases, an individual may have the requisite skills, but fail to appropriately demonstrate these skills because of maladaptive emotional or cognitive characteristics.

Bandura's social cognitive or social learning model illustrated briefly in chapter 2 has implications for how a treatment method might be selected when the social skills problem is caused by either a skill deficit or a competing maladaptive emotional or cognitive state. Bandura (1986) suggested that the acquisition of a new behavior involves a complex interaction between direct learning processes (e.g., observation, modeling, imitation, reinforcement) and cognitive processes that may facilitate or inhibit successful learning. Thus, we assume that both conditioning and cognition play key roles in the acquisition and performance of social skills.

Given these assumptions and conditions, it may be useful to determine, if possible, whether the socially incompetent behavior of a child stems primarily from a failure to acquire or a failure to perform the requisite skills. In reality, these two types of failures often are intertwined and quite difficult to separate. However, by carefully observing and evaluating a particular child's socially incompetent behavior, it may be possible to determine which type of failure is most important.

If a child appears unable to successfully perform or approximate the desired social skill behavior under any condition, it may be that it was never learned it in the first place. It should be assumed then that an acquisition deficit is operating. When this is the case, an attempt should be made to remediate the problem by identifying the specific skill deficit and systematically delivering social skills training using the instructional approach detailed later in this chapter.

If a child consistently demonstrates a particular social skill under one set of circumstances but fails to do so in other situations, it is quite possible that the desired behavior is in the child's repertoire, but is not being demonstrated because of maladaptive emotional and cognitive states. Thus, the existence of a performance deficit rather than an acquisition deficit could be assumed.

Another possibility, however, is that inadequate transfer training has occurred (transfer training issues of maintenance and generalization are dealt with later in this chapter). Assuming that a performance deficit exists because of maladaptive cognitive and emotional states rather than a failure to learn the skill, it is suggested that the therapist or trainer attempt to identify the source of the problem. Such identification will probably require a combination of directly observing the child in social settings and interviewing the child to assess his or her emotional and cognitive states. If maladaptive emotional or cognitive states are identified (or strongly presumed because of direct evidence), then it is most useful to plan the social skills training sessions with specific affective and cognitive goals, such as identifying negative or self-defeating thinking patterns, or dealing with such difficult emotions as anger, depression, or frustration. Alternatively, the therapist/trainer may wish individually to teach the child effective cognitive or affective strategies prior to or in conjunction with the social skills training intervention. The best resources for affective and cognitive interventions are found mainly in the area of treatments for depression (some excellent resources for child and adolescent populations include Clark, Lewinsohn, & Hops, 1990; Harrington, 1993; Stark, 1990).

Understanding Performance Conditions

Our discussion of acquisition versus performance of social skills would not be complete without at least a brief exploration of what is referred to as performance conditions. By definition, *performance conditions* are environmental factors that establish guidelines for specific social behaviors, such as when and where to initiate an interaction, how long the interaction should occur, and when the interaction should be terminated (Asher, Oden, & Gottman, 1977; Knapczyk & Rodes, 1996). Assuming that the therapist or trainer has identified a performance deficit as the source of a child's socially incompetent behavior, it may be useful to conduct a brief assessment of the performance conditions under which the child is expected to engage in social behavior. Perhaps what will be most needed is specific training in adapting to the demands of the environment. "When students fail to tailor their performance to the demands of the situation, their behavior can interrupt the natural flow of activities and attract negative attention" (Knapczyk & Rodes, 1996, p. 197).

According to Knapczyk and Rodes (1996), there are five important factors in performance conditions for social behaviors: time (when to engage in the behavior), location (where to engage in the behavior), people (with whom to engage in the behavior), amount (how much of the behavior is appropriate), and materials (whether or not there are specific materials needed for performance of the behavior). These five factors form the nucleus of any performance assessment of the conditions under which social skills are to be performed. Thus, when a therapist or trainer hypothesizes that a socially incompetent child is experiencing a performance deficit rather than an acquisition deficit, these five areas should be appraised briefly so that the intervention can include the right performance components, which will then become a key in generalization and maintenance of the social skills.

Additionally, Knapczyk and Rodes (1996) identified four general performance issues that should be considered as part of an evaluation of the performance conditions: whether the students use the target skill under the right conditions, under the wrong conditions, or better under some conditions than others, as well as whether they use the wrong behavior to respond to conditions. It is strongly recommended that before and during social skills training, therapists or trainers consider these four general performance issues and apply them to the specific children and circumstances with which they are working. The information in Table 4.1 may be a useful tool in this regard.

TABLE 4.1
Some General Questions Regarding Social Skills Performance Conditions

---

Are the Target Skills Being Used Under the Right Conditions?
    Is the target child cooperating during small group activities?
    Is the target child staying with students in his/her own group?
    Is the target child interacting during the total time allotted?
    Is the target child using materials appropriately?
Are the Target Skills Being Used Under the Wrong Conditions?
    Is the target child trying to interact with others not in the assigned group?
    Is the target child attempting to work cooperatively using materials or supplies not intended
        for that activity?
Are the Target Skills Being Used Better Under Some Conditions Than Others?
    Is the target child cooperating with classmates less effectively during specific times?
    Is the target child cooperating with classmates less effectively in specific settings?
    Is the target child cooperating with classmates less effectively when with certain types of
        classmates?
    Is the target child cooperating with classmates less effectively on different duration activities?
Are the Wrong Behaviors Being Used to Respond to Conditions?
    Is the target child talking about irrelevant topics during small group discussions?
    Is the target child getting off-task during activities?

DESIGNING A SOCIAL SKILLS
TRAINING PROGRAM

Before a social skills intervention is delivered, careful thought must go into the design of the program so that the intended effects are more likely to occur. This section deals with some basic planning and design issues that should be considered before the actual delivery of the social skills training intervention. Specifically, issues surrounding group composition and selection, and the desired number and length of sessions are addressed.

Advantages of Group Intervention

When possible, it is most desirable (and probably more effective) to implement social skills training interventions with small groups of students, which is the most common way that social skills training interventions in schools are delivered (Sheridan, 1995), because they are natural places for learning and using social skills (Elliott & Gresham, 1991). The popularity of the small group instruction format for teaching social skills to children and adolescents is not accidental. This format offers many advantages. Small groups can function as a microcosm of the larger environment, giving participants opportunities for staging and practice, interaction, and feedback that to some extent may parallel the natural environment. Through careful selection of participants, small groups can be specifically tailored to the training needs of the child and adolescent participants.

Of course, there are times and situations in which a small group-oriented social skills training intervention is not possible. For example, a therapist or trainer may not be available to lead the group, or when a particular child or adolescent needs treatment, it may be impossible for peers to be recruited for participation in the group intervention. In such cases, there are other alternatives including the use of a classroom-wide or school-wide social skills program embedded as a natural element of the curriculum or system (see chapter 5, this volume). Although this form of social skills training is a relatively new endeavor, it seems to offer some promise.

When a small group is not possible, another possible approach to social skills training involves individual sessions with a therapist or trainer and child or adolescent in need of treatment. Although the literature on individually based social skills training is quite scant and little empirical evidence exists to verify or disavow its effectiveness, we know that numerous clinicians utilize this treatment modality from time to time and often report successful results. Of course, given what is known regarding generalization and maintenance of social skills (addressed in detail later in this chapter), it would not be expected that individually based social skills training would be as effective as small-group forms of training. However, this may be a viable option for those situations in which small group training is not possible. For maximal effectiveness of individually based social skills training in counseling sessions, the therapist/trainer must provide a range of modeling and feedback similar to that found in the natural environment.

Group Composition and Selection of Participants

Several important factors in social skills training are associated with the general area of group composition and selection of students. Some of these factors are overviewed in this section: recommended numbers of participants and group leaders; age, developmental considerations, and gender composition of participants; recommended group composition characteristics; and the selective use of socially high functioning "confederates" in training groups.

Number of Participants and Group Leaders.   Each time a social skills training intervention is developed it must be decided how many child or adolescent participants to include in the group. An important related issue involves who will lead the group and specifically how many trainers should be included.

Definitive answers to either of these questions have simply not been addressed or developed through the vast empirical evidence on social skills training. However, the experience of numerous clinicians serves to provide some general guidelines that may be considered for group size and number of leaders.

Concerning the optimal number of child or adolescent participants, the training group should be large enough to create an actual social milieu, but not so large that it is approximates a classroom-type setting. The specific best answer to this question must be developed by the group leader(s), and it will need to take into account such factors as the mix of students and how difficult it may prove to effectively manage them. Sheridan (1995) recommended between four and eight students for optimal group size, whereas Elliott and Gresham (1991) recommended between three and six participants. We agree with these general ranges (i.e., between three and eight participants for most groups), with the possible caution that in some cases, having only three participants may inhibit social interaction and the optimal range of examples for modeling and feedback.

The number of therapist/trainers who should serve as group leaders is a somewhat more straightforward issue. Based on the authors' own clinical experiences as well as those of many colleagues, two is optimal and one is sufficient. Having two therapist or trainer co-leaders for a social skills training group appears to help maintain the needed structure and minimizes management problems, whereas having one leader has proven to be sufficient in most situations. In reality, a potential group leader many times may desire another therapist or trainer to help lead the group, but will have to work alone because no one else is available.

Age Range and Developmental Level.   Although it is desirable to provide a range of participants for social skills training groups so that generalization will be enhanced, developmental level is one area of potential participant difference in which group leaders must be extremely careful. The authors' experience and that of many colleagues indicates that child or adolescent participants in a general social skills training group should be within a reasonably common age range, perhaps 2 to 3 years at the most. Moving outside this general range, say by having 12- and 16-year-old participants in the same group, may prove to be a risky venture. The older participants may choose not to participate, whereas the younger subjects may not be able to role model some important social situations with older adolescents.

Related to age is the whole issue of developmental level, which is not always the same thing as age. Sheridan (1995) stated: "The format of group sessions requires cognitive and language abilities within the average range. . . . Students with below average cognitive abilities or very deficient processing capabilities will have a difficult time in social skills groups" (p. 48). In general, we agree with this assessment, although it is important to recognize that children or adolescents at lower developmental levels may still benefit from structured social skills training, providing it is designed specifically toward their developmental needs.

A directly relevant study in this area was conducted by Law, Brown, and Lester (1994), who found that organizing child participants into separate social skills training groups based on their communication abilities and needs optimized the beneficial effects of the intervention. Accordingly, clinicians may apply the same general rule that we suggested for age range within groups: It makes sense to have group members within a range of 2 to 3 years' equivalence in the developmental areas of intellectual ability and verbal communication skills.

Gender Composition.   Gender composition of social skills training groups has received little attention in the literature. Many, if not most, therapists or trainers conducting social skills training in group settings tend to develop mixed-gender groups. However, some clinicians may feel that it is better to develop an all-girls or all-boys group for various reasons.

For most training groups, we agree with Sheridan (1995), who stated: "There is no reason why boys and girls should not be included in the same group" (p. 48). It makes good sense to use mixed-gender groups for most social skills training because it will make the training setting more like the natural setting, thus enhancing the probability of generalization. Another advantage of mixed-gender training groups is that boys and girls will be better able to learn how members of the opposite gender may feel, think, and behave in specific social situations. Assuming that mixed-gender groups are to be used, it is important to have an adequate composition of both boys and girls. Sheridan (1995) suggested that "at least two or three females or two or three males" should be included in any group, a recommended number that also has important implications for enhancing generalization (i.e., providing a range of models and examples).

Homogeneous Versus Heterogenous Grouping. Another composition issue that will need to be addressed is how diverse or similar the participants should be in terms of the types of social skills deficits they exhibit. In the literature this particular issue is usually referred to in terms of homogeneous versus heterogeneous grouping.

Although heterogeneous grouping (selecting students with varying types of social skills abilities and deficits) may make some intuitive sense so far as providing a range of examples to facilitate generalization, the only thing that is clear in this area is that "the evidence is not yet in, despite years of research on selection and grouping practices that would suggest unequivocally that *either* homogeneous *or* heterogeneous grouping is clearly superior" (Goldstein, Sprafkin, Gershaw, & Klein, 1980, p. 58). Thus, potential group leaders should aim for a group composition that appears to meet best the training needs of their group and their own concerns about teaching and management. Elliott and Gresham (1990) suggested that both types of skill grouping may offer certain advantages. Developing groups in which participants have similar social skill deficits may permit a focus on the specific issues of concern, whereas having more diverse types of skills and problems within a group may allow students to serve as positive role models in particular ways for each other.

Use of High Functioning Participants. A final area of concern regarding group composition is an often overlooked but potentially critical issue: Should the training group consist only of children or adolescents with social skills deficits, or should socially high functioning participants also be recruited? Unfortunately, little or no specific empirical evidence exists on which to base such a decision. In typical practice, only participants who have deficits in social skills are targeted for inclusion in the training group. In many situations such a practice may be suitable, but in certain cases composing a group entirely of students with significant social skills deficits could backfire on the therapist or trainer. Specifically, children and adolescents with significant social skills deficits who also exhibit serious levels of antisocial behavior (e.g., many students who receive special education services under Individuals with Disabilities Education (IDEA) as seriously emotionally disturbed) may serve as substantially negative role models for one another in the training group.

TABLE 4.2
Recommendations for Composition and Selection of Participants
for Social Skills Training Groups

Number of Participants and Group Leaders
    Group size should typically range from no fewer than three to no more than eight partici-
        pants.
    One group leader is adequate, two group leaders is desirable

Age Range and Developmental Level of Participants
    It is desirable to have developmental levels of group members within no more than a 2- to 3-
        year range on such characteristics as intellectual ability and language skills.

Gender Composition of Social Skills Training Groups
    In most cases it is desirable to include both boys and girls in a training group.
    At least two or three members of each gender should be included in mixed-gender training
        groups.

Heterogeneous Versus Homogenous Grouping of Participants
    With regard to types of social skills deficits, there is no clear evidence that either heteroge-
        nous or homogenous grouping patterns are superior to each other.

Use of High Functioning Participants
    When groups have several participants with serious social skill deficits and behavioral–
        emotional disorders, it is desirable to include one or more high-functioning and well-
        adjusted "confederates" to provide positive peer modeling.

    The authors' combined clinical experiences working with groups composed entirely of children or adolescents with these characteristics have indicated that treatment gains under such circumstances appear to accrue more slowly and that the negative modeling that can occur may have such unintended effects as increasing antisocial statements within the group, making participation in the group aversive for some students, and exacerbating peer conflicts among group members. Moreover, it goes without saying that a group in which such problems escalate will result in frustrating and discouraging the therapist or trainer.

    Despite this gloomy forecast, there is a hopeful alternative. Some practitioners have found that keeping the numbers of seriously deficient and antisocial participants somewhat lower and then adding some *confederates* (highly socially competent participants) to the group can make a dramatic difference by reducing the modeling of antisocial behavior, maintaining order within the training group, and providing opportunities for positive modeling of social skills. Therefore, this procedure is recommended in certain cases, but with the caution that such high functioning participants will need to be carefully selected. They should be peers who are looked up to by other members of the training group, and they should be socially competent and sufficiently self-confident to function well within the group (particularly when having to deal with antisocial behavior within the group). Furthermore, they should be volunteers who would view such an experience as interesting and positive so that they will be able to model a positive attitude toward being in the group.

Number and Length of Sessions

Regardless of whether social skills training is delivered individually or within groups, and without respect to group size and composition, a therapist or trainer will need to make some preliminary decisions prior to training about how many sessions to hold and how long these sessions should be. As a general rule, sessions should be in the neighborhood of 45 minutes to 60 minutes in length. A shorter session tends to make it difficult to accomplish instructional objectives, and a longer session tends to diminish enthusiasm (and perhaps increase disruptiveness) of group participants. Of course, developmental factors should be considered along with the issue of session length. Younger and less mature children are generally not capable of attending and engaging as long as older and more mature children and may benefit from slightly shorter sessions (e.g., 30 minutes) held at more frequent intervals.

As was true for group size, no magic figure exists for determining an optimal number of training sessions. The answer to this question depends on how many specific social skills or general goal areas are being targeted. It is possible that some students will need training in only a few carefully circumscribed skills or areas, thus reducing the number of sessions that will be needed. In reality though, most children or adolescents with social skills deficits have multiple deficits, given the fact that social skills tend to be moderately to highly intercorrelated with each other (Merrell, 1993a, 1993b). Therefore, it is likely that several specific skills or goal areas will need to be targeted over several sessions during the intervention.

A related issue is how many skill areas will be taught and practiced in each session. Generally, the introduction of two to three skills per session is possible and desirable, assuming that a rapid pace and plenty of opportunities for practice are provided. The typical number of sessions per week is usually one (Sheridan, 1995), although some clinicians find that two sessions per week, when possible, helps to maximize treatment gains. Even though conducting two social skills training sessions per week may not be possible in many situations, this practice appears to offer some salient advantages associated with more opportunities for structured role-playing, modeling, and feedback.

NARROWING THE FOCUS: SELECTING
SOCIAL SKILLS FOR INTERVENTION

An essential planning task that must be carefully completed before social skills training interventions begin is selecting the specific social skills that will be targeted during training. It is certainly possible to identify a group of children or adolescents known to have social skills deficits and then expose them to a generic and broad social skills training intervention without targeting skill deficits unique to that group. However, such training is not likely to have the same impact as that aimed specifically at the unique constellation of social skill deficits exhibited within a selected group. In fact, developing and conducting behavioral interventions that are specifically problem- or deficit-matched has been identified as a best practice in working with children and adolescents who exhibit significant emotional or behavioral disorders (Peacock Hill Working Group, 1991).

Steps in Selecting Specific Social Skills for Intervention

Chapter 3 of this book is focused exclusively on assessment of social skills, a process that is critical not only for identifying children and adolescents with social skills deficits, but for targeting specific areas of social skills deficits as well. Thus, the first step in skill selection is conducting an assessment or screening of each child or adolescent who may potentially be targeted for intervention. For purposes such as formal classification and determination of service eligibility, a comprehensive multifactored assessment using at least two of the four general methods described in chapter 3 is recommended. However, if the screening and assessment goal is to identify potential social skills training participants and their particular skill deficits, a less comprehensive and less time-consuming process is recommended. Specifically, the completion of social skills rating scales (such as those reviewed in chapter 3) by teachers and parents with some additional interview or observational data as needed should be sufficient for this purpose.

After these brief assessment data are gathered, the next step is to screen potential participants. Normally, those with the greatest deficits in social skills should be given priority for training. Within this screening process, certain questions must be asked: "How many trainees can be accommodated?" "Which potential trainees are most in need of social skills training?" and "What is the most desirable mix of potential trainees?"

After selecting specific participants, the next step is reviewing the screening and assessment data to identify the most common deficit areas. Sheridan (1995) recommended a process of analyzing specific items from social skills rating scales, identifying the areas of greatest deficit for each participant, highlighting deficit areas consistent across participants, and then making a list of the eight skills that are the most problematic among the group. From this list then specific skills could be targeted for intervention. Such a process makes good sense, although the exact number of specific skill areas targeted may be somewhat flexible, depending on the time available for training.

Specific Skills Within the
Most Common Social Skills Dimensions

The discussion on classifying child and adolescent social skills in chapter 1 briefly overviewed the results of a comprehensive literature review and quali-

tative meta-analysis conducted by Caldarella and Merrell (1997) that identified five major dimensions of child and adolescent social skills. These five dimensions may serve as a basis for selecting specific social skill areas to target
for intervention, given that each dimension is composed of constituent skills
and child characteristics. In this section, these five major dimensions of child
and adolescent social skills are again presented, with the addition of the specific skills and characteristics of each domain. The skills are listed in de-
scending order of frequency, meaning that a skill or characteristic numbered
2 within a particular domain appeared more frequently in the literature review
and meta-analysis than those numbered 3 or higher.

Peer Relationship Skills.   The peer relationship dimension consists of social skills and characteristics reflecting a child or youth who is positive with
his or her peers. The specific skills and characteristics within this dimension
include these:

1. Compliments, praises, or applauds peers
2. Offers help or assistance to peers when needed
3. Invites peers to play or interact
4. Participates in discussions, talks with peers for extended periods
5. Stands up for rights of peers, defends a peer in trouble
6. Is sought out by peers to join activities, everyone likes to be with
7. Has skills or abilities admired by peers, participates skillfully with peers
8. Skillfully initiates or joins conversations with peers
9. Is sensitive to feelings of peers (empathy, sympathy)
10. Has good leadership skills, assumes leadership role in peer activities
11. Makes friends easily, has many friends
12. Has sense of humor, shares laughter with peers

Self-Management Skills.   The self-management dimension consists of skills
and characteristics reflecting a child or youth who is able to control his or her
temper, follow rules and limits, compromise with others, and receive criticism
well. Essentially, this dimension involves self-restraint. The specific skills and
characteristics of the self-management dimension include these:

1. Remains calm when problems arise, controls temper when angry
2. Follows rules, accepts imposed limits
3. Compromises with others when appropriate, compromises in conflicts
4. Receives criticism well, accepts criticism from others
5. Responds to teasing by ignoring peers, responds appropriately to teasing
6. Cooperates with others in a variety of situations

Academic Skills.   The academic dimension appears to be very much related to the classroom social milieu and includes skills reflecting a child or youth whom the teacher might call an independent and productive worker. The specific skills and characteristics of the academic skills dimension include these:

1. Accomplishes tasks or assignments independently, displays independent study skills
2. Completes individual seatwork and assigned tasks
3. Listens to and carries out teacher directions
4. Produces work of acceptable qualify for ability level, works up to potential
5. Uses free time appropriately
6. Is personally well organized (e.g., brings required materials to school, arrives at school on time)
7. Appropriately asks for assistance as needed, asks questions
8. Ignores peer distractions while working, functions well despite distractions

Compliance Skills.   The compliance dimension includes skills and characteristics reflecting a child who essentially gets along with others by appropriately following rules and expectations, using free time, and sharing things. The specific skills and characteristics of the compliance domain include these:

1. Follows instructions and directions
2. Follows rules
3. Appropriately uses free time
4. Shares toys, materials, and belongings
5. Responds appropriately to constructive criticism or when corrected
6. Finishes assignments, completes tasks
7. Puts toys, work, or property away

Assertion Skills.   The assertion dimension reflects children or youth who might be called outgoing or extroverted by others, and who exercise appropriate independence and social assertion in meeting their needs. The skills and characteristics within this dimension include these:

1. Initiates conversations with others
2. Acknowledges compliments
3. Invites peers to play, invites others
4. Says and does nice things for self, is self-confident
5. Makes friends
6. Questions unfair rules

7. Introduces self to new people
8. Appears confident with opposite sex
9. Expresses feelings when wronged
10. Appropriately joins ongoing activity/group

Task Analysis of Specific Social Skills

A careful examination of the specific social skills within each of the five major dimensions reveals that in many cases there is a final step that must be taken before training. Most social skills consist of several component tasks or steps that must be enacted to perform each skill. Thus, effectively training a child to "invite peers to play" (Skill 3 of the assertion dimension) may need to involve training them to enact several component tasks effectively. This process will involve what is commonly referred to as *task analysis* of social skills.

Reviewing task analysis of social behavior, Howell (1985) identified four dimensions for tasks: content, behavior, conditions, and criteria (accuracy and rate of proficiency). He also emphasized the contextual aspect of social behavior or the importance of understanding the social demands produced across different settings or situations. To produce the optimum treatment gains, it is exceedingly important to consider the various dimensions and contexts of social behavior while conducting training.

Many packaged social skills training programs contain task-analyzed components of specific social skills that are followed in a step-by-step manner during training. Such prepackaged lists can serve as helpful guidelines, particularly for inexperienced trainers, but some caution must be exercised. Because expectations and conditions for social behavior may vary across cultural–familial groups and institutional settings (Dygdon, 1993), the specific constituent tasks required to enact various social skills may need to be somewhat flexible. Therefore, it is recommended that after identifying the specific skills to be targeted during the social skills training intervention, the therapist or trainer should task analyze these skills to whatever level is most appropriate, taking into consideration the unique aspects of the population, culture, and settings.

The process of task analyzing specific social skills into their component parts need not be complicated or time consuming. Assuming that the therapist or trainer is familiar with the unique social expectations of the group participants within their common settings, a list could be intuitively generated quite easily. It also may be desirable to have training group participants help to break down specific skills into their component parts as part of the training session. Of course, more elaborate methods of task analysis, such as videotaping social behavior within naturalistic settings (Knapczyk & Rodes, 1996) are possible, and may be warranted under certain conditions. However, there are many advantages to keeping the process of task analysis simple.

Here is an example of a simple task analysis of a specific social skill: inviting peers to play (Skill 3 from the assertion domain). For the sake of contextual validity, it can be assumed that the children to be taught this skill are in the third grade at a midwestern elementary school.

Inviting Peers to Play

1. Choose an activity or game you would like to play.
2. Look for someone with whom you would like to play who is not busy doing something else.
3. Walk up to the person and look at him or her.
4. Say "Would you like play *(name of activity)* with me?"
5. If the answer is "yes," ask the person to go with you to the area where you want to play and start the game.
6. If the answer is "no," tell the person "okay" and look for someone else to play with.

This list of tasks is simple and straightforward, but certainly not exhaustive. If these is a desire to be more detail-oriented, much larger lists of discrete component tasks can be generated. However, in almost any case, exceedingly long lists of tasks or component behaviors are not needed, and may be too complicated for group members. The main point here is that creating a simple list of contextually valid component tasks and behaviors is an essential part of selecting specific skills for intervention, and it does not need to be an onerous chore.

IMPLEMENTING SOCIAL SKILLS TRAINING

To a naive observer, actually implementating a social skills training session with a group of children or adolescents may seem at first glance like a very straightforward and simple process. Also, because many manualized or packaged social skills training programs present training modules virtually as scripts to follow, an uninformed person might assume that conducting social skills training effectively is simply a matter of reading a script and filling in the blanks where necessary.

In reality, both of these assumptions are wrong. Effective delivery of a social skills training intervention is a sophisticated process that requires effective interpersonal clinical skills as well as complex sequencing of instructional design principles. This section overviews theoretical and practical aspects of delivering social skills training sessions effectively, including instructional design principles, an example of a scripted training outline, and details regarding practices required for maintenance and generalization of treatment gains.

General Instructional Principles
for Effective Social Skills Training

During the 1980s and 1990s there was a proliferation of manualized, packaged, social skills training interventions for children and adolescents, several of which have become quite popular and are widely used. Our review of social skills training programs in chapter 6 details many specifics of these programs. Although a number of important differences exist among available intervention programs, giving clinicians in the process of selecting a program a number of options, perhaps what is most striking about the available packaged programs are their similarities, which in most cases appear greater than any substantive differences. Although there may be a few notable exceptions, most manualized and packaged social skills training programs for children and adolescents seem to follow relatively similar instructional designs and processes. This high degree of similarity actually makes good sense because there is a large body of empirical evidence available on social skills training with children and adolescents, and several distinct effective practices in instructional principles are evident.

At a theoretical level, most social skills training programs aimed at children and adolescents appear to be somewhat behaviorally oriented in that they rely on basic principles of effective instruction derived through research on operant conditioning, social learning, and applied behavioral analysis (i.e., direct instruction programming). There also seems to be a moderate cognitive orientation in many training programs, particularly those aimed at older children and adolescents who may be advanced enough in their cognitive development to benefit from this type of orientation. In actual practice, most widely used programs and texts on social skills training appear to blend behavioral and cognitive approaches to instruction. Some examples and summary comments on general instructional principles for social skills training are provided in this section.

In the popular Skillstreaming series of social skills training guides and in related publications, Arnold Goldstein and his colleagues (Goldstein, 1988; Goldstein et al., 1980; McGinnis & Goldstein, 1984) have refined a set of instructional principles based on what they term the *structured learning* approach. This set of principles is quite behaviorally oriented, consisting of four major components: modeling, role playing, performance feedback, and transfer training. The *modeling* component of instruction consists of the trainees' being provided with numerous examples of a person performing the social skill behaviors to be learned. The modeling is typically performed by both the therapist or trainer and group members. The *role-playing* component of structured learning involves giving the trainees opportunities and encouragement to practice the targeted behaviors that were modeled. During role-playing, trainees are provided with positive feedback about their performance, with the intent that this feedback (most of which should be positive) will help shape behavior to become more and more similar to the behavior of the model. This is the *performance feedback* phase of instruction. The *transfer of training* component is embedded throughout most aspects of training, and consists of procedures designed to increase the likelihood that newly learned social skills will be applied correctly in settings outside the training setting.

In their *Social Skills Intervention Guide,* Elliott and Gresham (1991) also detailed a set of instructional principles for social skills training that are clearly sequenced and mainly behavioral in nature. The social skills training model includes four major components: promoting social skills acquisition, enhancing skill performance, removing interfering problem behaviors, and facilitating generalization. The *promoting social skills acquisition* phase involves various procedures by which initial learning of social skills is enhanced, such as modeling, coaching, behavioral rehearsal, and social problem solving, a technique in which the participants are presented with a potential social problem and asked to develop an appropriate solution. The *enhancing skill performance* phase is designed to enhance the trainees' performance of previously acquired social skills, and includes such steps as peer initiation strategies, cuing and prompting, reinforcement, and various incentive systems (e.g., contracts and group contingencies). Based on the notion that social skills training may sometimes fail to achieve the desired effect because of problem behaviors, the *removing interfering problem behaviors* component includes both reinforcement-based and reductive strategies for creating an optimum learning environment. Finally, the *facilitating generalization* component, like the transfer of training component, is to help ensure that newly acquired skills actually will be used in other settings.

In their excellent book on assessment and instruction of social skills, Elksnin and Elksnin (1995) compare and contrast three types of instructional approaches: social problem-solving, skills-specific, and combination. According to Elksnin and Elksnin, instructional principles of *social problem-solving* approaches are aimed at teaching general behaviors rather than discrete skills, with the intent that "once mastered, cognitive-interpersonal problem-solving skills can improve social behavior" (p. 76). Accordingly, all problem-solving approaches aim to teach students to define the problem, identify alternatives, determine solutions, and self-evaluate effectiveness. The general instructional principles within this framework are based mainly on a cognitive behavioral theoretical foundation and include modeling and instruction from a positive model, task performance and overt verbal self-appraisal, and a gradual fading from overt to covert self-instruction by learners as they perform the requisite social skill behaviors. In this, *skill-specific* approaches are considered to be extensions of applied behavioral analysis wherein skills are task analyzed, broken down into their constituent parts, and taught to learners step by step using modeling and role playing. *Combination* approaches, according to Elksnin and Elksnin, combine the use of social problem-solving and skills-specific approaches. In their view, both the structured learning approach and Elliott and Gresham's training model constitute combination approaches.

Cartledge and Milburn (1995) outlined effective instructional principles and processes for teaching social skills based on their demonstrated effectiveness in the literature and without regard to their theoretical grounding. In this review, three general areas of instructional programming were identified.

The first instructional principle was use of *social learning modeling and role-playing*. Like other instructional models that incorporate modeling and role-playing, this principle is based on Bandura's (1986) social learning theory. According to Cartledge and Milburn, the essential components of this instructional principle include giving instructions, identifying skill components, presenting a model, skill performance, feedback, reinforcement, and opportunities for practice.

The second effective instructional principle is referred to as *coaching*, which is like modeling but which may involve more verbal interactions and one-on-one as well as group instruction.

The third essential set of instructional principles for social skills training is the broad area of *cognitive and affective methods*. Cognitive and affective methods include such aspects as social perception (ability to interpret accurately a social situation), communication (including role-taking and empathy), affective behavior (ability to appropriately express and interpret emotions), cognitive approaches (altering belief systems, modifying self-statements, and effective problem solving).

Although the theoretical foundations on which these three areas of instructional principles are built may be disparate at times, they are not viewed as being mutually exclusive, and in Cartledge and Milburn's view, effective social skills instruction may involve all three areas.

In summary, although various guides to social skills instruction stress particular aspects or instructional principles that are somewhat unique and may derive from diverse theoretical foundations, there is obviously a great deal of overlap of instructional principles among specific training programs. There may be times and situations in which it may be necessary to program instruction quite narrowly, but in the total picture, all of the empirically validated instructional principles and components in various models have their appropriate place and use. Like Cartledge and Milburn (1995), the authors do not view these different models of instruction as being mutually exclusive or necessarily incompatible. To a great extent, the specific instructional principles and strategies selected for social skills training will depend on the specific training situation, and will of necessity be based on the developmental level of the children or adolescents for whom the intervention is designed. For example, instruction for early elementary and younger children will need to rely more heavily on behavioral methods because children at this level typically do not have the cognitive and affective maturity to benefit much from cognitive instructional programming. Likewise, cognitively mature older children and adolescents should almost always have cognitive and affective instructional programming as part of their social skills intervention.

Because each of the four models or sources in this discussion of general instructional principles for effective social skills training contained many similarities but some important differences, it may be useful to look at the various principles for effective instruction in a combined manner. Thus, Table 4.3 includes the authors' synthesis of the major instructional programming principles for social skills training derived from various theoretical models and training programs.

Example of a Social Skills Training Outline

Many manualized and packaged social skills training programs provide detailed outlines or scripts that group leaders may use in the actual delivery of the training sequences. Ideally, such scripts or outlines should be based on a carefully conceptualized instructional theory for social skills training, but this, unfortunately, is not always the case. The authors maintain that although packaged intervention outlines or scripts are sometimes quite useful, particularly for a beginning therapist or trainer, they are not necessarily requisite for effective training. it is also maintained that because of the wide diversity and complexity and social skills, intervention populations, and potential settings, most packaged training outlines or scripts will have some limitations from time to time. An effective therapist or trainer will therefore need to have the knowledge and skills to develop his or her own treatment outlines or to modify existing packaged outlines.

It is not the purpose of this volume to provide scripted outlines for teaching the major categories of social skills. Rather, its intent is to provide therapists or trainers with the background and conceptual framework to develop their own outlines to meet the particular training needs of their child or adolescent clients and the settings wherein they work. The material presented earlier in this chapter should provide some conceptual background for creating a self-styled and individualized training outline.

There are many possible ways in which such an outline may be developed. For the sake of providing a concrete example, the authors developed a semiscripted outline for the social skill of *beginning a conversation* that is based on the instructional principles detailed earlier in this section. This particular outline was developed with midelementary-age children in mind. Table 4.4 provides this outline, which may be used as a model for developing individualized, semiscripted outlines for virtually any social skills training goal with a wide range of populations and settings.

TABLE 4.3
A Synthesized Model of Principles for Effective Instruction
in Social Skills Training

Introduction Problem Definition
　Group leader presents problem situations and assists participants in defining the problem.
　Group leader assists participants in generating alternatives problem solving.

Identification of Solutions
　Specific instructions engaging in the desired social behavior are presented by group leader to participants.
　Group leader assists participants in identifying social skill components.

Modeling
　Group leader models the desired social behavior for participants.
　Both cognitive/verbal rehearsal component and behavioral enactment component are modeled by group leader.

Rehearsal and Role-Playing
　Participants are verbally guided through steps in enacting the desired social behavior.
　All participants are asked to perform the desired social skill through realistic and relevant role-play situations.

Performance Feedback
　Participants are reinforced for correct enactment of desired social behavior in role-play situation.
　Corrective feedback and additional modeling is provided when participants fail to enact desired social behavior in role-play situation.
　If corrective feedback was provided, participants are given additional opportunity for rehearsal and role-playing until desired social behavior is correctly enacted.

Removal of Problem Behaviors
　Problem behaviors interfering with acquisition and performance of social skills are eliminated through reinforcement-based and/or reductive procedures.

Self-Instruction and Self-Evaluation
　Participants are asked to "think aloud" during training modeled by group leader.
　Self-statements reflecting distorted thinking or belief systems are modified.
　Training sessions include a gradual shift from overt instruction and appraisal to self-instruction and appraisal.

Training for Generalization and Maintenance
　Throughout training, situations, behaviors, and role-players are made as realistic to natural social situations as possible.
　Appropriate homework assignments are given.
　Classroom teachers and parents are enlisted to monitor homework, encourage practice of skills, and provide feedback to participants.

Generalization and Maintenance

An important aspect of any social skills training intervention is proper planning and implementation for generalization across settings and for maintenance over time. Demonstrating an adequate mastery of in-session training objectives may be a critical part of any social skills intervention, but it certainly does not ensure that the targeted children or adolescents will demon-

TABLE 4.4

An Example of a Social Skills Training Outline
for the Beginning a Conversation

Introduce and Define the Problem

Today we are going to work on the skills needed to start a conversation with another person. What is a conversation? (Generate discussion with group members.)

Possible answers include (a) a way of talking with another person about something you are both interested in, (b) a way of communicating with another person by speaking and listening.

Have any of you ever seen someone trying to start a conversation the wrong way? What was that like? (Generate discussion of ineffective approaches to starting a conversation with group members.)

Why is it important to be able to start conversation with another person in a way that works well? (Assist group members in generating alternatives.)

Possible responses include (a) so you can make friends, (b) so you can learn about things from other people, (c) so you can tell other people something that is important to you.

Identify Solutions

This is how you begin a conversation:

look for the right time to start (don't interrupt).

greet the other person (say "hi").

look the other person in the eyes.

make sure they are listening to you (looking at you).

tell the other person what you wanted to say.

Now, I need you to help me go over the steps I just told you about. What are the important things to do to begin a conversation?

Assist group members in identifying the skill components; make sure each step is reviewed.

Model the Skills

Watch how I begin a conversation with another person using the five steps we just went over.

With your co-leader or one of the group members acting as the person you want to talk with, physically and verbally model the five steps.

Rehearse and Role-Play

Now I want each of you to try out these skills. First, let's review the five steps. (Briefly review each of the five steps from a chalkboard or poster.)

Now I want you to try it.

Have each group member take a turn at trying out the five steps for beginning a conversation, using other group members as the intended listener and providing prompting as needed.

Help group members choose appropriate and realistic situations for role-playing; facilitate selection of co-actors for role-playing that are similar to persons who would be encountered in the actual situation.

Provide Performance Feedback

(If the steps were correctly followed) That was great!

Point out the specific steps the participant correctly followed.

(If the steps were not followed correctly) That was a nice try, but there are still a few things we need to work on.

Point out the specific steps that the participant correctly followed and incorrectly followed; briefly model the steps needing correction and have the participant enact the steps again until he or she gets it right.

120

TABLE 4.4 *(Continued)*

Train for Self-Instruction and Self-Evaluation

Now, let's practice going over these steps when we are by ourselves.

Model covert rehearsal for self-instruction and prompting; have group members practice the same.

Now let's figure out how we know when we have begun a conversation the right way.

Provide brief training for self-evaluation: All the steps were followed, the conversation was successful, and a positive outcome occurred.

Train for Generalization and Maintenance

You have all done a good job working on the skills for beginning a conversation. I need each of you to practice this skill over the next few days, and then let the group know how it went next time we meet. Let's talk about some places and situations where you could practice beginning a conversation.

Help group members generate ideas for people and situations for which they can practice the skill steps; get specific verbal commitments from each group member with the expectation that they will report on their experience at the next meeting.

---

strate their newly mastered social skills in other settings, or that they will maintain mastery of these skills over time. In fact, the issues of generalization and maintenance in social skills training constitute not only a potentially serious obstacle for therapists/trainers, but are an area of serious scholarly inquiry, and much has been written on the topic (Chandler, Lubeck, & Fowler, 1992; DuPaul & Eckert, 1994; Fox & McEvoy, 1993; Moore, 1994).

Generalization and maintenance of any gains produced through social skills training does not usually occur incidentally or by accident. Instead, careful planning and attention to what is referred to as *transfer training* must be an integral part of the intervention from the very beginning. In a classic review of issues related to generalization in behavioral programming, Stokes and Baer (1977) convincingly asserted that sameness forms the basis for generalization. In other words, for optimum likelihood of generalization, the training setting must be similar to the settings in which generalization is desired in almost every respect. Maintenance of skills over time actually constitutes a specific type of generalization and appears to be enhanced not only by overlearning but by appropriate generalization to various settings outside of training. Thus, generalization and maintenance of behavioral gains accrued through social skills training are integrally linked and interdependent.

In terms of specific approaches and techniques to enhance generalization and maintenance, there appears to be a great deal of similarity among training manuals and packaged programs. For purposes of the discussion of generalization and maintenance in this chapter, suggestions are overviewed from four representative sources (two popular packaged training programs and two texts on social skills training), then their major points and similarities are summarized.

In the popular Skillstreaming program for teaching social skills, Goldstein and his colleagues (Goldstein et al., 1980) built in five specific elements for transfer of training, in other words, for generalization and maintenance. These elements include general principles (giving the trainee general principles that govern performance in both the training and real-life settings), response availability/overlearning (increasing the rate of original learning to increase the likelihood that responses will transfer to other situations), stimulus variability (employing a variety of stimuli such as models, trainers, and role-playing situations in the training setting), and real-life reinforcement (ensuring that once trainees attempt to apply their new skills in the real-life setting, they are reinforced for producing appropriate responses and given corrective feedback when their responses are less than appropriate). These five elements for transfer of training are integral aspects of the structured learning approach used in Skillstreaming.

Likewise, the Tough Kid Social Skills program (Sheridan, 1995), which is also based on structured behavioral principles for teaching skills, employs built-in components to increase the likelihood of generalization and maintenance. Four specific components for generalization are built in to the Tough Kid curriculum, including recognition (help trainees recognize situations in which the newly learned skills can be used), reinforcement (initially reinforce all attempts at using positive social skills, gradually shaping the reinforcement pattern to correct responses after a sufficient degree of learning and utilization has occurred), prompting (remind or prompt trainees when they have opportunities to know positive social skills, but for some reason, fail to use them), and modeling (when trainees fail to follow prompts in session or in the real life setting, the trainer demonstrates and acts out the appropriate steps for them to follow). In addition to these four basic steps, the Tough Kid training approach involves *providing feedback and instruction* to trainees if they fail to attempt a skill or if their attempts are unsuccessful. These components for generalization and maintenance are integrated into the Tough Kid training modules as well as the Skills Sheets (student handouts).

In their discussion of maintenance and generalization issues, Elksnin and Elksnin (1995) described six major components of generalization and maintenance that should be included in any social skills training intervention. These components include sequential modification (modifying the sequence of training sessions so that they are more likely to simulate real life settings); introduction to natural maintaining contingencies (increase the likelihood that trainees will receive reinforcement in the natural setting for engaging in positive social skills by making the training setting and contingencies as similar as possible to the natural setting and its reinforcement contingencies); train loosely (teaching more than one social skill per session, not requiring mastery before introducing new skills, and teaching skills more frequently but for shorter periods of time so that social skills learning is not contingent on tightly structured and inflexible stimulus conditions); use indiscriminable contingencies (make reinforcement contingencies less discriminable through using intermittent and thin reinforcement schedules and by delaying reinforcement, thus requiring a high rate of responding); program common stimuli (gradually making training settings increasingly like natural settings); and mediate generalization and train to generalize (using cognitive mediators such as self-talk, self-reinforcement, and self-monitoring). Elksnin and Elksnin also recommended *assigning homework* and *soliciting family support* as training components that may have the collateral effect of generalizing and maintaining newly acquired or mastered social skills.

In their comprehensive book on social skills training, Cartledge and Milburn (1995) devoted an entire chapter exclusively to generalization and maintenance issues. Their treatment of these issues is sophisticated and detailed, thus making a simplified itemized breakdown of recommended maintenance and generalization practices difficult. However, their discussion and recommendations can be broken down into five general areas, each containing several constituent factors. These five areas are outlined and discussed in somewhat more detail than the recommendations for generalization and maintenance from the previous three sources.

Aspects of Training.   According to Cartledge and Milburn (1995), "The ways in which social behaviors are taught appear to influence whether the new behaviors will occur in settings beyond the training site and whether they will occur with persons other than the trainer" (p. 119). Two specific strategies in this regard are offered. *Training in different settings* (actually, multiple settings) is recommended so that a wide range of stimulus exemplars are employed during training. The end result of such a tactic is that trainees should be able to generalize their newly acquired skills to a variety of new settings more easily than if training occurred only under set and rigid conditions. Use of analogue conditions is also recommended as an aspect of training to be considered. Recognizing that teaching new social skills in the natural environment is ideal but sometimes unrealistic, creating analogue conditions so that the training setting approximates the natural setting as closely as possible may also enhance generalization and maintenance.

Training With Different People.   It is recommended that more than one social skills trainer be utilized "to avoid the possibility that new behaviors will remain under the control of [only] one trainer and will fail to generalize" (Cartledge & Milburn, 1995, p. 122). In addition to the standard use of a therapist or trainer in teaching social skills, it is recommended that training with different people include the following three categories: teachers, parents, and peers. The use of individuals in these three categories to assist with training not only reduces the chance that newly acquired social skills will be under the stimulus control of only one trainer, but it also facilitates generalization across settings and time, given the varied environments in which these potential allies to training reside.

Training Mediators.   These are specifically referred to by Cartledge and Milburn (1995) as *cognitive mediators* "to assist the child in maintaining appropriate behaviors in settings, times, and conditions beyond those explicitly involved in training" (p. 127). Language is considered to be something that can be programmed to mediate behavior across conditions and to effect the natural contingencies of reinforcement. To simplify how this is actually put into effect, trainees are taught to use effective social communication skills (through language) that are likely to be reciprocated by others and thus serve as reinforcers. Additionally, the use of expectations as mediators may enhance generalization. Essentially, if child and adolescent trainees develop cognitive expectancies of success in their future social interactions, they will be more likely to generalize training gains. The therapist or trainer can play an important role in helping trainees develop positive cognitive expectancies by providing effective skill training, projecting a positive model, helping the child or adolescent trainees to develop confidence in their ability to use the new skills, and suggesting how these new skills will help them in the future.

Contingencies of Reinforcement.   Cartledge and Milburn (1995) contended that "the principle factors supporting maintenance of social skills over time are the contingencies of reinforcement operating in the settings where the social skills [will] be expressed" (p. 131). Thus, the nature of reinforcement (i.e., the contingencies of reinforcement) must be changed. *Changing the timing of reinforcement* so that newly acquired social skills are immediately reinforced initially, but later reinforced less predictably, may be one way of using the contingencies of reinforcement for generalization purposes. *Changing the nature of reinforcement* (moving from artificial reinforcement to natural reinforcement) and *changing the source of reinforcement* (making reinforcement increasingly less contingent on the therapist/trainer and more contingent on sources within the natural environment) are other recommended ways of changing the contingencies of reinforcement to enhance generalization and maintenance of social skills.

Developing Self-Management Skills.   This recommendation is based on the premise that "perhaps the most effective source for reinforcement is the child" (Cartledge & Milburn, 1995, p. 136). Many training sources for teaching self-management to children and adolescents are available in the applied behavior analysis literature, and there are many similarities among them. However, according to Cartledge and Milburn, successfully developing self-management skills for children and adolescents as part of social skills training involves adopting standards (developing effective criteria for goal difficulty, goal proximity, and performance feedback), self-monitoring (learning how to observe and record one's own behavior), self-evaluation (teaching the child or adolescent to apply some evaluative criteria in rating the success of his or her behavior), and self-reinforcement (providing self-selected rewards or internalized positive self-statements after successful performance. In summary, for social skills learned through a structured intervention to truly generalize across time, persons, and settings, the child or adolescent trainees must learn to manage their cognitions and behaviors so that reliance on only external forces for generalization is reduced.

By comparing the four sources for enhancing the generalization and maintenance of social skills, it is obvious that what each set of authors is stating about this area has substantial overlap with the major points of the other authors. In fact, many of the differences among sources are fairly cosmetic, and it is clear that in some cases, different terms are used to propose essentially similar concepts. The key factors in generalization and maintenance appear to differ the most in terms of specific details or nuances. However, each model appears to have many commendable aspects. Therefore, perhaps the best way to understand and use the principles of generalization and maintenance in social skills training is to take an integrated approach, considering the major overlapping and unique points from the four sets of authors. In Table 4.5 an outline of the integration or synthesis of these authors' major suggestions and points for generalization and maintenance in social skills training is provided by the authors of this volume.

EVALUATING SOCIAL SKILLS TRAINING INTERVENTIONS

Unfortunately, many social skills training interventions fail to monitor treatment progress during and after intervention. Because of time constraints, difficulty in obtaining cooperation from possible social informants, other demands, a lack of understanding the important role of evaluation, or a lack of knowing how to evaluate, many therapists or trainers simply choose to ignore the issue.

Failure to conduct basic evaluation procedures during and after treatment is unfortunate because evaluation is a process that may yield valuable information regarding what aspects of social skills training are working effectively, and which need modification to increase treatment efficacy. This concluding section provides some suggestions for realistic, simple, and straightforward monitoring of treatment gains during and after social skills training, and for overall evaluation of training efficacy.

TABLE 4.5
A Consolidated Approach to Best Practices in Promoting
Generalization and Maintenance in Social Skills Training

Learning Principles and Response Sets
   Teach trainees general performance principles that govern all settings.
   Have trainees overlearn skills.

Make Training Settings Like Real Life Settings
   Modify sequence of training to make it more similar to natural environment.
   Make contingencies in training setting similar to those in natural settings.
   Make stimuli in training settings increasingly similar to natural stimuli.

Vary Training Stimuli
   Employ a variety of models, trainers, situations, and settings.
   Maintain unstructured stimulus conditions during training.

Effective Use of Reinforcement
   Use basic principles of shaping.
   Change the timing, nature, and source of reinforcement over time.
   Make reinforcement increasingly less predictable.
   Ensure that trainees receive reinforcement for new skills in natural settings.

Therapist/Trainer Mediation
   Help trainees recognize situations in which new skills can be used.
   Prompt trainees when they have opportunities to perform new skills.
   Demonstrate/act out appropriate steps for skills when trainee fails to do so.
   Provide corrective feedback and instruction when needed.

Cognitive Mediation
   Teach social communication skills that will be reinforcing in natural setting.
   Help trainees develop positive expectations regarding their social skills.

Self-Management Skills
   Gradually shift responsibility to trainees.
   Teach trainees to self-monitor, self-evaluate, and self-reinforce.

Basic Types of Evaluation

Many types of program evaluation models have been developed and refined for use in educational and clinical settings, but two main distinctions of evaluation types consistently surface (Worthen, Borg, & White, 1993). The first distinction is whether the program evaluation is internal or external. An *internal* evaluation is one conducted by individuals directly involved in and thus highly familiar with the educational or clinical program, whereas an *external* evaluation is typically conducted by individuals outside the program, usually for the purpose of maintaining objectivity and avoiding judgment biases. A good case can be made for either internal or external evaluation of programs in particular situations. However, for most social skills training interventions, the authors maintain that internal evaluation is more pragmatic and realistic. Typically, the purpose of evaluating a social skills training intervention is to determine if the intervention has been successful, and to develop strategies for improving it if needed. Thus, there is less concern regarding vested interests and biases of the evaluator, who in this case is simply attempting to determine whether the intervention he or she has been conducting is effective and can be improved.

The second distinction that is usually made in models of program evaluation is between summative evaluation and formative evaluation (Worthen et al., 1993). In most conceptualizations, *summative* evaluation is a process conducted after a program is developed or implemented that provides information regarding the overall value or worth of the program. In social skills training, a summative evaluation would involve an overall determination of whether the intervention resulted in the desired behavioral changes and whether it could be viewed as successful. *Formative* evaluation, however, is a process conducted during the development or implementation of a program and aimed at determining how the program may be improved. In social skills training, a formative evaluation would aim to determine whether specific aspects of the intervention delivery or teaching could be improved along the way, rather than decide whether the program had an overall beneficial effect.

Ideally, social skills training programs could benefit from both summative and formative evaluation processes. Summative evaluation may be important in determining whether the overall objectives of the training were met, whereas formative evaluation may be useful in making modifications and improvements along the way while the training program is being delivered. If the social skills training intervention is being conducted strictly for clinical purposes (which will be true in most cases) rather than as part of a formal research investigation, both summative and formative evaluation processes can be utilized in a fairly straightforward and simple way. This type of program evaluation does not necessarily have to be difficult, costly, or time consuming.

Selecting and Developing Evaluation Tools

Once the general purposes for evaluating a social skills training intervention have been clarified, appropriate tools will need to be selected or developed. For most basic program evaluations, the tools may simply be social skills rating scales that were used to determine who was in need of social skills training and what skills should be targeted, such as any of the instruments that were reviewed in chapter 3. For a summative evaluation, the rating scale completed by parents or teachers prior to implementing the training program could be administration again after the intervention (a simple pretest–posttest design), and treatment gains could be gauged by identifying the differences between the two administrations. Standardized social skills rating scales could also be used in a combination summative–formative evaluation by administering them one or two times during the intervention process to gauge treatment gains along the way and to make changes where they are deemed necessary to optimize treatment progress.

Of course, standardized social skills rating scales, although they have many advantages for assessment and screening, also have some disadvantages when used for program evaluation purposes. Three levels of analysis typically are possible in behavioral research: micro, molar, and macro. In analyzing social behavior, the *micro* level of analysis might involve some very discrete and specific behaviors, such as whether a participant is making eye contact as part of a sequence of social approach behaviors. The *molar* level of analysis is slightly more broad, and can be illustrated by measuring whether a participant was able to successfully carry out an entire sequence of behaviors, such as whether they successfully approached a peer and made an invitation to play. The *macro* level is the most broad, and can be illustrated by having a rater determine to what extent a participant is typically successful in initiating peer interaction skills.

Given this breakdown in types of analysis, it is clear that most standardized norm-referenced social skills rating scales are geared largely toward the macro level. They are very useful for making overall judgments or distinctions regarding social behavior, but may be somewhat less useful for gauging specific types of skills progress during the intervention. Moreover, it is also obvious that for most purposes involving evaluation of social skills interventions, the micro level of analysis is too fine, and may yield information that is not very useful for basic formative evaluation purposes, although it may be critical for certain research goals. Therefore, analysis at the molar level will probably need to be an important part of any social skills intervention evaluation where formative evaluation is being pursued, whereas analysis at the macro level (e.g., standardized rating scales) will be most useful in pursuing summative types of evaluation goals.

If summative and formative evaluations of a social skills training intervention are being pursued simultaneously as suggested earlier, the combined use of standardized social skills rating scales and simple evaluation instruments developed by the therapist or trainer specifically for the type of training that is being conducted is recommended. The standardized social skills rating instruments are probably best utilized as entrance and exit measures (preintervention and postintervention), whereas the formative instruments developed by the trainer are best utilized as weekly probes, and they can be completed more than once a week if time and resources allow.

In developing brief instruments to be used frequently throughout the intervention for formative evaluation purposes, a wide range of possibilities exist. These specific types of measures developed by the group leader for frequent formative evaluation will of necessity need to vary depending on the specific type of intervention being conducted, the setting(s) for intervention, the availability of other social informants, and the developmental level of participants. Some potential examples of brief formative evaluation measures are listed as follows:

1. A brief teacher or parent rating scale that includes only items specifically tied to the range of social skills being targeted in the intervention (Fig. 4.1)

SOCIAL SKILLS EVALUATION FORM

STUDENT NAME:

DATE:

TEACHER: The student whose name is listed at the top of this form has been participating in a social skills training group that has been aimed at increasing positive interpersonal skills with peers. We need your help to determine how much progress we have made in this group. Please estimate how often the above-named student is exhibiting each of the 10 behaviors or characteristics listed below, *during the past two weeks*. Circle the number that best reflects his or her social skills during this period, using the following rating criteria:

0 = Never   1 = Sometimes   2 = Frequently

Offers help to other students when needed	0	1	2
Effectively participates in group discussions and activities	0	1	2
Understands other students problems and needs	0	1	2
Invites other students to participate in activities	0	1	2
Interacts with a wide variety of peers	0	1	2
Skillfully initiates or joins conversations with peers	0	1	2
Is sensitive to feelings of other students	0	1	2
Appropriately enters ongoing activities with peers	0	1	2
Compliments others' attributes and accomplishments	0	1	2
Is appropriately assertive when he/she needs to be	0	1	2

FIG. 4.1.   Example of a brief teacher rating scale for formative evaluation that includes only items specifically tied to the range of social skills targeted in the intervention. *Note.* From *School Social Behavior Scales*, by K. W. Merrell, 1993, Austin, TX: Pro-Ed. Copyright © 1993 by Pro-Ed. Adapted with permission.

2. A brief teacher or parent report that provides a gauge of participant engagement in social behaviors being specifically targeted during that week of training (Fig. 4.2)

3. A direct observation protocol completed by group leaders during or after each training session to determine whether specific target behaviors were initiated by participants (Fig. 4.3)

These examples of rating forms and protocols may be useful in providing models for formative evaluation instruments devloped by the group leader. Again, it is important to remember that these examples represent only a few narrow possibilities.

SOCIAL SKILLS EVALUATION FORM

STUDENT NAME:

WEEK:

TEACHER: The student whose name is listed at the top of this form has been participating in a social skills training group. This week we have been working on skills related to interpersonal sensitivity and empathy with peers. We need your help to determine how much progress we are making. Please estimate how often the above-named student has exhibited each of the five behaviors characteristics listed below, *during this past week*. Circle the number that best reflects his or her social skills during this period, using the following rating criteria:

0 = Never	1 = Sometimes	2 = Frequently

Offers help to other students when needed	0	1	2
Understands other students problems and needs	0	1	2
Invites other students to participate in activities	0	1	2
Is sensitive to feelings of other students	0	1	2
Compliments others' attributes and accomplishments	0	1	2

FIG. 4.2. Example of a brief teacher or parent report that provides a gauge of participant engagement in social behaviors specifically targeted during that week of training. *Note.* From *School Social Behavior Scales,* by K. W. Merrell, 1993, Austin, TX: Pro-Ed. Copyright © 1993 by Pro-Ed. Adapted with permission.

SOCIAL SKILLS OBSERVATION FORM

Name of Child:

Date of Training Session:

Skills Worked on During This Session:

OBSERVATION CODES:
Y = yes, N = no, NA = not applicable or no opportunity for observation

---

Made a positive comment to a peer	Y	N	NA
Participated effectively in role-plays	Y	N	NA
Appropriately critiqued another participant following a role-play	Y	N	NA
Made eye contact with group leader	Y	N	NA
Made eye contact with peers	Y	N	NA
Accepted corrective feedback appropriately	Y	N	NA
Smiled at an appropriate time	Y	N	NA

FIG. 4.3.   A direct observation protocol completed by group leaders during or following each training session to determine whether specific target behaviors were initiated by participants during the training session.

Evaluation of "Consumer Satisfaction"

A final issue to consider in this discussion of evaluating social skills training interventions is that it may be useful to expand the scope of evaluation beyond whether social behavior treatment gains were made. Some of the best potential evaluation information may be obtained directly from the child and adolescent participants. Specifically, the participants may provide valuable information about aspects of the intervention they liked and did not like, ways to make social skills training more interesting and fun for participants, whether the incentives were valued and reinforcing, and to what extent they enjoyed their participation in the training program. A simple questionnaire, exit interview, or both with each participant aimed at obtaining this type of information may prove to be well worth the effort in terms of making improvements in subsequent social skills training interventions.

SUMMARY

Distinctions are often drawn between social skills acquisition (the process of learning or acquiring new social behaviors) and social skills performance (actually demonstrating social behaviors that have been previously acquired). Because various social learning theories presume that differences between acquisition and performance deficits have implications for how the intervention should be implemented, it may be important to ascertain first why the target child is not engaging in positive social behaviors. It may also be important to conduct a brief determination of situational performance conditions under which the child is expected to interact socially, because the performance deficit may be closely tied to environmental constraints.

To be optimally effective, a social skills training intervention must be designed carefully rather than haphazardly. Some design issues that should be considered include group composition and selection of participants and the optimal number and length of social skills training sessions. In designing any effective social skills training intervention, it is important to define carefully the social skills that should be targeted. Essentially, any behavioral intervention should be specifically problem matched or deficit matched.

Building on the meta-analysis of child and adolescent social skills introduced in chapter 1 and combining this taxonomy with the principles of task analysis, a framework for narrowing the social skills that should be targeted for intervention is presented. Effective implementation of social skills training interventions requires that therapists or trainers possess excellent interpersonal and clinical skills and that they have a solid understanding of instructional design principles shown to be important in enhancing social behavior. The authors suggest an integrated, synthesized model of instructional principles for social skills training programs, along with examples of how these general principles can be used to create a semiscripted outline for virtually any social skill to be taught in a structured training intervention.

To be maximally effective outside as well as inside the training setting, social skills interventions also must be planned carefully so that treatment gains will be more likely to generalize to different settings and across time. Certain instructional and treatment practices are more likely to result in generalization and maintenance of social skills, and a consolidated approach to this problem, such as that outlined in Table 4.5, will help to maximize these practices. Finally, the use of both summative and formative approaches for evaluating a social skills training intervention is an additional recommended practice that may enhance its effectiveness.

Social Skills Training
as an Intervention
for Specific Problems,
Populations, and Settings

Chapter 4 focused on the general training of social skills and an accompanying basic model for use in developing and implementing training. This chapter builds on chapter 4 by focusing on specific groups of children who are commonly the target of social skills interventions. This chapter aims to serve as a partial review of the literature on the effectiveness of social skills training with specific groups of children as well as provides practical suggestions for developing social skills interventions for children and adolescents with particular common characteristics of social–emotional behavior. Readers should refer back to chapter 4 for more detailed information on the specific technology of conducting social skills training. The information in chapter 4 applies to any of the specific groups discussed in the present chapter.

As discussed in chapter 4, group interventions are most desirable and most effective for children with social skill deficits. Thus, the research and interventions discussed in this chapter involve predominately small-group interventions, although a separate section on classwide and schoolwide interventions is included.

RATIONALE FOR TARGETING SOCIAL SKILLS
TRAINING AT SPECIFIC PROBLEMS,
POPULATIONS, AND SETTINGS

As already seen, not all social skills problems are of the same type, so not all children will require or respond to the same type of social skills interventions.

Social skills training is often regarded as a general intervention or preventive effort for broad groups of children such as rejected or neglected children. But it is also becoming more commonly used as one component in comprehensive programs to remediate specific problems such as depression, or to prevent problems within a specific population (e.g., low income or at-risk children) or setting (e.g., the classroom or school setting).

Although much research on using social skills training as an intervention has focused on externalizing problems, particularly aggressive and acting-out behaviors, studies have also examined the use of social skills training to remediate internalizing problems such as depression and social withdrawal or social anxiety. In addition, social skills training is now more commonly seen as one component in multicomponent prevention or intervention activities aimed at decreasing delinquency, drug use, school drop out, and so forth. Obviously, social skills training cannot solve all the social–emotional problems of children and adolescents. However, when used in conjunction with other techniques, social skills training often is one component in an effective treatment program for problems ranging from depression to attention deficit hyperactivity disorder (ADHD).

Many commercially available social skills programs are generic in nature, although there may be some discussion of their use with different populations of children. (See chapter 6 for a more complete review of commercially available programs and their target populations.) Thus, it may appear that there is no need to target social skills training to specific populations. In fact, when the differences among children in need of social skill interventions are examined, it makes logical sense to tailor programs to specific populations.

Although some components of social skills training may be generic and apply just as well to depressed as to antisocial children, there are important differences across populations of children in types of deficits seen and the types of improvements that can be expected. This variety makes effective social skills training a more individualized, less generic activity than it often seems. Furthermore, narrowing the group of children so that all in a social skills training group have similar social deficits can make for a more effective, more cohesive group because all children will need to learn many of the same social skills. Thus, the group can be geared toward increasing one certain set of social competencies.

One way in which social skills training is often tailored to the specific needs of a certain population is by using social skills training as one component in a broader treatment plan. For example, with depressed children, it is unlikely that social skills training would be used alone without any other intervention. Cognitive restructuring and other such tasks are commonplace in working with this group of children. Almost all depression studies reviewed for this chapter incorporated some other treatment techniques (such as cognitive restructuring) with this target population. Thus, for depressed students, the social skills training may be interwoven through a treatment program that includes several other components. This type of intervention may be quite different from that needed for a group of aggressive children, especially when decreasing socially aggressive behavior is a primary focus of the group.

Social skills training may be better seen as a category of interventions rather than one intervention. In fact, some research supports the use of a more individualized, less standardized approach to social skills training (Bulkeley & Cramer, 1994). Furthermore, if researchers clarify they group of children their interventions are targeting, practitioners will be better able to match the needs of their clients to the literature on effectiveness for a certain population. Unfortunately, much of the literature on social skills training is vague about the specific problems of the participants. The literature base is growing, however, and our knowledge base of how to best teach social skills to a variety of different populations likely will continue to enlarge.

SOCIAL SKILLS TRAINING AND EXTERNALIZING PROBLEMS

Social skills training has long been used with children exhibiting externalizing problems, or acting out undercontrolled behavior. Much of the research on social skills training has involved children with nonspecific externalizing problems, those who are rejected by other students or who exhibit some behavioral difficulties within the classroom. This section focuses on two specific categories of externalizing behavioral problems: antisocial–aggressive behavior and ADHD. In reviewing the literature for this section, an attempt was made to include only information that directly relates to these populations and problems. Obviously, much of the information covered in chapter 4 and other studies on the more general category of rejected children may also be relevant to this section. Also, much of the literature on social skills training with antisocial–aggressive youth can be applied to children with ADHD. Although it is clear that many children with ADHD have social skill deficits and that social skills training is often advocated for these children, there is much less literature on the use of social skills training with this group compared to antisocial–aggressive children.

Antisocial-Aggressive Behavior and Conduct Disorders

Children exhibiting aggressive or antisocial behaviors are often involved in social skills training because of their difficulties with social interactions and social problem solving. Many of the behaviors exhibited by antisocial–aggressive or conduct-disordered children stem from social inadequacies. Children with conduct disorders or other aggressive behavior disorders are thought to have deficiencies in perceiving and evaluating social cues, which cause them to have deficits in their prosocial behaviors (Merrell, 1994a). In addition, aggressive children often do not use relevant social cues; they make negative or hostile attributions about the intent of others in ambiguous situations; they generate fewer and less effective solutions to social problems; and they expect rewards from aggressive behaviors (Akhtar & Bradley, 1991; Crick & Dodge, 1994; Hinshaw & Anderson, 1996). This conglomeration of social difficulties makes such children a prime target group for social skills training.

Social skills training with aggressive children has generally taken two routes. One route is the structured learning approach advocated by Goldstein and his colleagues (Goldstein, Glick, Reiner, Zimmerman, & Coultry, 1987; Goldstein et al., 1980). As was detailed in chapter 4, this approach involves the use of modeling, role playing, performance feedback, and transfer of training that is typical in many of the commercially available social skill training programs. In this type of training, specific skill behaviors are taught through these procedures.

The other route for social skills training commonly used with aggressive children is cognitive problem-solving training. This approach focuses more on changing the thinking processes of aggressive children and less on teaching specific skills. In this type of intervention, children are taught to generate and evaluate solutions, then form a plan of action. Kazdin (1987) outlined five characteristics of the cognitive problem-solving approach in working with aggressive children:

1. The focus is on children's thought processes, not behavioral acts (as is true with the structured learning approach).
2. A step-by-step approach is used in combination with self-instructions.
3. Structured tasks are used to teach skills.
4. The therapist or trainer is an active participant through modeling, providing feedback, etc.
5. Several procedures such as modeling, role playing, and reinforcement are used.

As can be seen from this description, some overlap exists between the two general methods, but the problem-solving method focuses more on the thought processes of aggressive children, and the structured learning approach has its focus on the specific behaviors of these children.

Although many outcome studies have found positive effects for both types of social skills training for antisocial–aggressive children, in general, the effects have been modest in terms of practical significance. Treatment gains made with antisocial–aggressive children and youth are often small or moderate, often are not seen across settings, and often do not generalize well over time.

A review of studies using the cognitive problem-solving method found positive but somewhat limited effects for this type of intervention (Stern & Fodor,

1989). Kazdin (1987) concluded that because of the marginal clinically significant effects, this intervention "has not been shown to be an effective treatment for antisocial behavior" (p. 194).

Limited effects also have been found for the structured learning approach to social skills training as an intervention for aggressive behavior. Goldstein and Pentz (1984) concluded in a review of outcome studies utilizing the structured learning approach that "skill acquisition is a reliable outcome, but the social validity of this consistent result is tempered substantially by the frequent failure—or at least indeterminacy—of transfer and maintenance" (p. 318). Another review of studies utilizing any type of social skills interventions for behaviorally disordered children also found significant improvements in some, but not all, measures of social competence (Zaragoza, Vaughn, & McIntosh, 1991).

For example, across studies in this review it was a common finding that peer ratings were the most resistant to change. In general, parent and teacher ratings, but not peer ratings, were likely to improve after intervention. To improve the effectiveness of social skills programs for antisocial–aggressive children it is suggested that a more individualized approach must be used. Because not all aggressive children exhibit the same social deficits, an effort should be made to tailor programs to the specific deficits a child has and target the specific context in which a child exhibits these problems (Akhtar & Bradley, 1991).

Although one may not see large gains in appropriate social behaviors or large decreases in inappropriate aggressive behaviors, many studies do indicate that social skills training can have some positive impact on children exhibiting aggressive behavior in a variety of settings including schools, outpatient clinics, and inpatient treatment centers. Social skills training may have more impact in certain areas (e.g., classroom behavior) than others, and maintenance of the behavior change may vary across time and settings. Changes and generalization may also vary depending on the original training procedures used. The studies cited next offer some suggestions on what changes may be expected with the severely antisocial–aggressive population and what trainers can do to achieve the best results possible.

As mentioned before, peer or social acceptance seems to be one of the more difficult things to improve with antisocial–aggressive children and adolescents, who are typically rated extremely low on sociometric measures. Even after social skills training that results in other positive changes, peer acceptance may not improve significantly (Lochman, Burch, Curry, & Lampron, 1984; Lovejoy & Routh, 1988). Even when changes are noted by teachers or through observational data, peer acceptance tends to remain low.

Whereas teachers may report positive changes in the behavior of antisocial–aggressive children, these changes may not generalize well over time. For example, in one study with aggressive children, parents and peers did not rate the children as having fewer externalizing problems after a social skills intervention, but teachers did rate the children more favorably. At a 3-month follow-up, teachers continued to rate the children more favorably than they did a control group of children who did not receive social skills training, but at a 9-month follow-up, even the changes noted by teachers were no longer statistically significant (Pepler, King, Craig, Byrd, & Bream, 1995). Findings such as these underscore the importance of designing and implementing social skills training interventions with maximum programming for generalization.

Although most studies indicate that peer acceptance is more difficult to change than teacher ratings, Hughes and Sullivan (1988) suggested that changes in peer attitudes are not adequately and accurately being assessed. To adequately assess whether peer acceptance has changed, they suggested that sociometric data should be collected from a new group of peers after treatment. This will help to determine if it is the consistently poor peer reputation that accounts in part for the rejection of these children, or whether these children, even after going through social skills training, still exhibit some behaviors that make them less desirable friends.

Obviously, this recommendation has practical limitations. It may be quite difficult to find a new group of peers that had no prior contact with the target child. However, it is important to realize that just because a child learns appropriate social skills and learns to apply these skills does not mean that this child will become socially accepted. Such a dilemma may present a problem for maintenance of behavior change if a child continues to interact with other antisocial–aggressive children purely because he or she continues to be rejected by other peers.

When working with antisocial–aggressive children, there are some practices that may be implemented to help improve the chance that peer relationships will improve. For example, one intervention study used both identified socially deficient children and same-sex nonidentified peers together in a social skills training group. Results indicated that the involvement of peers (compared to training with no peer involvement) along with coaching appropriate social skills did produce increased peer interactions and acceptance for the referred students. Simply coaching the children without the peer interactions did not produce improvements in peer acceptance, but peer interactions without coaching did produce some positive effects for peer acceptance, although these effects were time-limited (Bierman & Furman, 1984). Although this study did not focus specifically on antisocial–aggressive children, the inclusion of nonreferred peers in a group for aggressive children is a recommended practice.

Sheridan (1995) advocated that social skills groups for difficult children be supplemented with children who have less severe problems. As indicated in chapter 4, composing a social skills group entirely of children with antisocial behaviors may increase the chance that the children will serve as negative role models for each other. Thus it is recommended that nonreferred children also be included in a group so that positive role models exist for antisocial–aggressive children. Polyson and Kimball (1993) also suggested the use of nonreferred peers to enhance generalization in natural environments other than classrooms (e.g., the school playground).

Teaching children what to do as well as what not to do may also increase the likelihood that peer acceptance will increase. Bierman, Miller, and Stabb (1987) studied the effects of behavioral social skills training using positive instructions (what to do, with practice and praise for performing specific skills), negative prohibitions (what not to do, with reinforcement for general cooperative behavior rather than specific skills and response cost for violation of rules) and a combination of the two.

Results indicated that the positive instructions did not produce any immediate effects, but at a 6-week follow-up, these students both received and initiated more positive and fewer negative behaviors. The negative prohibitions produced some immediate effects for initiating fewer negative behaviors and receiving more positive responses. The only significant result at the follow-up was a reduced rate of initiating negative behaviors.

Although these improvements were noted in observed behavior, ratings of aggression by teachers and peers did not show any consistent improvement. Only students who received the combination of the negative prohibitions and positive instructions had an increase in peer acceptance ratings. The findings of this study indicate that to have immediate as well as longer lasting improvements in behavior, a combination of telling children what to do and what not to do may be the most effective. Polyson and Kimball (1993) also found that the combined approach of reducing aggressive behaviors and increasing incompatible prosocial behaviors is most likely to be effective with aggressive children.

As previously mentioned, generalization of treatment gains to real-life settings with severely antisocial–aggressive children is clearly a difficult challenge. The results of a study conducted by Kettlewell and Kausch (1983) provide an example of this challenge. These authors found that children who received social skills training performed better on the task used in training, reported less anger when completing this task, and had better problem-solving skills, but on a task similar to the training task but not actually used in training, there were no significant improvements in levels of anger or on frequency of aggressive acts or peer ratings of aggressiveness. The authors stated: "One must conclude that limited evidence exists for the generalization of treatment effects to the 'real-life' setting . . ." (p. 112).

Despite the difficulties, there are procedures to increase the chance of generalization. Covered in detail in chapter 4, these procedures perhaps provide the best hope for producing lasting positive changes across settings with severely antisocial–aggressive children and youth. For example, in a study using problem-solving training (generating and evaluating solutions to problems) to increase prosocial behavior, researchers found that the training produced only limited effects for aggressive boys. However, a generalization procedure that involved subjects completing a log to indicate if they had used problem-solving increased positive changes in the children's behavior (Guevremont & Foster, 1993).

An interesting technological twist on social skills training and the promotion of generalization is the use of virtual reality. Muscott and Gifford (1994) suggested that virtual reality technology can be used to simulate cooperative learning experiences and interactive role plays when social skills training is used for children with behavioral disorders. They cited several advantages of using such technology: ability to develop multiple experiences, ability to play out consequences (such as fighting) that are difficult to do in traditional role plays, and ability to change the nature of the experience. Obviously, this technology may not be practical in many settings (Muscott and Gifford state that the price for all needed equipment is approximately $15,000), but in the future it may become more commonplace and stimulate other uses of interactive technology in social skills training.

Social skills training is commonly thought of as an outpatient treatment, but it also has been used as one component of comprehensive inpatient treatment programs for aggressive children. In a study by Kazdin and colleagues (Kazdin, Esveldt-Dawson, French, & Unis, 1987), greater improvements were found for children in a problem-solving skills condition than in a relationship, client-centered therapy condition. Perhaps most important, these differences were maintained at a 1-year follow-up. As with outpatient treatment, however, although there were improvements, many of the children continued to exhibit more problems than a normative sample of children.

Another study (Kolko, Loar, & Sturnick, 1990) using an inpatient population found that training in social cognitive skills improved the social skills of these youth more significantly than participation in a social activity group (in which children were socialized in a semistructured environment but without the specific instruction and practice of social skills). The skills taught were chosen according to input and observations from staff members and, therefore, reflected the social skills these children lacked. This specific approach to social skills training (teaching skills children obviously lack that are clearly important in their social environment) rather than teaching general social skills is one way to make social skills interventions more socially valid and effective. It is recommend that this be done with any social skills group for antisocial–aggressive children.

Although social skills training is frequently used as a main treatment (often in combination with environmental manipulations) when working with aggressive or antisocial children, it also has been used successfully as one part of larger treatment packages. Interestingly, when used this way, social skills training and other treatment components may have positive impacts on variables other than social competence. Lochman (1992) conducted a study in which aggressive boys received either anger-coping therapy (incorporating cognitive–behavior social skills techniques) or no treatment. Boys who went through the anger-coping therapy did not demonstrate an improvement in classroom behavior, but they did have lower levels of substance use and higher levels of social problem-solving skills at 2½- to 3½-years posttreatment. Thus, just because the intervention did not significantly improve classroom behavior does not mean it produced no positive results. This study helps to point out the importance of collecting outcome data on multiple measures.

As seen from this discussion, severely antisocial–aggressive children and adolescents are often quite resistant to even the best-planned and implemented social skills interventions. This is a tough population! Although social skills interventions may produce some positive effects, aggressive and unpopular children generally improve less after social skills training than do withdrawn children (Schneider, 1992). Thus, someone working with both aggressive and withdrawn children should not develop unrealistic expectations for the same improvements in all students/clients.

Perhaps more importantly, the lack of large improvements across all outcome measures does not mean that social skills training should not be used with severely antisocial–aggressive children and adolescents. Notwithstanding the inherent difficulties with this population, social skills training still offers the hope of some meaningful therapeutic change, even if the increments of change are small. Children exhibiting aggressive and antisocial behaviors may improve after social skills training, but they may not improve to the level desired by teachers or parents: Their behaviors still may not fall within the average range. Furthermore, maintenance of changes over time is often an issue. As practitioners must realize, it is not uncommon for treatment gains to disappear within several months. To help overcome this problem, plans for generalization should be made, and the inclusion of booster sessions may be needed. Also, these children should be followed and assessed to determine if and when future intervention is necessary. Some practical suggestions for using social skills training with the antisocial–aggressive child and adolescent population are presented in Table 5.1.

ADHD

Children and adolescents with ADHD often have social problems. In fact, by some estimates, at least half of them have social problems with peers. Children with ADHD often are considered disruptive, unpredictable, and aggressive by others (Barkley, 1990). Typical social problems of children with ADHD include attempting to enter an ongoing social activity in an inappropriate way, not following standard rules of conversations and social activities, and a ten-

TABLE 5.1
Suggestions for Social Skills Training
With Antisocial–Aggressive Children and Adolescents

Include nonreferred children in the group to limit negative modeling, increase positive modeling, and increase probability that peer acceptance will improve.

Teach children what to do as well and what not to do. Consider using a response cost system or other behavioral interventions to decrease inappropriate behaviors.

Focus on teaching socially valid skills. Assess what skills children need to socialize effectively in their current environment and teach these skills.

Incorporate procedures for generalization across settings and across time.

Consider using follow-up "booster sessions" to help maintain gains made initial training.

Do not expect unrealistically large gains in appropriate social behavior. Recognize that peer acceptance is especially difficult to change with this population.

Collect outcome data on multiple measures. Because some behaviors are particularly resistant to change, multiple outcome measures are necessary to determine where changes occur.

Consider combining social skills training with other interventions (such as behavioral parent training) for maximum effectiveness.

---

dency to attempt to solve social problems through aggression (DuPaul & Stoner, 1994).

Social skills interventions have been used with ADHD children, not to treat their ADHD symptoms per se, but to increase their social competence and remediate the social skill problems that are so often a part of this disorder. Children with ADHD may not have skill *deficits*. (They may be able to state rules and steps for appropriate social behavior.) But they typically have problems performing the social skills they know. Thus, they are more likely to exhibit performance deficits rather than skill deficits (DuPaul & Stoner, 1994).

Although it is clear that many children with ADHD have problems with socially appropriate behavior, research on the effective use of social skills training with this specific population is quite sparse. In a review of 27 studies of social skills training effects on students with behavior problems, no studies were cited with ADHD students as a specific population (Zaragoza et al., 1991). As noted at the beginning of this section, likely much of the literature on aggressive children will also apply to children with ADHD, but it is difficult to know for sure without specific studies with the ADHD population.

As with antisocial–aggressive children, social skills training with ADHD children may involve behavioral social skills training (the structured learning approach) or cognitive problem solving. Because of the limited research on any type of social skills approach with ADHD children, it is difficult to draw conclusions about the effectiveness of these interventions. In a review of social skill deficits and ADHD, Landau and Moore (1991) discussed the use of behavioral and cognitive–behavioral interventions, but little was presented specifically on social skills training. For both types of training techniques, there appears to be a positive but limited effect on the social behaviors of children with ADHD. Because of the sparse research, though, no specific firm conclusions can be drawn at this time about the efficacy of social skills training interventions specifically with children and adolescents who have ADHD.

One study using social skills training as well as parent training did produce some positive effects on children with ADHD and their parents. This single subject design study ($n = 5$) used behavioral social skills training for children with ADHD along with a training group for the parents of the children. Improvements were found in social entry skills both during treatment and follow-up. Maintaining social interactions and problem-solving improvements, two other variables investigated, produced variable outcomes across subjects. Parent skills such as helping their child to solve problems, assisting their child in setting goals, and interacting with their child in a nonthreatening manner also increased. Ratings of behavioral and attention problems by parents and teachers also showed some improvement for most of the children in the study (Sheridan, Dee, Morgan, McCormick, & Walker, 1996). As with social skill interventions for antisocial–aggressive children, this study demonstrated that including additional procedures such as parent training can be helpful.

Guevremont (1990) developed a social skills training program specifically for children with ADHD. This program consists of three components: social skills and cognitive–behavioral training, generalization programming, and strategic peer involvement. The social skills training portion of the program covers four basic skills: social entry, conversational skills, conflict resolution and problem solving, and anger control. The generalization programming consists of activities incorporated within the training program (longer training, use of real-life scenarios, use of multiple and diverse training examples, self-monitoring homework, focus on relevant skills, and having booster sessions) as well as environmental support (developing ways for children to receive reinforcement for appropriate skills within the natural environment). The peer involvement (a form of generalization) is based on research indicating the difficulty in changing peer perceptions. Peer involvement is built into the program with the aim of producing greater peer acceptance.

Although in social skills training much of the focus is on what social skill deficits children have, Frederick and Olmi (1994) suggested that instead of looking only at the social deficits of children with ADHD, the social competencies of these children must also be observed. A number of children with ADHD do have difficulties with social interactions, but not all do. As Frederick and Olmi suggested, looking at these children with ADHD who are accepted by peers will give us a better indication of what social skills are necessary for children with ADHD to become socially accepted. Because these children have a number of difficulties other than social relationships, separating those difficulties related to social skills from those that are not should help target those specific skills that will increase social acceptance.

In a review of the literature on ADHD and social skills, Landau and Moore (1991) presented several suggestions for professionals working to increase the social competencies of children with ADHD. First, they noted the importance of paying attention to diagnoses in order to have the most homogeneous sample possible, and so that there can be better understanding and more confidence in how treatment findings in the literature relate to a specific group of students. These researchers also stressed the importance of using appropriate and socially valid selection procedures for children with ADHD who might take part in a social skills group. Training students in more specific skills that they lack (rather than general skills) is also suggested, so it becomes important to assess the social validity of such skills in the classroom, with peers, and with parents.

In keeping with the view of social skill deficits as one problem of children with ADHD, it is important to reduce other inappropriate behavior at the same time these children are being taught appropriate social skills. Landau and Moore (1991) also suggested that girls may require different intervention strategies than boys because of the typical difference in their presenting symptoms. This suggestion also would be applicable to the primarily inattentive type versus primarily hyperactive–impulsive type of ADHD. Children with the latter type may exhibit more acting-out behaviors and more behaviors similar to those of antisocial–aggressive children. Children with the inattentive type of ADHD may present with different social difficulties and require different social skill intervention strategies.

Unfortunately, the limited literature on social skills training specifically for the ADHD population makes it difficult to draw a large number of conclusions about optimal practices with this group of children and adolescents. However, the emerging but scant evidence in this area does appear to have some potentially promising implications for treatment. Several suggestions for working with children with ADHD are presented in Table 5.2, and the suggestions in Table 5.1 also would appear apt for the ADHD population.

TABLE 5.2
Suggestions for Social Skills Training With Children With ADHD

Identify children with ADHD who do not have social problems and examine how their social behaviors are different from ADHD children with social problems. Focus on training these skills.

Include in the social skills program procedures to reduce inappropriate behaviors typically seen in ADHD children.

Consider using social skills training as one component of a broader behavioral intervention program for children with ADHD.

Do not assume that all children with ADHD have similar social problems. Children with high levels of hyperactive and impulsive behaviors may have social problems similar to those of other "rejected" children, but this may not be as true of children showing primarily inattentive symptoms.

Include procedures to promote generalization.

SOCIAL SKILLS TRAINING
AND INTERNALIZING PROBLEMS

Although social skills training for children with disruptive behavior disorders has received the most attention in the literature as well as clinical work, internalizing problems are also conducive to social skills training. Social withdrawal is one obvious area in which social skills training may be beneficial. Such training is also commonly used as one component of treatment for depressed children. This section overviews the literature on social skills training with children and adolescents who have serious internalizing problems, along with some practical suggestions for implementing treatment specifically with this population.

Depression

A lack of social skills or competence has long been linked to childhood depression. Compared to their nondepressed peers, depressed children are less likely to have appropriate social skills and more likely to have a poor social self-concept and be inappropriately aggressive and impulsive in social situations. Depressed rather than nondepressed children face a greater chance of social rejection or isolation. Furthermore, their social problem solving seems to be impaired (Hammen & Rudolph, 1996). Typically, the use of social skills training with depressed children is more focused on alleviating the depression than on increasing social skills. It is believed that increasing social skills decreases the likelihood of depression. Thus it may be more correct to say that the focus is on alleviating depression by means of social skills training. In terms of research and outcome studies, this means that social competence typically is not used as an outcome measure. Instead, ratings of depression are the outcome measures. Because of this typical practice, social skills interventions are usually only one component of a treatment program for children and adolescents with depression. Because maladaptive cognitions are a hallmark of depression, the focus on social skills programs with depressed children may not aim solely to teach children the performance of certain behaviors but also show children how to change maladaptive cognitions that may be related to problems in social situations (Stark, Best, & Sellstrom, 1989).

Several studies have indicated that social skills training can effectively decrease depressive symptoms in children and adolescents. Reed (1994) used the Skillstreaming program as an intervention for depressed adolescents. A control art and imagery group was used as a comparison. Results showed that adolescents in the treatment group exhibited significantly less depressive symptoms after treatment. Notably, for the most part, this positive finding was more true of males than females. Many females did not improve, whereas the males continued to show improvement 6 to 8 weeks after treatment.

Reed (1994) suggested that these gender-based differential treatment effects were related to differing social competencies and expectations of males and females generally. Females are expected to be more competent socially, and their social groups may be more structured. This characteristic serves to render changes in social behavior of little practical importance for females. Males, though, may be more likely to improve their social standing when they improve their social functioning. Reed suggested that social skills training for depressed adolescents may need to differ for males and females, and that the more traditional approach to social skills training may be more beneficial for males.

Other studies (Butler, Mietzitis, Friedman, & Cole, 1980; Lewinsohn, Clarke, Hops, & Andrews, 1990; Stark, Reynolds, & Kaslow, 1987) have used social skills training as part of a broad intervention package for children with depression. Typically, the social skills component focuses on improving social interactions in general, and such programs tend to produce beneficial results. Because most programs of this nature include a number of other interventions (e.g., increasing pleasant activities, teaching self-management skills, relaxation training, etc.), it is often unclear to what extent the social skills component contributes to the improvement compared with the other intervention components. However, studies such as these clearly support the inclusion of a social skills training component in interventions for depressed children and adolescents.

In their review of treatments for depression, Dujovne, Barnard, and Rapoff (1995) reported that although training in social skills and interpersonal problem solving are often mentioned as possible treatment components for depressed children, little is known about the effectiveness of these types of training compared with other treatments for depression. Some evidence shows that social skills interventions (including interpersonal problem solving) do have positive effects for depressed children, but it is not clear if these methods are any more or less effective than other methods or whether they add to the effectiveness of a treatment program when used in conjunction with other methods.

Dujovne et al. (1995) suggested including operant/social-learning interventions as well as cognitive, social skills, and self-regulation approaches when treating depressed children. Within the social skills area it is suggested that role playing be done to teach children effective conversation and friendships skills such as starting a conversation, listening, asking and answering questions, and smiling.

In summary, although there are still many unanswered questions about the specific contributions of social skills training as a treatment component for depressed children and adolescents, it does seem to be a valid treatment component in its own right. Some specific suggestions on the use of social skills training with this population are presented in Table 5.3.

TABLE 5.3
Suggestions for Social Skills Training With Depressed Children

---

Incorporate other treatment approaches to depression such as cognitive restructuring, self-monitoring, etc.

Include children exhibiting similar types of social deficits in a group. Not all depressed children will have the same types of social problems.

Teach skills that will increase the chance that children will interact with others.

Recognize that males and females may respond differently to social skills training and may have different social difficulties related to their depression.

Social Withdrawal

Socially withdrawn children by nature experience difficulty with social relationships and tend to have a great deal of anxiety about social experiences. In addition to being shy or withdrawn and not interacting with others, these children are noted to have reduced social problem-solving skills compared with nonwithdrawn peers and are less likely to reinitiate social problem solving after failure (Stewart & Rubin, 1995).

Like other groups of children with social skills difficulties, withdrawn children may experience social skills problems due either to a skill deficit or a performance deficit. If such children have a skill deficit, they do not interact with others because they lack the social skills to do so. If the problem is a performance deficit, the children have the skills to interact with others but do not do so because competing negative emotional–cognitive states (e.g., anxiety or depression) prevent them from effectively interacting with others (Kratochwill & French, 1984).

The "competing emotions" rationale for social skills deficits suggests that other issues as well as social skill difficulties likely will need to be assessed and possibly treated for a socially withdrawn child to have optimal improvement. For example, if social withdrawal is due to anxiety, social skills training as well as anxiety reduction techniques may be the most effective treatment for the child.

Kratochwill and French (1984) also pointed out that social withdrawal may be a consequence (not a cause) of social incompetence. Perhaps children who have experienced negative social interaction or those who have been rejected by other children will become socially withdrawn and stop trying to initiate interactions. Intervention techniques different from those used with children who have never really tried to initiate social interactions may be used with these children.

Erwin's (1994) review of treatment studies using social skills training for isolated children concluded that such training can produce significant improvements in a number of social areas: level of social interaction, sociometric status, and problem-solving abilities. This review indicated that social skills training typically produces more significant effects for socially rather than nonsocially isolated children in terms of social interaction and sociometric status.

Other studies have also supported the use of social skills training with socially isolated or withdrawn children, although as with other social skills training groups, the results are somewhat mixed. In one study containing two separate outcome studies, one study found that social skills training improved teacher ratings of prosocial/on-task behavior but that there were no differences on sociometric ratings. The other outcome study found significant differences baesd on sociometric ratings (compared to control groups) but not on teacher ratings (Edleson & Rose, 1982). The authors of this study suggested that the 6 to 8 weeks allowed for the intervention program was not enough time. Informal teacher feedback to the authors indicated that the teachers were just beginning to see some changes in children at the end of treatment.

For more severe cases of social withdrawal (e.g., social phobia), social skills training has been used as one component in multicomponent treatment interventions (Albano, Marten, Holt, Heimberg, & Barlow, 1995). As with many interventions for depression that utilize social skills training, such training may not be the sole focus of treatment for more severe social phobias or anxiety disorders. As with the multicomponent treatment programs for children with depression, it is difficult to determine the impact of social skills training separately from the other components of such programs.

Although socially withdrawn or isolated children are a prime target for social skills training and may respond more positively to such training than other groups of children, a need still exists for more research on what makes a social skills program successful for this specific group of children. Nevertheless, there is a good deal of evidence to support the use of social skills training interventions with socially withdrawn children and adolescents. Some specific suggestions for conducting social skills training with withdrawn children are presented in Table 5.4.

SOCIAL SKILLS TRAINING AS A CLASSWIDE OR SCHOOLWIDE INTERVENTION

Most social skills training is conducted at the small group level, but it may also be implemented classwide or schoolwide, either as a sole intervention or in combination with a multicomponent intervention program. In fact, recently (since about 1990), there has been an increasing emphasis on using social skills training programs in whole classrooms or schools. Obviously, when implementing a program on a larger scale, there are additional considerations. One challenge when implementing classwide or schoolwide programs is de-

TABLE 5.4

Suggestions for Social Skills Training With Socially Withdrawn Children

Recognize that just because children are not interacting with others does not necessarily mean they do not have the appropriate skills. Other difficulties, such as anxiety or depression may prevent children from using social skills and lead to social withdrawal.

Recognize that social withdrawal may be a cause of social problems or a consequence of social difficulties. Different groups of children with social withdrawal may need different treatment approaches.

Consider combining social skills training with other interventions if social withdrawal is associated with a more severe anxiety disorder.

Ensure that children have adequate opportunities to practice skills in "real-life" settings in which they are most likely to experience difficulties with withdrawal or social anxiety.

ciding who should be in charge of the actual social skill training activities. Sheridan (1995) suggested that because many teachers may not feel prepared to teach social skills and because many school psychologists or school counselors may not have the time, it would be best for teachers to do the actual training while school psychologists, school counselors, and the like provide needed consultation and support. Obviously, before beginning a classwide or schoolwide program, all involved personnel need to be trained in the basics of teaching socials skills (e.g., effectively using modeling, role playing, etc.). Support staff should be available for teachers to consult about difficulties in implementing the program or specific students causing them problems.

In one school-based program with a specific focus on training teachers to work with students on conflict resolution in the natural classroom setting as events occurred, positive changes in children were seen, even though there was no specific social skills training curriculum (Adalbjarnardottir, 1993). Teachers took part in 20 training sessions held throughout the school year. These sessions focused both on theoretical issues and practical issues such as how to do certain tasks within the classroom. Although many school-based programs will not have the luxury of such extensive training with teachers, this program demonstrated that training teachers in techniques they can use in the classroom to promote prosocial skills can be an effective way to increase social competencies in children.

Schoolwide programs may present additional considerations beyond those presented with classwide programs. School commitment is particularly important (Sheridan, 1995). School administrators as well as teachers and other involved personnel must be supportive of the program. Although a schoolwide program would not be implemented without the approval of the school administrators, their active approval can set the tone for teachers and other staff, and they can provide funding for the programs and schedule time for certain activities.

Large-scale training activities present other difficulties. Because it is more difficult to monitor a whole classroom of students than a small group, classwide or schoolwide social skills training programs are often supplemented with other intervention procedures. For example, classwide reinforcement programs or token economy systems may be used both to reinforce appropriate social behavior and decrease and control any inappropriate behaviors (Connolly, Dowd, Criste, Nelson, & Tobias, 1995; Sheridan, 1995).

Although the additional planning and training needed for effective classwide or schoolwide programs may turn some away from these larger scale programs, there are advantages of using such programs rather than the traditional small-group format. One distinct advantage lies in the many opportunities to reinforce learned skills in the natural environment and promote the generalization of skills to the natural environment. Several social skills programs reviewed in chapter 6 incorporate classwide teaching of social skills along with the generalization of the skills taught to situations outside of the direct teaching situation (Connolly et al., 1995; Jackson, Jackson, & Monroe, 1983). In such programs, when a situation occurs that relates to social competence, the teacher or other school personnel can immediately relate what was learned in social skills training to what is currently happening. Because generalization and social validity are major concerns in the training of social skills, the classwide or schoolwide approach may be an optimal way for teaching skills and then focusing on their use and generalization.

Another advantage of the classwide or schoolwide approach is that children with differing levels of social status are taught together, thereby increasing the chances that those children low in social status will interact with higher status peers and become more accepted. One study used a classwide social skills training program with an emphasis specifically on peer situations and problem solving (Hepler & Rose, 1988). Children who participated in this intervention were rated more positively on peer sociometric techniques at a 4-week follow-up assessment, even though these findings were not present at posttesting 1 week after the treatment program was completed. Children with the lowest sociometric ratings (those who were rejected) also showed some significant improvement at follow-up. Most notably, they showed a decrease in the number of negative peer nominations they received compared to the control group. The authors suggested that the lack of change in sociometric ratings at the posttesting time may to due, in part, to the "rigidity of social status." More time may be needed for social status to change. Thus, the change is not seen until follow-up when children have been using the appropriate skills for a longer period of time. Although this program was implemented classwide in a school setting, it was not implemented by the classroom teachers. Many classwide and schoolwide programs will be implemented by teachers, as suggested earlier, but other programs may be implemented by school psychologists, school counselors, and the like.

One difficulty with traditional "pull-out" social skills training programs is that teachers cannot as easily supplement what is learned in the social skills lessons with experience in the child's natural school environment because the teachers are less integrally involved in training (if they are involved at all). Furthermore, if teachers are not involved, they may be less supportive of the program.

In one school-based intervention program in which teachers did not serve as trainers, positive effects were found, but only parents rated the students as having improved. Teachers and peers of the students did not see significant changes in the treatment group as compared with a control group (Verduyn, Lord, & Forrest, 1990). The authors of this study observed that the teachers were wary of the social skills training program when it was initially started and suggested that this may be one reason their ratings did not reflect changes. Subjective reports indicated the teachers did become more interested in the program as it progressed, and they saw some changes in children's behaviors.

By the end of the study, the teachers indicated that they felt social skills training was an important part of school curriculums, but not all teachers felt as though they were able to teach social skills adequately in the classroom. The subjective reports from this study indicated the importance of having those involved "buy into" the training program. In this case, because teachers were not actively involved in teaching social skills, their original lack of support for the program may not have had as strong effects as it would have if the teachers had implemented the program. Obviously, if teachers are to implement programs, they must receive adequate training and be provided with support and assistance. Even if teachers are not doing the social skills training themselves, there will be activities teachers can use in the classroom to promote the generalization of skills learned in the training groups, and they should be encouraged to become involved.

Social skills training at the classwide or schoolwide level may be part of a more comprehensive prevention or intervention program. For example, in one large schoolwide intervention program, social skills training was one component of the intervention program. This portion of the intervention involved providing teachers with training on how to teach social skills, then having all teachers implement social skills training as part of their classroom curriculum. This program as a whole had positive effects on a number of student variables (e.g., fewer referrals for discipline problems, fewer suspensions), but because of this program's comprehensive nature, it cannot be determined how the social skills component specifically related to the observed changes (Knoff & Batsche, 1995).

Another school-based program included social skills training as one component of a longitudinal program to reduce academic failure, delinquency, and drug abuse (O'Donnell, Hawkins, Catalano, Abbott, & Day, 1995). Social skills training was only a small part of this program. Classroom interventions, parent interventions, and child interventions (of which social skills training was the main component) were all included. Some positive effects were shown for subjects in this study, but overall, only girls showed stronger commitment to school and less drug abuse, and only boys showed an increase in social and academic skills.

Other variations on classwide or schoolwide programs involve doing some social skills training with all students and supplementing this with small group training for the students with the most social difficulties. Jones, Sheridan, and Binns (1993) outlined such a school-based social skills training program in which schoolwide social skills training was conducted along with treatment of specific students at highest risk for developing problems due to poor social skills. One important part of their program was the training of all school staff. This training was done in two phases: one was a two-part inservice phase to learn the purposes and procedures (including procedures for classroom training and generalization) of the social skills program, and the other used "booster sessions" to discuss the program after it had been in effect for several months.

The classroom-based portion of this program was implemented schoolwide, and was designed to teach skills useful to all students. The small-group training, for those at risk, was intended to be more intensive than the general classwide training. Generalization was promoted through school activities and home practice of the skills. School staff were trained in promoting generalization and reinforcing this when it occurred. Parents were encouraged to practice with their children at home the social skills learned in school.

No outcome data was presented on this program, but the authors did base their program on a review of the literature on social skills training. They also discussed the importance of evaluating all programs to evaluate changes. This program was geared specifically toward prevention of problems, not intervention. It was thought that if all students are provided with some social skills training, with the ones at highest risk for developing future problems given even more intense training, then the development of future problems related to the lack of social competence could be prevented.

As a whole, classwide or schoolwide programs seem to have some advantages, particularly related to generalization, over small-group interventions. However, it must be recognized that there is still little or no research evidence comparing the treatment efficacy of schoolwide or classroomwide interventions with traditional small-group social skills training. The disadvantages of such interventions relate more to the logistics of conducting such programs. Some specific suggestions for implementing social skills training programs at the class or school level are presented in Table 5.5.

TABLE 5.5

Suggestions for Classwide or Schoolwide Social Skills Training Programs

---

Decide who will be in charge of conducting the training. Typically this person will be the classroom teacher but it may be the school psychologist, school counselor, and so on.

Ensure that novice trainers are adequately prepared to teach social skills. Provide several training sessions before the social skills program is implemented.

Provide continuing support to trainers throughout the social skills program.

Consider combining the basic social skills training with other behavioral procedures (such as a token economy) to decrease inappropriate behaviors and reinforce the use of appropriate social skills.

Attend to situations in the natural environment that can be tied to the social skill lessons. Doing this will promote generalization and maintenance of the skills learned.

Consider supplementing classwide or schoolwide training with small group training for those children with more severe social deficits.

Consider using social skills training as one component of a preventive program, particularly with elementary school children.

EMPATHY TRAINING AND MORAL REASONING TRAINING

Training components that have sometimes been added to the basics of social skills training, particularly with antisocial–aggressive children and youth, are what have been referred to as *empathy training* and *moral reasoning training*. In fact, Goldstein and his colleagues (Goldstein et al., 1987) incorporated moral reasoning into their Anger Replacement Training (ART) program, which is intended for specific use with aggressive adolescents. The ART program is a three-pronged program in which social skills (utilizing Goldstein's structured learning approach), anger control, and moral reasoning are all emphasized. This three-pronged approach is seen as addressing the behavioral, affective, and cognitive factors related to aggression.

The moral reasoning portion of this program has its foundations in Kolhberg's work. As Goldstein et al. (1987) stated: "It is apparent that Moral Education involves at least three conditions that are believed to enhance moral reasoning—role taking opportunities through reciprocal social interaction, cognitive conflict regarding genuine moral dilemmas, and exposure to the next higher stage of reasoning" (p. 113). Moral education uses moral dilemmas that group members consider, discuss, examine their reasoning, and take an individual position. The rationale for such moral discussion groups is that they will lead to changes in moral behavior. Moral reasoning seems to be related to both antisocial behavior and prosocial behavior, thus presenting a rationale for its inclusion in the ART program. Although others have discussed the use of moral reasoning, Goldstein and his colleagues appear to be the first to incorporate moral reasoning training into a comprehensive social skills program.

Empathy training, or learning to empathize or see another's position, is an additional concept that Goldstein and colleagues have incorporated into broad social skills curriculums (Goldstein, 1988). Although an exact definition of *empathy training,* and why empathy training should be incorporated into social skills programs, is still somewhat vague, the basic rationale for its inclusion is that, as with moral reasoning training, there is a positive relation between empathy skills and prosocial skills, and a negative relation between empathy skills and antisocial–aggressive behavior. Several studies examining the effects of empathy training found positive effects for children. For example, empathy training was shown to be associated with an increase in positive social behaviors and a more positive self-evaluation for both aggressive and nonaggressive students (Feshbach, 1983; Feshbach & Feshbach, 1982).

Although moral reasoning training and empathy training are not new ideas, few guidelines exist showing how to incorporate such training into a comprehensive social skills program and little information on what benefits this type of training adds to a program. Practitioners may want to consider adding such components to their programs while recognizing that these training methods are still somewhat experimental and intended to supplement rather than replace other social skills training methods.

SUMMARY

As noted throughout this chapter, social skills training can have positive effects for children with a variety of problems ranging from antisocial–aggressive behavior to depression. Besides its application to a wide variety of populations, social skills training can also be used in different settings including small groups at outpatient treatment centers or schools, inpatient treatment centers, and the regular school classroom setting.

As some sections of this chapter have shown, positive treatment effects often are not as strong as we would like them to be, particularly when working with highly intractable problems such as antisocial–aggressive behavior/conduct disorder. Then, are these programs effective and useful?

Ogilvy (1994) suggested that to determine if a social skills training program has been effective, three criteria must be met: "a) the programme has successfully taught the specific skills targeted; b) the skills taught have generalised to real life settings and the effects are maintained over time; c) these specific skills have made a difference to the child's life in terms of some socially valued outcome" (p. 79). Ogilvy observed that research to date supports the use of social skills training as a component in a program to bring about change, but not as the sole intervention, particularly when attempting to improve peer relationships and sociometric status. Clearly, this is what research with specific populations, particularly antisocial–aggressive children and youth, also has indicated. Ogilvy stated that when targeting a specific problem, social skills interventions should be combined with other appropriate interventions, such as including peers to some extent if one focus of the training is to improve relationships with peers. Many programs have done this, particularly programs for internalizing disorders, such as depression, for which social skills training is only one component.

Maintenance over time, which has been alluded to throughout this chapter and discussed in detail in chapter 4, needs more investigation with all target populations and within all settings. Hughes and Sullivan (1988) reported that 50% (19 of 38) of social skills outcome studies identified in their review investigated maintenance over time for 4 weeks or more, but only three studies reported following subjects for 6 months or longer. Obviously, effects of programs must generalize over longer periods of time, especially if the program is expected to make a difference in the child's life.

With these caveats in mind, the authors of this volume contend that clinicians who desire to conduct social skills training should not be overly discouraged by the lack of long-term follow-up data. After all, social skills training has a great deal of promise and potential as an important intervention. However, they should recognize that the best way to maintain changes seen at posttreatment is unclear. This state of affairs may be particularly true with the antisocial–aggressive population. As mentioned previously, trainers should continue to follow up periodically on children who have finished a social skills training experience and incorporate booster sessions when needed, no matter what population or setting is the target of the intervention.

The concerns of Ogilvy (1994) about the teaching of specific skills, the generalization of such skills, and the social validity of these skills are concerns for social skills training conducted with any population and within any setting. As noted in this chapter, some groups may respond better to social skills training (e.g., withdrawn children), and other populations may need more training for even moderate changes to be seen in the specific skills being taught. Ensuring that skills taught are socially valid for the group to whom they are being taught and having a plan for generalization is important for all populations. Classwide and schoolwide programs may provide some advantages in promoting generalization and increasing the social validity of skills being taught.

When planning a social skills intervention for a specific population, practitioners should take into account the best practices for working with a specific group and modify their groups to ensure initial learning and maintenance of skills to the best degree possible. The specific practical suggestions provided in Table 5.1 through Table 5.5 may be helpful in this regard. Practitioners, though, may need to have flexible expectations and training procedures for their different groups.

A Review of Selected
Social Skills Training Programs

The purpose of this final chapter is to present short descriptions and reviews of several commercially published social skills programs. This list of programs is not intended to be an exhaustive list. Instead, it is a sampling of the programs available to help education and mental health professionals teach social skills to school-age children. The programs included in this chapter (which are presented in no particular order) were selected after a number of catalogs devoted to educational and psychological publications and programs were reviewed. Programs were selected for inclusion if they appeared to specifically address teaching social skills to children and adolescents. Programs that did not target school-age children and adolescents (e.g., those programs targeted specifically to preschool-age or adult populations) were not included. Programs targeting a specific population (e.g., children with autism, children of divorced parents) were also not included, although programs targeted toward lower functioning children or children with mild-to-moderate disabilities in general were included. Programs included were those that focus specifically on the development of social skills and social competence (i.e., skills involved in interacting with others), not just those that deal with feelings, anger resolution, and the like, although these aspects are often included as part of a more complete social skills program.

These reviews are not intended to be critical reviews of the various social skills programs. They are meant to help clinicians who run social skills groups or engage in clinical work with socially impaired children gain a better knowledge of the variety of programs available and some of the populations toward whom these programs are geared. As readers peruse this chapter, they will see that there are many similarities among social skills programs. All programs are intended for use in teaching social skills to groups of children (although adaptations can be made for individual instruction with almost all programs), and all programs use the *structured learning* method (or some variation) of teaching social skills (direct instruction, modeling, rehearsal, feedback, and generalization work).

Although a great number of similarities exist among these programs, there are also differences. Not all programs will be equally effective for all clinicians, nor will they be equally effective for all populations of children. Thus, this chapter should be used as a guide to help choose the program that will best meet the needs of each individual clinician and his or her population of children with social skills deficits.

THE SKILLSTREAMING SERIES
AND RELATED TRAINING PROGRAMS

Publisher: Research Press
                   PO Box 9177
                   Champaign, IL 61826

Skillstreaming in Early Childhood: Teaching Prosocial Skills to the Preschool and Kindergarten Child

Authors: Ellen McGinnis and Arnold P. Goldstein

Publication Year: 1990

Skillstreaming the Elementary School Child: A Guide for Teaching Prosocial Skills

Authors: Ellen McGinnis, Arnold P. Goldstein, Robert P. Sprafkin, and N. Jane Gershaw

Publication Year: 1984

Skillstreaming the Adolescent: A Structured Learning Approach to Teaching Prosocial Skills

Authors: Arnold P. Goldstein, Robert P. Sprafkin, N. Jane Gershaw, and Paul Klein

Publication Year: 1980

The Skillstreaming program includes three books outlining the Skillstreaming structured learning method for teaching prosocial skills. The three books are almost identical in their layout, and the general information is presented with obvious adaptations for children of different age levels. Although the specific prosocial skills to be taught vary somewhat at the three age levels, there are many similarities in the types of skills and in the presentation of training methods.

The Skillstreaming method is based on the structured learning model. Each skill presented in this program is broken down into its component behaviors, and guidelines for the use of modeling, role playing, performance feedback, and transfer training to teach the skills are presented. Each Skillstreaming book overviews these components and some of the research related to the use of these activities. Also included in each book is a discussion of informal assessment methods that can help group leaders identify children who may be appropriate for a Skillstreaming group as well as the individual strengths and weaknesses of each group participant. Examples of informal assessment forms are included. There is also a chapter in each book devoted to behavior management issues in the context of the skillstreaming group.

The Skillstreaming lessons are intended to be taught in a group format, and the skills and methods for teaching these skills are geared toward this format. The authors do indicate that the skills may be taught to individual children but that it would be difficult, if not impossible, to stick with the format for modeling and role playing with only a clinician and a child. Thus, when using this curriculum, it will be best to stay with the group format recommended by the authors.

At the preschool level (ages 3–6) there are 40 prosocial skills divided into six categories of behaviors: beginning social skills, school-related skills, friendship-making skills, dealing with feelings, alternatives to aggression, and dealing with stress. Each skill is broken down into two to four steps, and these steps as well as suggested role-play situations, comments, and related activities are included. For example, Asking Someone to Play (a friendship-making skill) contains these steps: *Decide if you want to, Decide who,* and *Ask.* Steps for all skills are short and should be relatively easy for a young child to understand. The associated Program Forms Booklet includes handouts for each of the 40 skills with illustrations to aid the nonreaders in remembering the steps.

At the elementary school level, 60 prosocial skills are presented in five categories: classroom survival skills, friendship-making skills, skills for dealing with feelings, skill alternatives to aggression, and skills for dealing with stress. Each of these skills is broken into three to five steps, and these steps along with notes for discussion about each step are presented in the book. As with the preschool version, suggested modeling situations are included, as well as comments on the skill. The steps for each skill are longer than in the preschool version but are still short and concise. For example, Joining In (a friendship-making skill) consists of the following steps: *Decide if you want to join in, Decide what to say, Choose a good time,* and *Say it in a friendly way.*

At the adolescent level, 50 skills are presented divided in the following six categories: beginning social skills, advanced social skills, skills for dealing with feelings, skill alternatives to aggression, skills for dealing with stress, and planning skills. As with the elementary version, the steps for each skill (ranging from three to six) are presented and along with each step are notes for discussion, suggested modeling situations, and comments on the skill. The steps are still short and concise but are at a slightly higher level than those at the elementary level. For example, the skill of Joining In (an advanced social skill) consists of these steps: *Decide if you want to join in an activity others are doing, Decide the best way to join in, Choose the best time to join in,* and *Join in the activity.*

The Skillstreaming programs are intended to be used in school and clinic settings with almost any child. In fact, at the preschool level, the authors recommend that all children in the preschool or kindergarten class be involved in the skillstreaming program both to help prevent later social problems and so that peers with adequate skills can serve as models for those with skill deficits. At the elementary and adolescent level it is recommended that children with similar types of deficits be included in a group.

The Skillstreaming manuals are easy to read and the skill lessons are presented one per page. Unlike some other manuals, these do not present scripts for group leaders to follow, although they do present some example group scripts that the beginning group leader may find helpful. The Notes for Discussion presented right next to each skill step should be helpful to leaders in stimulating discussion and incorporating different activities into the group.

Aggression Replacement Training:
A Comprehensive Intervention for Aggressive Youth

Authors: Arnold P. Goldstein, Barry Glick, Scott Reiner, Deborah Zimmerman, and Thomas M. Coultry

Publication Year: 1987

Closely related to the family of Skillstreaming intervention materials, Aggression Replacement Training (ART) is a three-pronged program designed to be used specifically with juvenile delinquents or other adolescents experiencing significant behavioral problems and a notable lack of prosocial behaviors. The three components of this program are these: structured learning procedures to enhance prosocial skills, anger-control training to decrease aggressive and angry behaviors, and moral education to overcome more egocentric, primitive styles of reasoning.

The structured learning component of this program is adapted directly from the adolescent Skillstreaming program. Instead of 50 prosocial skills, though, only 10 are included in ART. These 10 skills were included by the authors based on the particular relevance of the skill to the type of participant targeted by this program and the extent to which the skills enhance motivation and participation in the group.

The anger-control portion of ART is a set of 10 lessons intended to help adolescents understand what makes them angry and learn how to reduce their anger and aggression. As with the structured learning component, modeling, role playing, and performance feedback are used to help teach these anger-reduction skills. The participants are taught to recognize what makes them mad and to develop ways of reducing the anger in order to consider alternative responses.

The third component of this package, moral education, is taught through dilemma discussion intended to increase moral reasoning and provide an opportunity for group participants to use the reasoning skills learned in the structured learning and anger-control portions of this program. The dilemmas for use in these discussions are presented in the manual. Each component of ART is described in detail, and there is a trainer's manual chapter for each of the three components that leads one though the general steps for conducting such a group.

This is one of the few social skills programs directed specifically at the juvenile delinquent population. The actual social skills section of this curriculum is identical to that of the Skillstreaming programs (although only the 10 specific skills are targeted here), but the additional components of this program make for a unique combination targeted toward a particularly difficult group of children.

The Prepare Curriculum:
Teaching Prosocial Competencies

Author: Arnold P. Goldstein

Publication Year: 1988

Also related to the Skillstreaming programs, The Prepare Curriculum is intended to be used with elementary- and high school-age children who have deficits in prosocial behavior, either by being aggressive and antisocial or withdrawn and socially isolated. This curriculum consists of 10 courses, many of which are similar (or identical) to the techniques presented in the Skillstreaming and ART manuals. The courses offer training in these areas: problem-solving, interpersonal skills, situational perception, anger control, moral reasoning, stress management, empathy, recruiting supportive models, cooperation, and understanding and using groups. Each of these 10 courses consists of a varying number of session outlines. Although the courses are presented in a suggested order, most do not build on earlier courses, and group leaders could be somewhat flexible in choosing what courses to present and in which order. Each course has a chapter describing the skills to be taught, an outline of research related to effective teaching of these skills, and brief outlines of sessions. As mentioned earlier, there is considerable overlap between the Prepare Curriculum and the Skillstreaming and Anger-Replacement Therapy curriculums. For example, the Interpersonal Skills Training course of the Prepare Curriculum is the adolescent version of the Skillstreaming program.

The Prepare Curriculum is a very complete curriculum and covers a wider variety of prosocial behaviors than most other social skills training programs. Because the curriculum is so complete, counselors and psychologists most likely will find themselves choosing from the various courses the skills they feel are most relevant to their particular group of students.

THE CULTURE AND LIFESTYLE APPROPRIATE SOCIAL SKILLS INTERVENTION CURRICULUM (CLASSIC): A PROGRAM FOR SOCIALLY VALID SOCIAL SKILLS TRAINING

Author: Judith A. Dygdon

Publication Year: 1993

Publisher: John Wiley & Sons, Inc.
                     615 Third Avenue
                     New York, NY 10158–0012

The CLASSIC is a behaviorally oriented social skills curriculum of 15 lessons (each lasting approximately 75 min) designed for children and adolescents of average intelligence. The author indicates that the program may be used with other children, but that adaptations may need to be made. The CLASSIC program is geared toward small-group instruction, and the author suggests that the group have coleaders rather than a single leader. The scripts for the CLASSIC program were developed with children between the ages of 10 and 14 in mind, but as the author indicates, with some modifications in wording and developmental level of examples, this program could be used with both younger and older children.

The CLASSIC program is intended to be useful across differing cultural groups and with children exhibiting a variety of social skills problems, from aggressive–antisocial behavior to social withdrawal. An important goal of the CLASSIC is to be socially valid, to actually enable children to be more accepted by their peers, not simply to teach social skills. Because the emphasis is on cross-cultural appropriateness and social validity, target behaviors or goals are identified somewhat differently than in other social skills programs. There are no set target behaviors. Instead, the group identifies behaviors that are socially acceptable in their particular social environment. This is done by group members generating lists of behaviors exhibited both by children they like and those they do not like. These lists are generated early in the program, and frequent reference is made back to them in later lessons.

The majority of the CLASSIC manual (pp. 39–151) is devoted to lesson plans for the 15 sessions. These plans explain what should be prepared for each session and what equipment will be needed. The chapter before the plans contains strategies on effectively using skills such as modeling, role playing, and so forth. Included in the lesson plans are detailed scripts of what the group leaders should say in each lesson. In addition, the author supplies notes to the leader on what to do during group sessions. The actual lessons differ somewhat from those presented in other social skills programs in that there are no set skills to be role played and practiced. Instead, there are general skills to be learned and applied to various settings.

The first few sessions are spent identifying acceptable, likable behaviors and unacceptable behaviors. The next several sessions are spent discussing nonverbal behaviors, and the remainder of the sessions are given to discussing social problem solving and the use of social skills in different situations. Throughout the last half of the CLASSIC there is a focus on these steps: Relax, Set a goal, Make a list, and Check it out. The Check it out portion involves referring back to the list of acceptable and unacceptable behaviors to see if potential solutions encompass any of them. Also included is an evaluation of negative consequences.

The CLASSIC is interesting and somewhat different from the more typical programs because it lacks specific target skills. Whether this type of program (with group members generating the appropriate social skills to learn) is more socially valid than a traditional social skills program is unclear. No empirical evidence is given to show that this program is more effective than other programs. The leader scripts are a bit cumbersome to read through because they mix leader scripts (what to say) with instructions to the leader (what to do). Most likely after reading through this section several times and training several groups, a leader would be better prepared to adapt the specifics of the scripts to fit his or her own style.

METACOGNITIVE APPROACH
TO SOCIAL SKILLS TRAINING:
A PROGRAM FOR GRADES 4–12

Authors: Jan Sheinker and Alan Sheinker
Publication Year: 1988
Publisher: Aspen Publishers, Inc.
                   7201 McKinney Circle
                   Frederick, MD 21701

The Metacognitive Approach to Social Skills Training (MASST) is intended to teach children in elementary school, middle school, and high school to be self-directive and to self-monitor, self-evaluate, and self-correct. This curriculum is lengthy, but, as the authors indicate, not all lessons must be used: Leaders could select only those lessons most relevant to their target population.

The total package consists of 40 units divided into five parts: *Who am I? Self-concept; Where am I going? Goal setting; How will I become the person I choose to be? How do I get what I want from others and from myself? Who is in charge?* Each of these five parts is then divided into sections, each section into units, and each unit into lessons. For example, Part Four is "How do I get what I want from others and myself?" This part has four sections. Section A is "How I get friendship," and under this section there are two units with four lessons each. The bulk of the manual (pp. 25–250) consists of these lesson plans.

Each unit begins with goals for the leader and students as well as things to remember while teaching the lessons (e.g., encourage students to self-evaluate and self-correct). Each lesson outlines activities and discussions and gives homework suggestions. Verbatim scripts are not included, but specific steps are outlined for the leader instead. These steps are ordered to provide general guidelines that the group leader can follow in conducting each group session. Each lesson outlined occupies about half a page. Many lessons have associated worksheets, either for homework purposes or for use within the lesson. All worksheets are contained in an appendix (pp. 258–362) and may be reproduced for use in conducting these groups.

As the authors indicate, each lesson will take approximately 40 minutes. They recommend holding the group at least twice a week, thus covering two lessons per week. Getting through the whole curriculum would require 8 or 9 months, and the curriculum would be included as part of the regular classroom curriculum. Because having a social skills group for 8 or 9 months is not practical outside the classroom, the authors present an outline of lessons that can be used for shorter curriculums (from 4–18 weeks).

The authors indicate that this program is appropriate for almost any school-age child, whether the child is in the regular classroom, in a gifted placement, or in an alternative educational or special education classroom. It is cautioned, though, that this program is not appropriate for dealing with overt antisocial behavior. If children have severe acting-out or social problems it is recommended that they first go through a program that teaches basic behavioral and interactive skills before beginning the MASST program. Because of the wide age range targeted by this curriculum (grades 4–12), not all lessons will be appropriate for all students. In the first section of the manual, the authors recommend lessons for use with elementary, middle, and high school children. In addition, each lesson is coded with E (elementary school: 4–6), J (junior high and upper middle grades: 7–9), and H (high school: 10–12) to indicate the level toward which each lesson is geared with many lessons coded as being appropriate for all age groups.

The MASST curriculum and lessons are based on the idea that internal control is needed for problem solving and responsible behavior. Students are taught to evaluate social situations, generate behavioral choices, and predict outcomes. The group leader uses questions to guide this process and thinking out loud as a form of modeling. Students are expected to practice and apply the skills learned in the group.

For some people, one drawback to this program may be the type and expense of equipment needed. The authors break the equipment needs into two categories: essential and optional. Even the essential equipment includes things such as a tape recorder and instant camera. The optional equipment includes a video camera. As more classrooms become equipped with such materials, this may not be an issue in the classroom, but outside of the classroom setting it may be difficult for many clinicians to access such materials.

TEACHING SOCIAL SKILLS:
A PRACTICAL INSTRUCTIONAL APPROACH

Authors: Robert Rutherford, Jane Chipman, Samuel DiGangi, and Kathryn Anderson

Publication Date: 1992

Publisher: Exceptional Innovations
                  PO Box 6085
                  Ann Arbor, MI 48106

This social skills package is intended for use primarily by teachers in teaching elementary school children prosocial behaviors through self-management, which includes the components of self-monitoring, self-reinforcement, and self-evaluation. Three types of problem behaviors are discussed: withdrawn, immature, and aggressive. The distinction is also made between children who can't perform a behavior (they have never before demonstrated the behavior) and children who won't perform a behavior (they are not currently demonstrating the desired behavior).

The first chapter discusses five basic interventions for the can't children (identifying prosocial behaviors, modeling prosocial behavior, role playing, reinforcing appropriate behavior, and teaching self-control) and two for the won't children (providing clear expectations and fine-tuning the five steps outlined for the can't children). Most of the manual (pp. 11–180) contains outlines of ways to teach 23 prosocial behaviors. For each behavior, interventions for withdrawn, immature, and aggressive children are presented separately, and within those categories, the problem both of children who can't and of those who won't are discussed separately. Rather than specific interventions, these are general guidelines and a discussion of the general interventions and key things to note with the particular type of socially deficient child. This program is much less specific about exactly what to do or how to do it than other programs are. Each section begins with a brief discussion of environmental assessment, which is intended to help the teacher determine what environmental factors may be contributing to the behavior and whether it is a case of the child's not having the skills or one of the child's currently not using the skills. A large appendix in the manual consists of record cards intended for use with some of the interventions. These record cards are designed to aid children in the monitoring and evaluation of the behaviors. The use of record cards is incorporated into the general intervention guidelines where their purpose and rationale is explained.

This program is unique in its separation of session outlines into the different categories of behaviors: aggressive, immature, withdrawn. This separation may help the group leader dealing with a specific population of students, but the general interventions suggested are much the same across all types of socially deficient children and for both the can't and the won't children.

THE TOUGH KID SOCIAL SKILLS BOOK

Author: Susan M. Sheridan
Publication Date: 1995
Publisher: Sopris-West
                 1140 Boston Ave.
                 Longmont, CO 80501

The Tough Kid social skills curriculum builds on an earlier work, *The Tough Kid Book* (Rhode, Jenson, & Reavis, 1992), which has proven to be a very popular behavioral intervention guide for use with antisocial and other difficult children. A "tough kid" is someone who "displays excesses in noncompliance and aggression, and deficits in self-management, academic, and social skills" (p. 1). As the name of this Tough Kid program suggests, the focus is on teaching appropriate social skills.

Chapter 1 in the manual comprises a description of tough kids and the kind of behavioral problems they might exhibit as well as their typical interactions with peers. Chapter 2 is an in-depth discussion of assessing of social skills: methods to use, examples of ways to use different methods, and forms (sociometric forms, surveys, and observational coding systems). The remainder of the manual addresses issues in developing and setting up a social skills group and provides summaries of what might be covered in the group.

As with other social skills programs, the Tough Kid program is intended for use in a group format, most preferably in a small-group format, although it can be used with whole classrooms of children. Also, as with other social skills programs, the Tough Kid program uses instruction, modeling, role playing, and feedback to teach the skills to children in the group. The manual includes a general discussion of these principles and highlights the steps in the effective use of these techniques.

Part two of the manual provides outlines of sessions using the Tough Kid model. Three basic types of social skills are addressed: social entry, maintaining interactions, and solving problems. The outlines do not include exact scripts the leaders should follow, but detail the lessons that should be addressed in each session and provide suggestions for activities and scenarios to role play. There are 11 core session outlines as well as opening session, last session, and booster session outlines. Skill sheets to be used teaching these lessons also are included in the manual.

Unlike most social skill program manuals, this manual devotes more time to general discussion of issues related to teaching social skills (e.g., assessing social skills, leading a social skills group) than to the session outlines. By the time leaders get to the session outlines, they should have a good grasp of the basics in teaching social skills (assuming, of course, the first part of the manual was read). The actual session outlines are easy to follow, and in addition to the outline of session components and activities, there are guidelines for how much time should be spent in each activity. The addition of the skill sheets (which list the skill steps for each lesson) is a nice feature of this program.

THE ASSIST PROGRAM:
AFFECTIVE–SOCIAL SKILLS:
INSTRUCTIONAL STRATEGIES
AND TECHNIQUES

Author: Pat Huggins

Publication Date: 1990–1995

Publisher:˙   Sopris-West
                     1140 Boston Ave.
                     Longmont, CO 80501

The ASSIST program consists of 9 separate books covering a variety of issues that teachers and other school personnel may confront in elementary schools. The books focus primarily on teaching friendship skills, self-esteem, anger-management, and cooperation skills. For the purposes of this chapter, only two of the nine books are reviewed: *Teaching Friendship Skills* (primary version) and *Teaching Cooperation Skills*.

The Teaching Friendship Skills curriculum is intended to be used by school personnel working to increase the social competence of elementary school-age children. The primary version is intended to be used with children in Grades 1 through 3. There also is an intermediate version with lessons tailored toward children in Grades 4 through 6. The curriculum utilizes discussions, modeling, role play, performance feedback, and maintenance and transfer training to teach these skills. In the primary version there are eight lessons. Each lesson consists of a script (the lesson presentation) and all transparencies, handouts, and so forth that will be needed for the lesson. The transparencies are used to better demonstrate to the class what is being discussed. Supplemental activities following the same theme as the lesson are also included. Appendices in this manual contain suggestions for books that may be used to help teach social skills, games that may be played that promote social skills, school-wide activities for increasing friendship skills, and posters that may be used in the classroom that relate to social skills.

The Teaching Cooperation Skills manual consists of 11 lessons primarily geared toward teaching children to work in the classroom in cooperative learning groups. Lessons address such topics as these: dealing with conflict in groups, learning to negotiate, and learning how to listen to others. As with the friendship skills curriculum, each lesson contains a script for the teacher and various transparencies, handouts, and so forth to be used in teaching the lesson.

These curriculums seem especially geared toward general school-age children, those with no great deficits in social skills but who could benefit from lessons on the basics of social skills. The lessons are set up in such a way that a teacher (or counselor who came in once a week) could easily teach them to the whole class. A small-group format does not seem necessary and is not indicated by the authors. For children with more severe social deficits, this curriculum most likely will not address the problems adequately.

SOCIAL SKILLS INTERVENTION GUIDE: PRACTICAL STRATEGIES FOR SOCIAL SKILLS TRAINING

Authors: Stephen N. Elliott and Frank M. Gresham

Publication Date: 1991

Publisher: American Guidance Service
                  Circle Pines, MN 55014-1796

This social skills intervention package was written to be used with the Social Skills Rating System (SSRS), an instrument designed for the assessment of social skills in children reviewed in chapter 3. The Social Skills Intervention program can be used by clinicians to develop intervention techniques after a child has been identified as having social skills deficits. It is intended to be used with children in Grades 1 through 10 who have some identified social skills deficit or are at risk for social problems. This program covers social skills in five domains (matching the five areas assessed by the SSRS): *cooperation, assertion, responsibility, empathy,* and *self-control.* As with other social skills packages, this program is intended for use with groups of children. The authors specify that having three to six children in the group is ideal.

Before the authors begin discussing the specific social skills to be taught within this program, they provide a lengthy review in chapter 3 of basic intervention strategies and treatment procedures. This chapter briefly covers the main components of a social skills training program (instruction, rehearsal, feedback/reinforcement, and reduction of problem behaviors) and then goes into more detail about specific learning techniques that can be used in the treatment of social skills deficits. For example, the authors cover the use of modeling and behavioral rehearsal but also discuss things such as differential reinforcement, response cost, and other behavioral methods. Not only does the reader get a review of basic procedures used in social skills training but there is also a review of many behavioral techniques that can be used in settings other than the social skills group.

The chapter on implementing social skills programs uses case examples to highlight the linking of assessment to intervention and intervention planning itself. This chapter provides some useful information on topics ranging from requesting parental consent for children's participation in groups to guidelines for sequencing the skills to be taught. Evaluating progress (along with a sample progress record) is also covered.

Section two of this book provides the specifics for implementing a social skills program. Within the five domains, 43 separate social skills are covered, although the authors recommend limiting the number of skills to be taught to approximately 1 per week. The information for each lesson in broken down into five instructional categories (which are briefly discussed before the individual lessons are presented): Tell, Show, Do, Follow-Through and Practice, and Generalization. The Tell phase involves introducing and defining the skill. The Show phase makes use of modeling and role playing. The Do phase requires the children to define and practice the skill. The Follow-Through and Practice phase involves periodic review of the skill and having students take part in activities outside the group setting. In the Generalization phase an attempt is made to have children internalize the skill learned by tying it to their activities and experiences. Word for word instructions are not specified, but instead, the user is given a specific outline of topics for discussion related to the social skill to be taught.

The detailed discussion of behavioral interventions adds to this program. Not only are behavioral management techniques discussed in detail, but tables of guidelines are also provided for easy reference. The actual social skill lessons are outlined well, with enough detail for leaders to complete the different steps easily.

GETTING ALONG WITH OTHERS: TEACHING SOCIAL EFFECTIVENESS TO CHILDREN

Authors: Nancy F. Jackson, Donald A. Jackson, and Cathy Monroe

Publication Date: 1983

Publisher: Research Press
                      2612 North Mattis Ave
                      Champaign, IL 61821

This program is divided into two different manuals: a program guide and a skill lessons and activities book. The skill lessons and activities book contains specifics on what to do and say in sessions as well as forms that may be used with participants. The program guide contains a general overview of the program and training lessons. It is suggested that users read and study this before implementing the social skills program. There are also companion videotapes that can be ordered to provide additional instructions for leaders as they learn the skills covered in the program guide. This social skills program is geared toward the elementary school-age child, although the authors indicate that with accommodations, the program could be used with students of other ages.

An underlying assumption of this program is that the group leader's interactions with the children have a major impact on the acquisition of skills. Thus, there is a focus on interactional style that often is not seen in other social skills programs. This program also operates under the assumption that the children involved have a social skills acquisition deficit, not that they have difficulties applying skills that they already know (i.e., a performance deficit).

This program is based on a demonstration model initially developed by the authors at a community health center and then introduced in other settings. The authors' evaluations of the program indicate its effectiveness, particularly with children who have moderate problems and obvious social skills deficits. The authors cite research supportive both of changes in child behavior and changes in parent and teacher satisfaction with the child's social skills.

The program guide is quite detailed in covering what leaders should learn and know before beginning a social skills group. In fact, a training schedule is outlined, and for some activities a training partner is needed. According to the training schedule, the total training time needed is approximately 15 hours, including seven 1-hour meetings with a partner. The authors indicate that users of this program should learn both "techniques for interacting with children that can make each social encounter an episode for teaching social skills and tightly organized skill introduction sequences" (p. 1).

Throughout this social skills program there is an emphasis not just on skill lessons, but also on applying skills in real-life settings such as free-play activities and snack time. This book contains information and learning activities on topics such as identifying target behaviors and using behavioral teaching techniques (e.g., positive feedback and ignoring/attending), as well as specifics on how to implement the skill lessons. The program guide contains one of the most complete training guides incorporated with any social skills program.

It is suggested that the social skills lessons be taught twice weekly for 2 hours at a time but the authors recognize that adaptations may need to be made. Some of the adaptations suggested include substituting naturally occurring events for those in which skills are practiced (e.g., using lunch time instead of having a snack time incorporated into the group; using recess as a free-play time). There are a total of 17 sessions outlined in the skill lessons book. When used in a small-group format, it is suggested that 6 to 8 children be included and that there be two leaders.

Each session consists of seven components, some of which may be substituted with naturally occurring events. The first component in each session involves Homework Completion and Free Play. Children who bring completed homework are allowed free play time; those who did not complete their homework must complete it. A group homework review then occurs. Next is Relaxation Training. After this comes the actual skill lesson. Each skill lesson covers a social skill such as following directions, starting a conversation, handling name-calling and teasing, and the like. After the skill lesson, students are provided with a snack time. Children must earn their snack, and this time is intended to be used for further practice and reinforcement of social skills. After snack time, an activity time occurs in which children practice what they learned during the lesson. The last part of the session consists of filling out Home Notes (which go home to parents and review the lesson of the day, tell how the child did, and ask the parents to complete a brief section on the child's performance at home with the lesson objectives) and the assignment of homework.

THE WELL-MANAGED CLASSROOM:
PROMOTING STUDENT SUCCESS
THROUGH SOCIAL SKILLS INSTRUCTION

Authors: Theresa Connolly, Tom Dowd, Andrea Criste, Cathy
                  Nelson, and Lisa Tobias

Publication Date: 1995

Publisher: The Boys Town Press
                  Father Flanagan's Boys' Home
                  Boys Town, NE 68010

As the title of this book suggests, this is not purely a social skills program but also a classroom management program. The book is intended to help teachers learn better behavior management strategies in the classroom through social skills instruction. This book is based on the Boys Town Education Model, which includes four components: social skills curriculum, teaching interactions, motivational systems, and administrative intervention. The educational model is based on applied behavior analysis and social learning theory. The social skills curriculum consists of 16 skills. These skills are taught in part through teaching interactions, which include teaching in a variety of natural school settings including the classroom, hallway, and offices. Teaching interactions are used when a student performs an undesirable behavior. The teacher uses a brief instructional sequence right after the behavior occurs.

This manual is different from most other social skills program manuals in that there is not much discussion about the specific social skills to be taught. Instead, more general information (about teaching strategies and classroom management) is presented. For example, chapter 3 covers building and maintaining positive teacher–student relationships. Before even discussing the social skills to be taught, the authors devote a chapter to problem solving in general and basic behavioral principles and interventions such as reinforcement, shaping, response cost, and so forth. Chapter 6 is the only chapter that focuses directly on the social skills curriculum. Each of the 16 skills is listed with procedures, but there is no script for the teacher and no discussion regarding the skill. The authors indicate that each skill should be taught one at a time. The rest of the manual focuses on issues in the classroom related to instruction in general and the teaching of social skills in particular. For example, chapter 8 covers how to give a rationale for behaviors and discusses when to use rationales, and chapter 9 discusses the use of effective praise. Chapter 10 is on preventive teaching, which involves a more planned method to teach the 16 social skills. The sequence the teacher is to use in teaching a skill is outlined and includes eight steps: introduce skill, describe appropriate behavior, give rationale, request acknowledgment, practice, give feedback, provide positive consequence, and establish future follow-up practice. Other chapters discuss dealing with ongoing behavior problems, behavior contracting, and working with parents.

Because of the emphasis on classroom behavioral issues, this curriculum is obviously most appropriate for teachers and may be best used by teachers interested in combining the teaching of social skills with a more broad approach to classroom discipline.

TEACHING SOCIAL SKILLS TO YOUTH: A CURRICULUM FOR CHILD-CARE PROVIDERS

Authors: Tom Dowd and Jeff Tierney
Publication Date: 1992
Publisher: The Boys Town Press
                   Father Flanagan's Boys' Home
                   Boys Town, NE 68010

This program is based on the Boys Town Family Home treatment program and is intended to be used by almost anyone who has contact with children: parents, teachers, child care providers, and others. The first portion of this manual includes an overview of social skills and the techniques that can be used in teaching them. The second portion details 182 specific social skills that can be taught to children and adolescents.

The manual begins with an overview of what social skills are and why they are important. Also discussed are some correlates of social skills deficiencies such as aggression, mental health disorders, and loneliness. The authors discuss analyzing social behavior through antecedents and consequences, and using this information to determine deficits in social skills. Techniques for teaching prosocial behaviors are covered, and the authors provide examples of teaching interactions. Techniques for teaching skills both to children individually and in groups are covered. The individual techniques include using a planned teaching interaction as well as teaching methods throughout naturally occurring incidents to promote use and generalization of the skills. The planned teaching interactions are similar to those of other social skills training programs and include introducing the skill, demonstrating the skill, practicing the skill, and providing feedback. Generalization is then promoted through acknowledging use of appropriate social skills in everyday interactions and using corrective teaching to intervene when a child is displaying negative social behavior. The teaching of social skills in a group is also covered, and the methods outlined here are similar to the individual planned teaching interactions and teaching methods in other group-based social skills programs. The basic components include these: introducing the skill, modeling the skill, role playing, positive consequences for participation, and assignments to promote generalization.

The 182 social skills covered in this manual are divided into levels: basic, intermediate, advanced, and complex. There are 8 basic skills, such as Accepting "no" for an answer and Introducing yourself. The 56 intermediate skills include skills such as Greeting others, Showing appreciation, and Waiting your turn. There are 81 advanced skills that include Dealing with fear, Making restitution, and Responding to teasing. The 37 complex skills include Conflict resolution, Goal-setting, and Seeking professional assistance. Appendixes are also provided that group these skills by specific behavior problems (e.g., serious conflicts with authority members, peer interaction problems) and specific situations (e.g., classroom behavior and academic performance, friendship, and dating). The description of each social skill consists of the steps that should be followed to successfully complete the skill. For example, the steps in responding to teasing are described thus: "Remain calm but serious, assertively ask the person to stop teasing, if the person doesn't stop, ignore the other person or remove yourself, if the teasing stops, thank the other person for stopping and explain how teasing makes you feel, report continued teasing or hazing to an adult" (p. 206).

Because each social skill is simply presented with its different steps, users of this program must be familiar with the teaching techniques covered in the first portion of this manual. The skills presented in this manual do not have to be taught in a specific order nor do all skills need to be taught. Professionals using this program could choose the skills that are relevant for the specific individuals or groups targeted for training, although it would be wise to ensure knowledge and use of the basic skills before moving on to those that are more complicated.

SOCIAL SKILLS FOR SCHOOL AND COMMUNITY: SYSTEMATIC INSTRUCTION FOR CHILDREN AND YOUTH WITH COGNITIVE DELAYS

Authors: Laurence R. Sargent

Publication Date: 1991

Publisher: Division on Mental Retardation,
                  Council for Exceptional Children
                  1920 Association Dr.
                  Preston, VA 22091-1589

This social skills program is targeted specifically toward children with cognitive delays. As the author stated in the beginning of the manual, children with cognitive delays are also more likely on the whole to have learning deficits that impair the development of social skills, and to have behaviors that others find annoying. Thus, there is a particular need for interventions to increase the prosocial skills of this population.

Before getting to the specific social skills lessons, the author discusses direct instruction of social skills and addresses some specific issues regarding the use of this model with children who have cognitive disabilities. Most of the manual consists of social skills lessons divided into the following age groups: primary (ages 5–8), intermediate (ages 9–12), middle school/junior high, and senior high. In the initial discussion of social skills and social competence, the idea of proactive instruction is stressed, that is, teaching necessary skills before children experience negative consequences from not having the skills or from having inappropriate versions of the skills. The lessons follow a direct instruction format with six identified procedures: establish the need (help students understand need for skill), identify skill components, model the skill, role play the skill, practice, generalize and transfer.

For each of the 100 lessons an objective is presented and followed by specific performance criteria. These criteria list the cluster of behaviors children should exhibit when they are able to adequately perform the skill. After this, procedures for teaching the behavior are presented. These procedures are broken down into the aforementioned six parts. The group leader is provided with a fairly detailed outline of what should be covered in each session without the directness of an exact script. Homework forms are included in an appendix. These forms require little writing. They consist primarily of yes–no questions, but some of the questions may be too difficult for children with cognitive delays to read on their own.

This program is very similar to most other social skills programs with its use of the direct instruction format, but it is geared toward a specific population of students (i.e., those with cognitive delays). As such, this program may be quite helpful to those professionals working with children who have mental retardation or other forms of cognitive delays. Although some of the skills presented in the manual would be appropriate for any child (e.g., gaining teacher attention), other skills are more specific to this target population (e.g., drinking from the water fountain appropriately). As a whole, the skills presented in this program address many different areas in which children with cognitive delays may have difficulties with appropriate behavior.

THE WALKER SOCIAL SKILLS CURRICULUMS

The ACCEPTS Program

Authors: Hill M. Walker, Scott McConnell, Deborah Holmes, Bonnie Todis, Jackie Walker, and Nancy Golden

Publication Date: 1988

Publisher: Pro-Ed
8700 Shoal Creek Blvd
Austin, TX 78757–6897

The ACCESS Program

Authors: Hill M. Walker, Bonnie Todis, Deborah Holmes, and Gary Horton

Publication Date: 1988

Publisher: Pro-Ed
8700 Shoal Creek Blvd
Austin, TX 78757–6897

The ACCEPTS (A Curriculum for Children's Effective Peer and Teacher Skills) and the ACCESS (Adolescent Curriculum for Communication and Effective Social Skills) programs are designed to teach prosocial skills to students with mild to moderate disabilities. Both programs are based on direct instruction techniques. As stated in the introduction of the ACCEPTS manual, the primary goal of this program is to "prepare handicapped children to enter and perform satisfactorily within less restrictive settings. A secondary goal is to directly teach skills that facilitate classroom adjustment and contribute to peer acceptance" (p. v). As such, there are two general categories of social skills addressed in this curriculum: those that facilitate classroom adjustment and those that facilitate social competence with peers.

A goal of the ACCEPTS program is not only to facilitate positive peer interactions but to allow children with disabilities to gain the social skills necessary for interacting appropriately with both disabled and nondisabled students in a general education setting (i.e., away from a self-contained room). Potential candidates for involvement in the ACCEPTS program are those children who lack classroom competencies or those who lack basic social competence in their peer interactions.

The ACCEPTS curriculum is divided into teaching scripts that cover five different areas: classroom skills, basic interaction skills, getting along, making friends, and coping skills. In each area various skills are presented, broken down into steps, and taught by the direct instruction method. These teaching steps include a definition and discussion of the behavior, positive and negative examples, modeling, and role playing. Video scenes accompany many of these teaching scripts to demonstrate appropriate and inappropriate social skills applicable to the lesson being taught. Although the authors provide alternative tasks to use instead, users of this curriculum are urged to use the videotaped scenes. An appendix in the manual lists the skills taught through the videotaped vignettes, and the group leader may choose to model the examples rather than use the videotape. In addition to the teaching skills part of the ACCEPTS manual, there is also a brief section on using behavioral management principles to promote the use of the social skills in natural settings. Both classroom and playground behavior management systems are presented.

The ACCESS program is an upward extension of the ACCEPTS program and is intended for use in teaching social skills to middle- and high school-age children with either moderate or mild disabilities. This program consists of 31 lessons broken down into three areas of skills: peer-related, adult-related, and self-related. Peer-related skills are skills important for children to have in order to interact appropriately with other children in classroom and work situations. For example, Listening and Greeting other people are two peer-related skills included in this program. Adult-related skills are those that are more important in situations controlled by adults (e.g., Following classroom rules, Doing quality work). Self-related skills are those that allow one to manage aspects of everyday life (e.g., Being organized, Using self-control).

The teacher's manual for the ACCESS program contains scripts for each lesson. These scripts are interesting because, in addition to having the group leader's words and actions scripted out, student responses to questions are also included. This process may be helpful to a group leader because it lets the leader know the response that must be obtained. However, the way the manual lays this out is somewhat difficult to follow. Also included in the teacher's manual are cards that provide role play scenarios for use in teaching the different skills.

In addition to the teacher's manual for the ACCESS program, there is also a student study guide containing outlines of the lessons and student contracts related to the use of these skills. The student study guide contains fairly detailed outlines of the lessons, and the authors make the point that this program will be most effective for children if they have a fourth- or fifth-grade reading level.

As with the Social Skills for School and Community program, the Walker curricula take the basic concept of direct instruction for social skills and apply this methodology to the population of children and adolescents with mild to moderate disabilities. As such, these manuals provide similar instruction to that of other programs but more specifically target the skills needed by children with handicaps.

CONCLUDING COMMENTS

As can be seen from the social skills programs covered in this chapter, there are a number of programs available for teaching social skills to children. As stated at the beginning of this chapter, this list was not meant to be all inclusive. The reader has most likely noticed from the descriptions of these programs that most include many of the same components. A closer examination of the actual program materials reveals that most programs cover many of the same skills. Thus, to some extent, it should not matter which program one uses because there is so much overlap. However, there are some differences in programs that may make a certain program more suitable for a particular group of children or for a certain professional involved in teaching social skills. Table 6.1 provides a summary of the programs and some brief comments on their content and usability.

Although the manuals indicate that some programs can be adapted for children of varying ability levels, two programs covered in this chapter are written specifically for use with children who are lower functioning and may be most useful when working with this specific population. These programs are Social Skills for School and Community and The Walker Social Skills curriculums. Many curriculums are geared toward the child with mild behavioral problems, although some are more specifically targeted toward children with more severe behavioral problems along with their social deficits. Most notably, the Aggression Replacement Training program was developed specifically for use with the juvenile delinquent population.

The targeted age ranges of the programs vary somewhat, but many programs have skill components appropriate for children in elementary school through high school. Some programs were developed for a specific age range (such as the CLASSIC and Getting Along with Others), but even such programs may be adapted for other age ranges.

Although most of these programs are very similar in terms of the skills they discuss and the manner of instruction they emphasize, there is a great deal of variety in how much direction is given to leaders. Some programs (e.g., the CLASSIC) have detailed structured scripts of what a group leader should say. Other programs (e.g., the Skillstreaming series) contain only the skill steps and some brief suggestions for group leaders. One type is not necessarily better than the other, but leaders may prefer one particular method of presentation. Obviously, an experienced clinician would not read directly from a manual no matter how detailed the script was, and most leaders will develop their own style with any program they choose.

The programs also differ somewhat on how much "extra" information they include, particularly, information on social skills in general, on the direct instruction technique, and on managing behavior problems. Some programs go into this type of material in great detail (e.g., the Tough Kids program), whereas other programs mainly present the social skills to be taught. It seems as though for many group leaders such background information would be helpful, enabling them to lead a more effective group by knowing the rationale behind the methods and ways of dealing with group disruption. Obviously, some group leaders will have obtained this information elsewhere, and for them, this extra material may not be necessary.

Although readers might desire a recommendation of what program is best, such a recommendation would be illusory. All programs cover the basics of teaching social skills. Some have a large number of skills that may be more useful for classroom teachers who plan to make social skills training part of their curriculum. Other programs have a small number of skills and may be more appropriate for the professional involved in time-limited groups. The authors hope that this chapter allows readers to become familiar with a number of social skills programs from which they can then choose the program that best fits their unique needs.

TABLE 6.1

Brief Overview of Commercially Published Social Skills Training Programs

Title	Author(s)	Age/Population	Comments
Skillstreaming in Early Childhood	McGinnis and Goldstein	• Ages 3–6 • General population	• Good overview of structured learning and the basics in conducting social skills groups. • Skills are presented with their steps and some suggestions for group discussion are included for each step.
Skillstreaming the Elementary School Child	McGinnis, Goldstein, Sprafkin, and Gershaw	• Elementary school • General population	
Skillstreaming the Adolescent	Goldstein, Sprafkin, Gershaw, and Klein	• Adolescents • General population	• Each of these three programs is very similar but the skills and the level of skills are geared toward the specific age group (preschool children, elementary school children, and adolescents)
Aggression Replacement Training	Goldstein, Glick, Reiner, Zimmerman, and Coultry	• Adolescents • Juvenile delinquents or adolescents with significant behavior problems	• Combines components of the Skillstreaming program with anger-control teaching and moral education.
The Prepare Curriculum	Goldstein	• School age students	• Divides social skills training into 10 course areas • Large manual with much overlap with the Skillstreaming and Aggression-replacement training
The Cultural and Lifestyle Appropriate Social Skills Intervention Curriculum (CLASSIC)	Dygon	• Children ages 10–14 of average intelligence (population developed for) • Can be modified for others	• Emphasis on cross-cultural issues • No set target behaviors so groups can develop target behaviors specific to that culture/population • Detailed session outlines

TABLE 6.1 (Continued)

Title	Author(s)	Age/Population	Comments
Metacognitive approach to social skills training	Sheinker and Sheinker	• Grades 4–12	• Lengthy curriculum but can select skills to be taught • Lesson outlines with specific steps for leader included • Worksheets contained in manual • Not recommended for children with overt antisocial behavior
Teaching Social Skills	Rutherford, Chipman, DiGangi, and Anderson	• Elementary school children	• Differentiates between children who "can't" and "won't" perform a skill • Differentiates among children who are withdrawn, immature, and aggressive. • Skill interventions for each of these groups
The Tough Kid Social Skills Book	Sheridan	• Students between ages 8–12 (population developed for)	• Program is targeted specifically at the "tough kid" (i.e., someone who is deficit in social skills as well as being noncompliant and aggressive) • A number of reproducible handouts and worksheets are included.
The ASSIST Program	Huggins	• Elementary school children	• Nine books included in this series, two have a focus on social skills (Teaching Friendship Skills and Teaching Cooperation Skills) • More appropriate for the average child in large group instruction format • Less appropriate for children with particular social skill deficits

(Continued)

TABLE 6.1 (*Continued*)

Title	Author(s)	Age/Population	Comments
Social Skills Intervention Guide	Elliott and Gresham	• Grades 1–10	• Manual includes a lengthy review on intervention strategies and treatment procedures • Outlines of topics for possible discussion provided
The Well-Managed Classroom	Connolly, Dowd, Criste, Nelson, and Tobias	• School-age children • In a classroom setting	• Program focuses not just on social skills but also on general classroom management • Social skills are taught within a structured format as well as within natural settings • Intended to be used primarily by classroom teachers
Teaching Social Skills to Youth	Dowd and Tierney	• Children of any age	• Program covers a number of social skills, which are divided into basic, intermediate, advanced and complex skills • No set curriculum—can pick and choose the skills to teach • The use of planned teaching and corrective teaching (to intervene when an inappropriate behavior is being displayed in the natural setting) is discussed
Getting along with others	Jackson, Jackson, and Monroe	• Elementary school students	• Program contains two books: a program guide and a skill lessons and activities book • Program guide outlines a training course for group leaders to be followed before starting a group • Focus on applying skills in real-life situations and use of the skills in these situations are emphasized

TABLE 6.1 (*Continued*)

Title	Author(s)	Age/Population	Comments
Social Skills for School and Community	Sargent	• Elementary though High School students • Students with cognitive delays	• Specifically for children with cognitive delays • Detailed leader scripts and homework forms included
The Walker Social Skills Curriculum: The ACCEPTS Program	Walker, McConnell, Holmes, Todis, Walker, and Golden	• Elementary school students • Students with mild to moderate disabilities	• Focuses on skills that facilitate classroom competencies and adjustment and those that facilitate social competencies • Videos can be purchased to go along with teaching the skills
The Walker Social Skills Program: The ACCESS Program	Walker, Todis, Holmes, and Horton	• Middle and high school students • Students with mild to moderate disabilities	• Manuals include leader scripts and appropriate child responses • ACCESS program also has a Student Study Guide

References

Achenbach, T. M., & Edelbrock, C. S. (1981). Behavioral problems and competencies reported by parents of normal and disturbed children aged four through sixteen. *Monographs for the Society for Research in Child Development, 46* (1 Serial, No. 88).

Achenbach, T. M., & Edelbrock, C. S. (1983). Taxonomic issues in child psychopathology. In T. H. Ollendick & M. Herson (Eds.), *Handbook of child psychopathology.* New York: Plenum.

Achenbach, T. M., & Edelbrock, C. S. (1984). Psychopathology of childhood. *Annual Review of Psychology, 35,* 227–256.

Achenbach, T. M., McConaughy, S. H., & Howell, C. T. (1987). Child/adolescent behavioral and emotional problems: Implications of cross-informant correlations for situational specificity. *Psychological Bulletin, 101,* 213–232.

Adalbjarnardottir, S. (1993). Promoting children's social growth in the schools: An intervention study. *Journal of Applied Developmental Psychology, 14,* 461–484.

Akhtar, N., & Bradley, E. J. (1991). Social information processing deficits of aggressive children: Present findings and implications for social skills training. *Clinical Psychology Review, 11,* 621–644.

Albano, M., Marten, P. A., Holt, C. S., Heimberg, R. G., & Barlow, D. H. (1995). Cognitive-behavioral group treatment for social phobia in adolescents: A preliminary study. *Journal of Nervous and Mental Disease, 183,* 649–656.

Alessi, G. (1988). Direct observation methods for emotional/behavior problems. In E. S. Shapiro & T. R. Kratochwill (Eds.), *Behavioral assessment in schools: Conceptual foundations and practical applications* (pp. 14–75). New York: Guilford.

American Association on Mental Retardation (1992). *Mental retardation: Definition, classification, and systems of support* (9th ed.). Washington, DC: American Association on Mental Retardation.

American Psychiatric Association. (1994). *Diagnostic and statistical manual of mental disorders* (4th ed.). Washington DC: American Psychiatric Association.

Argyle, M. (1981). *Social skills and health.* London: Metheun.

Arkes, H. R. (1981). Impediments to accurate clinical judgment and possible ways to minimize their impact. *Journal of Consulting and Clinical Psychology, 49,* 323–330.

Asher, S. R., Oden, S., & Gottman, J. (1977). Children's friendships in school settings. In L. Katz, M. Glockner, S. Goodman, & N. Spencer (Eds.), *Current topics in early childhood education.* Norwood, NJ: Ablex.

Asher, S. R., & Parker, J. G. (1989). Significance of peer relationship problems in childhood. In B. H. Schneider, G. Attili, J. Nadel, & R. P. Weissberg (Eds.), *Social competence in developmental perspective* (pp. 5–23). Boston: Kluwer.

Asher, S. R., & Taylor, A. R. (1981). The social outcomes of mainstreaming: Sociometric assessment and beyond. *Exceptional Children Quarterly, 1,* 13–30.

Asher, S. R., & Wheeler, V. A. (1985). Children's loneliness: A comparison of rejected and neglected peer status. *Journal of Consulting and Clinical Psychology, 53,* 500–505.

Axelson, J. A. (1993). *Counseling and development in a multicultural society* (2nd ed.). Pacific Grove, CA: Brooks/Cole.

Bandura, A. (1978). The self system in reciprocal determinism. *American Psychologist, 33,* 344–358.

Bandura, A. (1986). *Social foundations of thought and action.* Englewood Cliffs, NJ: Prentice-Hall.

Barkley, R. A. (1990). *Attention deficit hyperactivity disorder: A handbook for diagnosis and treatment.* New York: Guilford.

Barnett, D. W., & Zucker, K. B. (1990). *The personal and social assessment of children.* Boston: Allyn & Bacon.

Barton, E. J., & Ascione, F. R. (1984). Direct observation. In T. H. Ollendick & M. Herson (Eds.), *Child behavioral assessment: Principles and procedures* (pp. 166–194). New York: Pergammon Press.

Bell, N. J., & Carver, W. A. (1980). A reevaluation of gender label effects: Expectant mothers' responses to infants. *Child Development, 51,* 925–927.

Bell-Dolan, D. J., Reaven, N. M., & Peterson, L. (1993). Depression and social functioning: A multidimensional study of the linkages. *Journal of Clinical Child Psychology, 22,* 306–315.

Bierman, K. L., & Furman, W. (1984). The effects of social skills training and peer involvement on the social adjustment of preadolescents. *Child Development, 55,* 151–162.

Bierman, K. L., Miller, C. L., & Stabb, S. D. (1987). Improving the social behavior and peer acceptance of rejected boys: Effects of social skills training with instructions and prohibitions. *Journal of Consulting and Clinical Psychology, 55,* 194–200.

Bloom, B. L. (1968). An ecological analysis of psychiatric hospitalization. *Multivariate Behavioral Research, 3,* 423–463.

Boggs, S. R., & Eyberg, S. (1990). Interview techniques and establishing rapport. In L. M. LaGreca (Ed.), *Through the eyes of the child* (pp. 85–108). Boston: Allyn & Bacon.

Bower, E. (1969). *Early identification of emotionally handicapped children in school* (2nd ed.). Springfield, IL: Thomas.

Bracken, B. A. (1992). *Multidimensional Self-Concept Scale.* Austin, TX: Pro-Ed.

Bracken, B. A. (1993). *Assessment of Interpersonal Relations.* Austin, TX: Pro-Ed.

Bracken, B. A., Keith, L. K., & Walker, K. C. (1994). Assessment of preschool behavior and social-emotional functioning: A review of thirteen third-party instruments. *Assessment in Rehabilitation and Exceptionality, 1,* 331–346.

Brinton, B., & Fujiki, M. (1982). A comparison of request-response sequences in the discourse of normal and language-disordered children. *Journal of Speech and Hearing Disorders, 47,* 57–62.

Broekhoff, J. (1977). A search for relationships: Sociological and social-psychological considerations. *The Academy Papers, 11,* 45–55.

Bruininks, R. H., Woodcock, R. W., Weatherman, R. F., & Hill, B. K. (1984). *Scales of Independent Behavior*. Allen, TX: DLM Teaching Resources.

Bruner, J. (1977). Early social interaction and language acquisition. In H. Schaffer (Ed.), *Studies in mother-infant interaction* (pp. 271–289). London: Academic Press.

Bryan, T., Pearl, R., Donahue, M., & Pflaum, T. (1983). The Chicago Institute for the Study of Learning Disabilities. *Exceptional Education Quarterly, 4*, 1–23.

Bryant, B., Trower, P., Yardley, K., Urbieta, H., & Letemendia, F. T. (1976). A survey of social inadequacy among psychiatric outpatients. *Psychological Medicine, 6*, 101–112.

Bulkeley, R., & Cramer, D. (1994). Social skills training with young adolescents: Group and individual approaches in a school setting. *Journal of Adolescence, 17*, 521–531.

Butler, L., Mietzitis, S., Friedman, R., & Cole, E. (1980). The effect of two school-based intervention programs on depressive symptoms in preadolescents. *American Educational Research Journal, 17*, 111–119.

Caldarella, P., & Merrell, K. W. (1997). Common dimensions of social skills of children and adolescents: A taxonomy of positive behaviors. *School Psychology Review, 26*, 265–279.

Cartledge, G., & Milburn, J. F. (1986). Selecting social skills. In G. Cartledge & J. F. Milburn (Eds.), *Teaching social skills to children* (2nd ed.) (pp. 7–28). New York: Pergamon Press.

Cartledge, G., & Milburn, J. F. (1995). *Teaching social skills to children and youth: Innovative approaches* (3rd ed.). Needham Heights, MA: Allyn & Bacon.

Center, D. B., & Wascom, A. M. (1986). Teacher perceptions of social behavior in learning disabled and normal children and youth. *Journal of Learning Disabilities, 19*, 420–425.

Chandler, L. K., Lubeck, R. C., & Fowler, S. A. (1992). Generalization and maintenance of preschool children's social skills: A critical review and analysis. *Journal of Applied Behavior Analysis, 25*, 415–428.

Chin-Perez, G., Hartman, D., Park, H. S., & Sacks, S. L. (1986). Maximizing social contact for secondary students with severe handicaps. *Journal of the Association for Persons with Severe Handicaps, 11*, 118–124.

Clarke, G., Lewinsohn, P., & Hops, H. (1990). *The adolescent coping with depression course*. Eugene, OR: Castalia.

Coie, J. D., Dodge, K. A., & Cappotelli, H. (1982). Dimensions and types of social status: A cross-age perspective. *Developmental Psychology, 18*, 557–570.

Cole, D. A., & Carpentieri, S. (1990). Social status and the comorbidity of child depression and conduct disorder. *Journal of Consulting and Clinical Psychology, 58*, 748–757.

Combs, M. L., & Slaby, O. A. (1977). Social skills training with children. In B. B. Lahey & A. E. Kazdin (Eds.), *Advances in clinical child psychology* (pp. 161–201). New York: Plenum.

Conger, J. C., & Keane, S. P. (1981). Social skills intervention in the treatment of isolated or withdrawn children. *Psychological Bulletin, 90*, 478–495.

Connolly, T., Dowd, T., Criste, A., Nelson, C., & Tobias, L. (1995). *The well-managed classroom: Promoting success through social skill instruction*. Boys Town, NE: Boys Town Press.

Cowen, E. L., Pederson, A., Babigan, H., Izzo, L. D., & Trost, M. A. (1973). Long-term follow-up of early detected vulnerable children. *Journal of Consulting and Clinical Psychology, 41*, 438–446.

Craig, H., & Evans, J. (1989). Turn exchange characteristics of SLI children's simultaneous and non-simultaneous speech. *Journal of Speech and Hearing Disorders, 54*, 334–337.

Craig, H., & Gallagher, T. (1986). Interactive play: The frequency of related verbal responses. *Journal of Speech and Hearing Research, 62*, 474–482.

Crick, N. R., & Dodge, K. A. (1994). A review and reformulation of social information-processing mechanisms in children's social adjustment. *Psychological Bulletin, 115*, 74–101.

Dodge, K. A. (1980). Social cognition and children's aggressive behavior. *Child Development, 51*, 162–170.

Dodge, K. A. (1985). Facets of social interaction and the assessment of social competence in children. In B. H. Schneider, K. H. Rubin, & J. E. Ledingham (Eds.), *Children's peer relations: Issues in assessment and intervention* (pp. 3–22). New York: Springer-Verlag.

Dodge, K. A., & Frame, C. L. (1982). Social cognitive biases and deficits in aggressive boys. *Child Development, 53,* 620–635.

Doll, E. A. (1935). A genetic scale of social maturity. *The American Journal of Orthopsychiatry, 5,* 180–188.

Dowd, T., & Tierney, J. (1992). *Teaching social skills to youth: A curriculum for child-care providers.* Boys Town, NE: Boys Town Press.

Dujovne, V. F., Barnard, M. U., & Rapoff, M. A. (1995). Pharmacological and cognitive–behavioral approaches in the treatment of childhood depression: A review and critique. *Clinical Psychology Review, 15,* 589–611.

DuPaul, G. J., & Eckert, T. L. (1994). The effects of social skills curricula: Now you see them, now you don't. *School Psychology Quarterly, 9,* 113–132.

DuPaul, G. J., & Stoner, G. (1994). *ADHD in the schools: Assessment and intervention strategies.* New York: Guilford.

Dygdon, J. A. (1993). *The culture and lifestyle appropriate social skills curriculum: A program for socially valid social skills training.* New York: Wiley.

Edleson, J. L., & Rose, S. D. (1982). Investigations into the efficacy of short-term group social skills training for socially isolated children. *Child Behavior Therapy, 3*(2/3), 1–16.

Eisenberg, N. (1983). Sex-typed toy choices: What to they signify? In M. B. Liss (Ed.), *Social and cognitive skills: Sex roles and children's play* (pp. 45–70). New York: Academic Press.

Eisenberg, N., & Harris, J. D. (1984). Social competence: A developmental perspective. *School Psychology Review, 13,* 267–277.

Eisenberg, N., Murray, E., & Hite, T. (1982). Children's reasoning regarding sex-typed toy choices. *Child Development, 53,* 81–86.

Elksnin, L. K., & Elksnin, N. (1995). *Assessment and instruction of social skills.* San Diego, CA: Singular Publishing Group.

Elliott, S. N., & Gresham, F. M. (1991). *Social skills intervention guide: Practical strategies for social skills training.* Circle Pines, MN: American Guidance.

Emerson, E. N., Crowley, S. L., & Merrell, K. W. (1994). Convergent validity of the School Social Behavior Scales with the Child Behavior Checklist and Teacher's Report Form. *Journal of Psychoeducational Assessment, 12,* 372–380.

Erikson, E. (1963). *Childhood and society.* New York: Norton.

Erwin, P. G. (1994). Effectiveness of social skills training with children: A meta-analytic study. *Counseling Psychology Quarterly, 7,* 305–310.

Etaugh, C. (1983). Introduction: The influence of environmental factors on sex differences in children's play. In M. B. Liss (Ed.), *Social and cognitive skills: Sex roles and children's play* (pp. 1–19). New York: Academic Press.

Fagot, B. I. (1974). Reinforcing contingencies for sex-role behaviors: Effect of experience with children. *Child Development, 49,* 30–36.

Fagot, B. I. (1981). Male and female teachers: Do they treat boys and girls differently? *Sex Roles, 7,* 263–271.

Fagot, B. I., & Patterson, G. R. (1969). In-vivo analysis of reinforcing contingencies for sex-role behaviors in the preschool. *Developmental Psychology, 1,* 563–568.

Feshbach, N. D. (1983). Learning to care: A positive approach to child training and discipline. *Journal of Clinical Child Psychology, 12,* 266–271.

Feshbach, N. D., & Feshbach, S. (1982). Empathy training and the regulation of aggression: Potentialities and limitations. *Academic Psychology Bulletin, 4,* 399–413.

Foster, S. L., & Ritchey, W. L. (1979). Issues in the assessment of social competence in children. *Journal of Applied Behavior Analysis, 12,* 625–638.

Fox, J. L., & McEvoy, M. A. (1993). Assessing and enhancing generalization and social validity of social skills interventions with children and adolescents. *Behavior Modification, 17,* 339–366.

Frederick, B. P., & Olmi, D. J. (1994). Children with attention-deficit/hyperactivity disorder: A review of the literature on social skills deficits. *Psychology in the Schools, 31,* 288–296.

Fuchs, D., & Fuchs, L. S. (1994). Inclusive schools movement and the radicalization of special education reform. *Exceptional Children, 60,* 294–309.

Furman, W., & Bierman, K. L. (1982). Developmental changes in young children's conceptions of friendship. *Child Development, 54,* 549–556.

Gallagher, T., & Craig, H. (1984). Pragmatic assessment: Analysis of a highly frequent repeated utterance. *Journal of Speech and Hearing Disorders, 49,* 368–377.

Gardner, H. (1983). *Frames of mind.* New York: Basic Books.

Gesten, E. L. (1976). A health resources inventory: The development of a measure of the personal and social competence of primary-grade children. *Journal of Consulting and Clinical Psychology, 44,* 775–786.

Goldberg, D., & Huxley, P. (1980). *Mental illness in the community.* London: Tavistock Publications.

Goldstein, A. P. (1988). *The prepare curriculum: teaching prosocial competencies.* Champaign, IL: Research Press.

Goldstein, A. P., Glick, B., Reiner, S., Zimmerman, D., & Coultry, T. M. (1987). *Aggression replacement training: A comprehensive intervention for aggressive youth.* Champaign, IL: Research Press.

Goldstein, A. P., & Pentz, M. A. (1984). Psychological skill training and the aggressive adolescent. *School Psychology Review, 13,* 311–323.

Goldstein, A. P., Sprafkin, R. P., Gershaw, N. J., & Klein, P. (1980). *Skillstreaming the adolescent.* Champaign, IL: Research Press.

Goldstein, H., & Gallagher, T. M. (1992). Strategies for promoting the social-communicative competence of young children with specific language impairment. In S. R. Odom, S. L. McConnell, & M. A. McEvoy (eds.), *Social competence of young children with disabilities* (pp. 189–213). Baltimore: Brookes.

Goleman, D. (1994). *Emotional intelligence.* New York: Bantam.

Gottlieb, J. (1975). Public, peer, and professional attitudes toward mentally retarded persons. In M. J. Bagab & S. A. Richardson (Eds.), *The mentally retarded and society: A social science perspective* (pp. 99–125). Baltimore: University Park Press.

Gottlieb, J. (1981). Mainstreaming: Fulfilling the promise? *American Journal on Mental Deficiency, 86,* 115–126.

Gottman, J. M. (1983). How children become friends. *Monographs of the Society for Research in Child Development, 48* (3, Serial No. 201).

Gottman, J. M. (1986). The observation of social process. In J. M. Gottman & J. C. Parker (Eds.), *Conversations of friends: Speculation on affective development* (pp. 51–102). New York: Cambridge University Press.

Grenell, M. M., Glass, C. R., & Katz, K. S. (1987). Hyperactive children and peer interaction: Knowledge and performance of social skills. *Journal of Abnormal Child Psychology, 15,* 1–13.

Gresham, F. M. (1981). Social skills training with handicapped children. A review. *Review of Educational Research, 51,* 139–176.

Gresham, F. M. (1982). Misguided mainstreaming: The case for social skills training with handicapped children. *Exceptional Children, 48,* 422–433.

Gresham, F. M. (1986). Conceptual issues in the assessment of social competence in children. In

P. S. Strain, M. J. Guralnick, and H. M. Walker (Eds.), *Children's social behavior: Development, assessment, and modification* (pp. 143–179). New York: Academic Press.

Gresham, F. M., & Elliott, S. N. (1987). The relationship between adaptive behavior and social skills: Issues in definition and assessment. *The Journal of Special Education, 21*, 167–181.

Gresham, F. M., & Elliott, S. N. (1990). *The Social Skills Rating System*. Circle Pines, MN: American Guidance.

Gresham, F. M., Elliott, S. N., & Black, F. L. (1987). Teacher-rated social skills of mainstreamed mildly handicapped and nonhandicapped children. *School Psychology Review, 16*, 78–88.

Gresham, F. M., & MacMillan, D. L. (in press). Social competence and affective characteristics of students with mild disabilities. *Review of Educational Research*.

Gresham, F. M., & Reschly, D. J. (1987a). Dimensions of social competence: Method factors in the assessment of adaptive behavior, social skills, and peer acceptance. *Journal of School Psychology, 25*, 367–381.

Gresham, F. M., & Reschly, D. J. (1987b). Issues in the conceptualization, classification, and assessment of social skills in the mildly handicapped. In T. Kratochwill (Ed.), *Advances in school psychology* (pp. 203–264). Hillsdale, NJ: Lawrence Erlbaum Associates.

Grossman, H. J. (Ed.) (1983). *Classification in mental retardation*. Washington, DC: American Association on Mental Deficiency.

Guevremont, D. (1990). Social skills and peer relationship training. In R. A. Barkley, *Attention deficit hyperactivity disorder: A handbook for diagnosis and treatment* (pp. 540–572). New York: Guilford.

Guevremont, D. C., & Foster, S. L. (1993). Impact of social problem-solving training on aggressive boys: Skill acquisition, behavior change, and generalization. *Journal of Abnormal Child Psychology, 21*, 13–27.

Haager, D., & Vaughn, S. (1995). Parent, teacher, peer, and self-reports of the social competence of students with learning disabilities. *Journal of Learning Disabilities, 28*, 205–215, 231.

Hammen, C., & Rudolph, K. D. (1996). Childhood depression. In E. J. Mash & R. A. Barkley (Eds.), *Child psychopathology* (pp. 153–195). New York: Guilford.

Hargie, O., Saunders, C., & Dickson, D. (1987). *Social skills in interpersonalcommunication* (2nd ed.). London: Croom Helm.

Harrington, R. (1993). *Depressive disorder in childhood and adolescence*. New York: Wiley.

Harter, S. (1990). Issues in the assessment of the self-concept of children and adolescents. In A. M. LaGreca (Ed.), *Through the eyes of the child* (pp. 292–325). Boston: Allyn & Bacon.

Hartup, W. W. (1983). Peer relations. In E. M. Hetherington (Ed.), *Handbook of child psychology (Vol. 4): Socialization, personality, and social development* (pp. 103–198). New York: Wiley.

Hartup, W. W. (1984). The peer context in middle childhood. In W. A. Collins (Ed.), *Development during middle childhood: The years from six to twelve* (pp. 240–282). Washington, DC: National Academy Press.

Harway, M., & Moss, L. T. (1983). Sex differences: The evidence from biology. In M. B. Liss (Ed.), *Social and cognitive skills: Sex roles and children's play*. New York: Academic Press.

Hayvren, M., & Hymel, S. (1984). Ethical issues in sociometric testing: Impact of sociometric measures on interaction behavior. *Developmental Psychology, 20*, 844–849.

Hepler, J. B., & Rose, S. F. (1988). Evaluation of a multi-component group approach for improving the social skills of elementary school children. *Journal of Social Service Research, 11*(4), 1–18.

Hinshaw, S. P., & Anderson, C. A. (1996). Conduct and oppositional defiant disorders. In E. J. Mash & R. A. Barkley (Eds.), *Child Psychopathology* (pp. 113–149). New York: Guilford.

Hollinger, J. D. (1987). Social skills for behaviorally disordered children as preparation for mainstreaming: Theory, practice, and new directions. *Remedial and Special Education, 11*, 139–149.

Hops, H. (1983). Children's social competence and skill: Current research practices and future directions. *Behavior Therapy, 14,* 3–18.

Hops, H., & Finch, M. (1985). Social competence and skills: A reassessment. In B. H. Schneider, K. H. Rubin, and J. E. Ledingham (Eds.), *Children's peer relations: Issues in assessment and intervention* (pp. 23–39). New York: Springer-Verlag.

Horney, K. (1945). *Our inner conflicts.* New York: Norton.

Howell, K. W. (1985). A task-analytical approach to social behavior. *Remedial and Special Education, 6*(2), 24–30.

Huggins, P. (1990–1994). *Teaching cooperation skills.* Longmont, CO: Sopris-West.

Huggins, P. (1993–1995). *Teaching friendship skills: Primary version.* Longmont, CO: Sopris-West.

Hughes, J. N., & Baker, D. B. (1990). *The clinical child interview.* New York: Guilford.

Hughes, J. N., & Sullivan, K. A. (1988). Outcome assessment in social skills training with children. *Journal of School Psychology, 26,* 167–183.

Hundert, J., & Houghton, A. (1992). Promoting social interaction of children with disabilities in integrated preschools: A failure to generalize. *Exceptional Children, 58,* 311–320.

Interagency Committee on Learning Disabilities (1987). *Learning disabilities: A report to the U. S. Congress.* Bethesda, MD: National Institutes of Health.

Jackson, N. F., Jackson, D. A., & Monroe, C. (1983). *Getting along with others: Teaching social effectiveness to children.* Champaign, IL: Research Press.

Jentzsch, C. E. (1993). *The predictive validity of the Battelle Developmental Inventory as a measure of social-behavioral development for young children with disabilities.* Unpublished Masters thesis, Utah State University. Logan, UT.

Jentzsch, C. E., & Merrell, K. W. (1996). An investigation of the construct validity of the Preschool and Kindergarten Behavior Scales. *Diagnostique, 21*(2), 1–15.

Johnson, J. E., & Roopnarine, J. L. (1983). The preschool classroom and sex differences in children's play. In M. B. Liss (Ed.), *Social and cognitive skills: Sex roles and children's play* (pp. 193–218). New York: Academic Press.

Jones, R. N., Sheridan, S. M., & Binns, W. R. (1993). Schoolwide social skills training: Providing preventative services to children at-risk. *School Psychology Quarterly, 8,* 57–80.

Kamps, D. M., Leonard, B. R., Vernon, S., & Dugan, E. P. (1992). Teaching social skills to students with autism to increase peer interactions in an integrated first-grade classroom. *Journal of Applied Behavior Analysis, 25,* 281–288.

Kauffman, J. M. (1989). *Characteristics of behavior disorders of children and youth* (4th ed.). Columbus, OH: Merrill.

Kauffman, J. M. (1993). Special problems in the inclusion of students with emotional or behavioral disorders in general education classrooms and schools. *Special Education Perspectives, 2*(1), 23–28.

Kauffman, J. M. (1995). How we might achieve the radical reform of special education. In J. M. Kauffman & D. P. Hallahan (Eds.), *The illusion of full inclusion* (pp. 193–211). Austin, TX: Pro-Ed.

Kauffman, J. M., Semmell, M. I., & Agard, J. A. (1974). PRIME: An overview. *Education and Training for the Mentally Retarded, 9,* 107–112.

Kazdin, A. E. (1981). Behavioral observation. In M. Herson & A. S. Bellack (Eds.), *Behavioral assessment: A practical handbook* (pp. 101–124). New York: Pergamon.

Kazdin, A. E. (1982). *Single-case research designs: Methods for clinical and applied settings.* New York: Oxford University Press.

Kazdin, A. E. (1987). Treatment of antisocial behavior in children: Current status and future directions. *Psychological Bulletin, 102,* 187–203.

Kazdin, A. E., Esveldt-Dawson, K., French, N. H., & Unis, A. S. (1987). Problem-solving skills training and relationship therapy in the treatment of antisocial child behavior. *Journal of Consulting and Clinical Psychology, 55,* 76–85.

Keane, S. P., & Conger, J. C. (1981). The implications of communication development for social skills training. *Journal of Pediatric Psychology, 6,* 369–381.

Keller, H. R. (1986). Behavioral observation approaches to assessment. In H. Knoff (Ed.), *The assessment of child and adolescent personality* (pp. 353–397). New York: Gilford.

Kelly, J. A. (1982). *Social skills training: A practical guide for interventions.* New York: Springer.

Kettlewell, P. W., & Kausch, D. F. (1983). The generalization of the effects of a cognitive-behavioral treatment program for aggressive children. *Journal of Abnormal Child Psychology, 11,* 101–114.

Knapczyk, D. R., & Rodes, P. G. (1996). *Teaching social competence.* Pacific Grove, CA: Brooks/Cole.

Knoff, H. M., & Batsche, G. M. (1995). Projects ACHIEVE: Analyzing a school reform process for at-risk and underachieving students. *School Psychology Review, 24,* 579–603.

Kohlberg, L. (1969). Stage and sequence: The cognitive–developmental approach to socialization. In D. A. Goslin (Ed.), *Handbook of socialization theory and research.* Chicago: Rand-McNally.

Kolko, D. J., Loar, L. L., & Sturnick, D. (1990). Inpatient social–cognitive skills training groups with conduct disordered and attention deficit disordered children. *Journal of Child Psychology and Psychiatry and Allied Disciplines, 31,* 737–748.

Kratochwill, T. R., & French, D. C. (1984). Social skills training for withdrawn children. *School Psychology Review, 13,* 331–338.

LaGreca, A. M., & Vaughn, S. (1992). Social functioning of individuals with learning disabilities. *School Psychology Review, 21,* 340–347.

Lambert, N., & Windmiller, N. (1981). *AAMD Adaptive Behavior Scale—School Edition.* Monterey, CA: Publishers Test Service.

Landau, S., & Milich, R. (1988). Social communication patterns of attention-deficit-disordered boys. *Journal of Abnormal Child Psychology, 16,* 69–81.

Landau, S., & Milich, R. (1990). Assessment of children's social status and peer relations. In A. M. LaGreca (Ed.), *Through the eyes of the child* (pp. 259–291). Boston: Allyn & Bacon.

Landau, S., & Moore, L. A. (1991). Social skills deficits in children with attention-deficit hyperactivity disorder. *School Psychology Review, 20,* 235–251.

Law, J., Brown, G., & Lester, R. (1994). Speech and language therapy provision in a social education centre: The value of a "first step" assessment. *British Journal of Learning Disabilities, 22,* 66–69.

Lethermon, V. R., Williamson, D. A., Moody, S. C., Granberry, S. W., Lenauer, K. L., & Bodiford, C. B. (1984). Factors affecting the social validity of a role-play test of children's social skills. *Journal of Behavioral Assessment, 6,* 231–245.

Lethermon, V. R., Williamson, D. A., Moody, S. C., & Wozniak, P. (1986). Racial bias in behavioral assessment of children's social skills. *Journal of Psychopathology and Behavioral Assessment, 8,* 329–337.

Lewinsohn, P. (1974). A behavioral approach to depression. In R. Friedman & M. Katz (Eds.), *The psychology of depression: Contemporary theory and research.* Washington, DC: U. S. Government Printing Office.

Lewinsohn, P. M., Clarke, G. N., Hops, H., & Andrews, J. A. (1990). Cognitive-behavioral treatment for depressed adolescents. *Behavior Therapy, 21,* 385–401.

Libet, J., & Lewinsohn, P. M. (1973). The concept of social skill with special references to the behavior of depressed persons. *Journal of Consulting and Clinical Psychology, 40,* 304–312.

Lochman, J. E. (1992). Cognitive-behavioral intervention with aggressive boys: Three year follow-up and preventative effects. *Journal of Consulting and Clinical Psychology, 60,* 426–432.

Lochman, J. E., Burch, P. R., Curry, J. F., & Lampron, L. B. (1984). Treatment and generalization effects of cognitive-behavioral and goal-setting interventions with aggressive boys. *Journal of Consulting and Clinical Psychology, 52,* 915–916.

Loeber, R., Dishion, T. J., & Patterson, G. R. (1984). Multiple gating: A multistage assessment procedure for identifying youths at risk for delinquency. *Journal of Research in Crime and Delinquency, 21,* 7–32.

Lovejoy, M. C., & Routh, D. K. (1988). Behavior disordered children's social skills: Increased by training, but not sustained or reciprocated. *Child and Family Behavior Therapy, 10,* 15–27.

Maccoby, E. E., & Jacklin, C. N. (1974). *The psychology of sex differences.* Stanford, CA: Stanford University Press.

MacMillan, D. L., Gresham, F. M., & Forness, S. R. (1996). Full inclusion: An empirical perspective. *Behavioral Disorders, 21,* 145–159.

Martin, R. P. (1988). *Assessment of personality and behavior problems.* New York: Guilford.

Martin, R. P., Hooper, S., & Snow, J. (1986). Behavior rating scale approaches to personality assessment in children and adolescents. In H. Knoff (Ed.), *The assessment of child and adolescent personality* (pp. 309–351). New York: Guilford.

Masten, A. S., Morrison, P., & Pelligrini, D. S. (1985). A revised class play method of peer assessment. *Developmental Psychology, 21,* 523–533.

Mathews, W. S. (1977). Modes of transformation in the initiation of fantasy play. *Developmental Psychology, 13,* 212–216.

Matson, J. L. (1984). Issues in assessing social skills deficits and excesses in handicapped children. *Australia and New Zealand Journal of Developmental Disabilities, 10,* 203–207.

Matson, J. L. (1988). Teaching and training relevant community skills to mentally retarded persons. *Child and Youth Services, 10,* 107–121.

Matson, J. L., Compton, L. S., & Sevin, J. A. (1991). Comparison and item analysis of the MESSY for autistic and normal children. *Research in Developmental Disabilities, 12,* 361–369.

Matson, J. L., Esveldt-Dawson, K., & Kazdin, A. E. (1983). Validation of methods for assessing social skills in children. *Journal of Clinical Child Psychology, 12,* 174–180.

Matson, J. L., & Ollendick, T. H. (1988). *Enhancing children's social skills.* New York: Pergamon.

Matson, J. L., Rotatori, A. F., & Helsel, W. J. (1983). Development of a rating scale to measure social skills in children: The Matson Evaluation of Social Skills with Youngsters (MESSY). *Behavior Research and Therapy, 21,* 335–340.

McCandless, B., & Marshall, H. (1957). A picture sociometric technique for preschool children and its relation to teacher judgments of friendship. *Child Development, 28,* 139–148.

McCarver, R. B., & Campbell, V. A. (1987). Future developments in the concept and application of adaptive behavior. *The Journal of Special Education, 21,* 197–207.

McFall, R. M. (1982). A review and reformulation of the construct of social skills. *Behavioral Assessment, 4,* 1–33.

McGinnis, E., & Goldstein, A. P. (1984). *Skillstreaming for the elementary-age child.* Champaign, IL: Research Press.

McGinnis, E., & Goldstein, A. P. (1990). *Skillstreaming in early childhood: Teaching prosocial skills to the preschool and kindergarten child.* Champaign, IL: Research Press.

McGuire, J., & Priestley, P. (1981). *Life after school: A social skills curriculum.* Oxford: Pergamon.

McLoyd, V. C. (1980). Verbally expressed modes of transformation in the fantasy play of black preschool children. *Child Development, 51,* 1133–1139.

McMahon, C. M., Wacker, D. P., Sasso, G. M., & Melloy, K. J. (1994). Evaluation of the multiple effects of a social skill intervention. *Behavioral Disorders, 20,* 35–50.

Meehl, P. (1954). *Clinical vs. statistical prediction.* Minneapolis: University of Minnesota Press.

Meichenbaum, D., Butler, L., & Gruson, L. (1981). Toward a conceptual model of social competence. In J. D. Wyne & M. D. Smye (Eds.), *Social competence*. New York: Guilford.

Mercer, C. D., Hughes, C., & Mercer, A. R. (1985). Learning disability definitions used by state
education departments. *Learning Disability Quarterly, 8*, 45–55.

Mercer, J. R., Gomez-Palacio, M., & Padilla, E. (1986). The development of practical intelligence
in cross-cultural perspective. In R. J. Sternberg & R. K. Wagner (Eds.), *Practical intelligence*
(pp. 307–337). Cambridge, England: Cambridge University Press.

Merrell, K. W. (1989). Concurrent relationships between two behavior rating scales for teachers:
An examination of self-control, social competence, and school behavioral adjustment. *Psychology in the Schools, 26*, 267–271.

Merrell, K. W. (1991). Teacher ratings of social competence and behavioral adjustment: Differences between learning disabled, low-achieving, and typical students. *Journal of School Psychology, 29*, 207–217.

Merrell, K. W. (1993a). Using behavior rating scales to assess social skills and antisocial behavior
in school settings: Development of the school social behavior scales. *School Psychology Review, 22*, 115–133.

Merrell, K. W. (1993b). *School Social Behavior Scales*. Austin, TX: Pro-Ed.

Merrell, K. W. (1994a). *Assessment of behavioral, social, and emotional problems: Direct and
objective methods for use with children and adolescents*. White Plains, NY: Longman.

Merrell, K. W. (1994b). *Preschool and Kindergarten Behavior Scales*. Austin, TX: Pro-Ed.

Merrell, K. W. (1995a). An investigation of the relationship between social skills and internalizing
problems in early childhood: Construct validity of the Preschool and Kindergarten Behavior
Scales. *Journal of Psychoeducational Assessment, 13*, 230–240.

Merrell, K. W. (1995b). Relationships among early childhood behavior rating scales: Convergent
and discriminant construct validity of the Preschool and Kindergarten Behavior Scales. *Early
Education and Development, 6*, 253–264.

Merrell, K. W. (1996). Assessment of social skills and behavior problems in early childhood: The
Preschool and Kindergarten Behavior Scales. *Journal of Early Intervention, 20*, 132–145.

Merrell, K. W., & Gill, S. J. (1994). Using teacher ratings of social behavior to differentiate gifted
from non-gifted students. *Roeper Review, 16*(4), 286–289.

Merrell, K. W., Merz, J. M., Johnson, E. R., & Ring, E. N. (1992). Social competence of students
with mild handicaps and low achievement: A comparative study. *School Psychology Review,
21*, 125–137.

Merrell, K. W., Sanders, D. E., & Popinga, M. (1993). Teacher ratings of social behavior as a predictor of special education status: Discriminant validity of the School Social Behavior Scales.
Journal of Psychoeducational Assessment, 11, 220–231.

Merrell, K. W., & Shinn, M. R. (1990). Critical variables in the learning disabilities identification
process. *School Psychology Review, 19*, 74–82.

Michelson, L., Sugai, D., Wood, R., & Kazdin, A. E. (1983). *Social skills assessment and training with children: An empirical handbook*. New York: Plenum.

Milich, R., & Landau, S. (1984). A comparison of the social status and social behavior of aggressive and aggressive/withdrawn boys. *Journal of Abnormal Child Psychology, 12*, 277–288.

Moore, L. A. (1994). The effects of social skills curricula: Were they apparent initially? *School
Psychology Quarterly, 9*, 133–136.

Moreno, J. L. (1934). *Who shall survive?* Washington, DC: Nervous and Mental Disease Publishing.

Muscott, H. S., & Gifford, T. (1994). Virtual reality and social skills training for students with behavior disorders: Applications, challenges and promising practices. *Education and Treatment of Children, 17*, 417–434.

Mussen, P. H. (Ed.). (1970). *Carmichael's manual of child psychology* (Vol. 3). New York: Wiley.

National Institutes of Health. (1990). *Epidemiology of specific language impairment.* RFP NIH-DC-90–19. Washington, DC: Author.

Nientemp, E. G., & Cole, C. L. (1992). Teaching socially valid interaction responses to students with severe disabilities in an integrated school setting. *Journal of School Psychology, 30,* 343–354.

O'Donnell, J., Hawkins, J. D., Catalano, R. F., Abbott, R. D., & Day, L. E. (1995). Preventing school failure, drug use, and delinquency among low-income children: Long-term intervention in elementary schools. *American Journal of Orthopsychiatry, 65,* 87–100.

Ogilvy, C. M. (1994). Social skills training with children and adolescents: A review of the evidence of effectiveness. *Educational Psychology, 14,* 73–83.

O'Reilly, J. P., Tokuno, K. A., & Ebata, A. T. (1986). Cultural differences between Americans of Japanese and European ancestry in parental valuing of social competence. *Journal of Comparative Family Studies, 17,* 87–97.

Parke, H. S., Tappe, P., Carmeto, R., & Gaylord-Ross, R. (1990). Social support and quality of life for learning disabled and mildly retarded youth in transition. In R. Gaylord-Ross, S. Siegel, H. S. Park, S. Sacks, & L. Goetz (Eds.), *Readings in ecosocial development* (pp. 293–328). San Francisco: San Francisco State University, Department of Special Education.

Parker, J., & Gottman, J. (1989). Social and emotional development in relational context. In T. Berndt & G. Ladd (Eds.), *Peer relationships in child development* (pp. 95–131). New York: Wiley.

Peacock Hill Working Group. (1991). Problems and promises in special education and related services for children and youth with emotional or behavioral disorders. *Behavioral Disorders, 16,* 299–313.

Pelligrini, D. (1980). Social cognition, competence, and adaptation in children under stress. In N. Gamezy (Ed.), *Studies of stress and coping in children.* Symposium conducted at the meeting of the American Psychological Association, Montreal, Canada.

Pepler, D. J., King, G., Craig, W., Byrd, B., & Bream, L. (1995). The development and evaluation of a multisystem social skills group training program for aggressive children. *Child and Youth Care Forum, 24,* 297–313.

Piaget, J. (1983). Piaget's theory. In P. H. Mussen (Ed.), *Handbook of child psychology* (Vol. 1). New York: Wiley.

Polyson, J., & Kimball, W. (1993). Social skills training with physically aggressive children. In A. J. Finch, W. M. Nelson, & E. S. Ott (Eds.), *Cognitive-behavioral procedures with children and adolescents: A practical guide* (pp. 206–232). Boston: Allyn & Bacon.

Quay, H. C. (1986). Classification. In H. C. Quay & J. S. Werry (Eds.), *Psychological disorders of childhood (3rd ed., pp. 1–34).* New York: Wiley.

Reed, M. K. (1994). Social skill training to reduce depression in adolescents. *Adolescence, 29,* 293–302.

Reid, J. B. (1982). Observer training in naturalistic research. In D. P. Hartmann (Ed.), *Using observers to study behavior* (pp. 37–50). San Francisco: Jossey-Bass.

Reid, J. B., Baldwin, D. B., Patterson, G. R., & Dishion, T. J. (1988). Observations in the assessment of childhood disorders. In M. Rutter, A. H. Tuma, & I. S. Lann (Eds.), *Assessment and diagnosis in child psychopathology* (pp. 156–195). New York: Guilford.

Reschly, D. J., & Gresham, F. M. (1981). *Use of social competence measures to facilitate parent and teacher involvement and nonbiased assessment.* Unpublished manuscript, Iowa State University, Ames.

Reynolds, C. R., & Kamphaus, R. W. (1992). *The Behavioral Assessment System for Children.* Circle Pines, MN: American Guidance Services.

Rhode, G., Jenson, W. R., & Reavis, H. K. (1992). *The tough kid book: Practical classroom management strategies.* Longmont, CO: Sopris-West.

Rime, B., Bouvy, H., Leborgne, B., & Rouillon, F. (1978). Psychopathy and non-verbal behaviour in an interpersonal situation. *Journal of Abnormal Psychology, 87,* 636–643.

Roff, M. (1961). Childhood social interactions and young adult bad conduct. *Journal of Abnormal and Social Psychology, 63,* 333–337.

Roff, M., Sells, B., & Golden, M. M. (1972). *Social adjustment and personality development in children.* Minneapolis: University of Minnesota Press.

Rourke, B. P., & Fuerst, D. R. (1992). Psychosocial dimensions of learning disability subtypes: Neuropsychological studies in the Windsor Laboratory. *School Psychology Review, 21,* 361–374.

Rubin, K. H., & Ross, H. S. (1982). Some reflections on the state of the art: The study of peer relationships and social skills. In K. H. Rubin & H. S. Ross (Eds.), *Peer relationships and social skills in childhood* (pp. 1–8). New York: Springer-Verlag.

Rule, S., Stowitschek, J. J., Innocenti, M., & Striefel, S. (1987). The Social Integration Program: An analysis of the effects of mainstreaming handicapped children into day care centers. *Education and Treatment of Children, 10,* 175–192.

Rutherford, R., Chipman, J., DiGangi, S., & Anderson, K. (1992). *Teaching social skills: A practical instructional approach.* Ann Arbor, MI: Exceptional Innovations.

Sargent, L. R. (1991). *Social skills for school and community: Systematic instruction for children and youth with cognitive delays.* Reston, VA: Division on Mental Retardation, Council for Exceptional Children.

Sattler, J. M. (1988). *Assessment of children* (3rd ed.). San Diego: Jerome M. Sattler.

Schlundt, D., & McFall, R. (1985). New directions in the assessment of social competence and skills. In L. L'Aabate & M. Milan (Eds.), *Handbook of social skills training and research.* New York: Wiley.

Schneider, B. H. (1992). Didactic methods for enhancing children's peer relations. A quantitative review. *Clinical Psychology Review, 12,* 363–382.

Schneider, B. H., Rubin, K. H., & Ledingham, J. (1985). *Children's peer relations: Issues in assessment and intervention.* New York: Springer-Verlag.

Schumaker, J., Deshler, D., Alley, G., & Warner, M. (1983). Toward the development of an intervention model for learning-disabled adolescents: The University of Kansas Institute for Research on Learning Disabilities. *Exceptional Education Quarterly, 4,* 44–47.

Selman, R. L. (1981). The child as a friendship philosopher. In S. R. Asher & J. M. Gottman (Eds.), *The development of children's friendship* (pp. 242–272). Cambridge, England: Cambridge University Press.

Shapiro, E. S., & Skinner, C. H. (1990). Best practices in observation and ecological assessment. In A. Thomas & J. Grimes (Eds.), *Best practices in school psychology—II* (pp. 507–518). Washington, DC: National Association of School Psychologists.

Sheinker, J., & Sheinker, A. (1988). *Metacognitive approach to social skills training: A program for grades 4–12.* Frederick, MD: Aspen.

Sheridan, S. M. (1995). *The tough kid social skills book.* Longmont, CO: Sopris West.

Sheridan, S. M., Dee, C. C., Morgan, J. C., McCormick, M. E., & Walker, D. (1996). A multimethod intervention for social skills deficits in children with ADHD and their parents. *School Psychology Review, 25,* 57–76.

Shure, M., & Spivack, G. (1980). Interpersonal problem solving as a mediator of behavioral adjustment in preschool and kindergarten children. *Journal of Applied Developmental Psychology, 1,* 29–44.

Snell, M. E. (1991). Schools are for all kids: The importance of integration for students with severe disabilities and their peers. In J. W. Lloyd, A. C. Repp, & N. N. Singh (Eds.), *The Regular Education Initiative: Alternative perspectives on concepts, issues, and models* (pp. 133–148). Sycamore, IL: Sycamore.

Stainback, S., & Stainback, W. (1992). Schools as inclusive communities. In W. Stainback & S. Stainback (Eds.), *Controversial issues confronting special education* (pp. 29–43). Boston: Allyn & Bacon.

Stainback, W., & Stainback, S. (1984). A rationale for the merger of special and regular education. *Exceptional Children, 51,* 102–111.

Stark, K. D. (1990). *Childhood depression: School-based interventions.* New York: Guilford.

Stark, K. D., Best, L. R., & Sellstrom, E. A. (1989). A cognitive-behavioral approach to the treatment of childhood depression. In J. N. Hughes & R. J. Hall (Eds.), *Cognitive behavioral psychology in the schools: A comprehensive handbook* (pp. 389–433). New York: Guilford.

Stark, K. D., Reynolds, W. M., & Kaslow, N. J. (1987). A comparison of the relative efficacy of self-control therapy and a behavioral problem-solving therapy for depression in children. *Journal of Abnormal Child Psychology, 15,* 91–113.

Stephens, T. M. (1978). *Social skills in the classroom.* Columbus, OH: Cedars Press.

Stern, J. B., & Fodor, I. G. (1989). Anger control in children: A review of social skills and cognitive behavioral approaches to dealing with aggressive children. *Child and Family Behavior Therapy, 11,* 1–20.

Sternberg, R. J. (1986). The nature and scope of practical intelligence. In R. J. Sterberg & R. A. Wagner (Eds.), *Practical Intelligence* (pp. 1–12). Cambridge, England: Cambridge University Press.

Stewart, S. L., & Rubin, K. H. (1995). The social problem-solving skills of anxious-withdrawn children. *Development and Psychopathology, 7,* 323–336.

Stokes, T. F., & Baer, D. M. (1977). In implicit technology of generalization. *Journal of Applied Behavior Analysis, 19,* 349–367.

Strain, P. S. (1983). Identification of social skill curriculum targets for severely handicapped children in mainstream preschools. *Applied Research in Mental Retardation, 4,* 369–382.

Stumme, V. S., Gresham, F. M., & Scott, N. A. (1982). Validity of social behavior assessment in discriminating emotionally disturbed and nonhandicapped students. *Journal of Behavioral Assessment, 4,* 327–341.

Sue, D. W., & Sue, D. (1990). *Counseling the culturally different* (2nd ed.). New York: Wiley.

Swanson, H. L., & Malone, S. (1992). Social skills and learning disabilities: A meta-analysis of the literature. *School Psychology Review, 21,* 427–443.

Thorndike, E. L. (1920). Intelligence and its uses. *Harpers Magazine, 140,* 227–235.

Trower, P. M. (1979). Fundamentals of interpersonal behavior: A social-psychological perspective. In A. S. Bellack & M. Herson (Eds.), *Research and practice in social skills training.* New York: Plenum.

Turner, S. M., Beidel, D. C., Herson, M., & Bellack, A. S. (1984). Effects of race on ratings of social skill. *Journal of Consulting and Clinical Psychology, 52,* 474–475.

Ullman, C. A. (1975). Teachers, peers, and tests as predictors of adjustment. *Journal of Educational Psychology, 48,* 257–267.

Vaughn, S. (1987). TLC—Teaching, learning, and caring: Teaching interpersonal problem-solving skills to behaviorally disordered adolescents. *The Pointer, 31,* 25–30.

Veldman, D. J., & Sheffield, J. R. (1979). The scaling of sociometric nominations. *Educational and Psychological Measurement, 39,* 99–106.

Verduyn, C. M., Lord, W., & Forrest, G. C. (1990). Social skills training in schools: An evaluation study. *Journal of Adolescence, 13,* 3–16.

Vosk, B., Forehand, R. Parker, J. B., & Rickard, J. (1982). A multimethod comparison of popular and unpopular children. *Developmental Psychology, 18,* 571–575.

Wahler, R. G., & Dumas, J. E. (1986). "A chip off the old block": Some interpersonal characteristics of coercive children across generations. In P. S. Strain, M. J. Guralnick, & H. M. Walker (Eds.), *Children's social behavior: Development, assessment, and modification* (pp. 49–91). New York: Academic Press.

Wahler, R. G., & Fox, J. J. (1982). Setting events in applied behavior analysis: Toward a conceptual and methodological expansion. *Journal of Applied Behavior Analysis, 14,* 327–338.

Wahler, R. G., Hughey, J. B., & Gordon, J. S. (1981). Chronic patterns of mother-child coercion: Some differences between insular and noninsular families. *Analysis and intervention in developmental disabilities, 1,* 145–156.

Walker, H. M., Colvin, G. R., & Ramsey, E. R. (1995). *Antisocial behavior in school settings.* Pacific Grove, CA: Brooks/Cole.

Walker, H. M., & Hops, H. (1976). Increasing academic achievement by reinforcing direct academic and/or facilitating nonacademic responses. *Journal of Educational Psychology, 68,* 218–225.

Walker, H. M., McConnell, S., Holmes, D., Todis, B., Walker, J., & Golden, N. (1988). *The Walker Social Skills Curriculum: The ACCEPTS program.* Austin, TX: Pro-Ed.

Walker, H. M., & McConnell, S. R. (1995). *The Walker-McConnell Scales of Social Competence and School Adjustment.* San Diego: Singular Publishing.

Walker, H. M., & Severson, H. R. (1991). *Systematic Screening for Behavior Disorders.* Longmont, CO: Sopris West.

Walker, H. M., Steiber, S., & Eisert, D. (1991). Teacher ratings of adolescent social skills: Psychometric characteristics and factorial replicability. *School Psychology Review, 20,* 301–314.

Walker, H. M., Todis, B., Holmes, D., & Horton, G. (1988). *The Walker social skills curriculum: The ACCESS program (adolescent curriculum for communication and effective social skills).* Austin, TX: Pro-Ed.

Whalen, C. K., Henker, B., Collins, B. E., & Granger, D. (1987). Peer perceptions of hyperactivity and medication effects. *Child Development, 58,* 816–828.

Wiggins, J. S. (1981). Clinical and statistical prediction: Where are we and where do we go from here? *Clinical Psychology Review, 1,* 3–18.

Wing, J. K. (1978). *Schizophrenia: Towards a new synthesis.* New York: Academic Press.

Wolpe, J., & Lazarus, A. (1966). *Behavior therapy techniques.* New York: Pergamon.

Worthen, B. R., Borg, W. R., & White, K. R. (1993). *Measurement and evaluation in the schools: A practical guide.* White Plains, NY: Longman.

Young, K. R., & West, R. P. (1984). *Parent training: Social skills manual.* Logan, UT: Utah State University, Department of Special Education.

Zaragoza, N., Vaughn, S., & McIntosh, R. (1991). Social skills interventions and children with behavior problems: A review. *Behavioral Disorders, 16,* 260–275.

Author Index

197

AUTHOR INDEX

Subject Index